CHALLENGING GOVERNANCE THEORY

From networks to hegemony

Jonathan S. Davies

First published in Great Britain in 2011 by

The Policy Press
University of Bristol
Fourth Floor
Beacon House
Queen's Road
Bristol BS8 1QU
UK

Tel +44 (0)117 331 4054
Fax +44 (0)117 331 4093
e-mail tpp-info@bristol.ac.uk
www.policypress.co.uk

North American office:
The Policy Press
c/o The University of Chicago Press
1427 East 60th Street
Chicago, IL 60637, USA

t: +1 773 702 7700
f: +1 773-702-9756
e:sales@press.uchicago.edu
www.press.uchicago.edu

British Library Cataloguing in Publication Data
A catalogue record for this book is available from the British Library.

Library of Congress Cataloging-in-Publication Data
A catalog record for this book has been requested.

ISBN 978 1 84742 614 7 paperback
ISBN 978 1 84742 615 4 hardcover

Cover design by Qube Design Associates, Bristol
Front cover: image kindly supplied by www.alamy.com
Printed and bound in Great Britain by Hobbs, Southampton
The Policy Press uses environmentally responsible print partners

FSC
www.fsc.org
MIX
Paper from responsible sources
FSC® C020438

'No one is doing networks' (Anonymous)

'I think we have gone slightly network mad' (Anonymous)[1]

'The centralized state machinery … entoils (inmeshes) the living civil society like a boa constrictor' (Karl Marx, 1871, *The Civil War in France*, 1st draft)[2]

---

[1] I am very grateful to Jan Hurst for allowing me to quote two insightful respondents from her doctoral study of governing networks.

[2] www.marxists.org/archive/marx/works/1871/civil-war-france/drafts/ch01.htm

For my mother,
Sonia Gerda Davies

Contents

List of tables

Preface

The claim that governance is increasingly about networks was becoming the established orthodoxy when I embarked on my graduate studies in the mid-1990s. My suspicions about this new orthodoxy were provoked immediately; partly by my dislike of postmodernism, partly because it ignored dramatic upward concentrations of wealth and power occurring at the same time and partly because empirical research seemed to contradict it. My work thereafter only fuelled this scepticism, ultimately suggesting the need for a completely different understanding of network governance. This volume pulls together various strands of critique by myself and others and advances an alternative based on a Marxist reading of Gramsci. Naturally, it draws liberally on my previously published work – the relevant sources are recorded in the list of references – but takes it in a new direction. The book argues that network governance is part of the hegemonic strategy of neoliberalism – the visionary, utopian and profoundly flawed regulative ideal of late capitalism. It was inspired by the debate about challenging orthodoxies and developing critical governance research that we have been having at the University of Warwick since 2008, culminating in the Critical Governance Conference in December 2010 (see http://go.warwick.ac.uk/orthodoxies).

I am very grateful to colleagues who helped me write the book. Colin Crouch, Mike Geddes and Helen Sullivan commented astutely on the draft manuscript and I hope to have done some justice to their insights. I thank other colleagues past and present in the International Centre for Governance and Public Management (IGPM) at Warwick for many stimulating discussions. I single out John Benington, Crispian Fuller, Kevin Morrell, Ines Newman and Penelope Tuck. Others who have been a source of great encouragement and inspiration in recent years include Steve Griggs, David Imbroscio, Chris Skelcher, Clarence Stone and David Wilson, and many friends at the Political Studies and Urban Affairs associations and the recent Critical Governance Conference. I am grateful too to the anonymous reviewer who made very valuable comments on the draft manuscript. The Policy Press have been model publishers and my thanks go particularly to my editor Emily Watt for encouraging me and keeping me on track. Many thanks are also due to her colleagues, Jessica Hughes, Kathryn King, Jo Morton, Charlotte Skelton and Laura Vickers, without whom the project would not have come to fruition. I am most grateful to The Policy Press for publishing my work. Otherwise, the usual disclaimers apply. I apologise for errors of fact and interpretation, which are solely mine.

Jonathan S. Davies
31 March 2011

Introduction

For a generation, scholars, politicians, officials, activists and public intellectuals have celebrated the transformative potential of networks across government, economy and society. The network is the leitmotif of postmodernist social science, encompassing everything from radical anti-foundationalism to neo-Marxism and everyday theories of governance, public administration and public policy. Network analysis is applied to a vast range of social phenomena, inter alia to describe, model, analyse, explain and justify them. From the radical left to the libertarian right, scholars celebrate networks alongside their antagonists in mainstream public administration and policy. International corporate elites depict themselves and their companies as networked and networking as the medium of innovation in the age of informational or knowledge capitalism (Boltanski and Chiapello, 2005a). Across much of the world, from the UK and the US to mainland Europe, Scandinavia, Mexico, South Africa and the Antipodes, and at every geopolitical scale from the neighbourhood to the global, networking is proselytised as the way to conduct governance, intergovernmental relations, management and relations between government and civil society – and indeed as the best way to organise resistance. In short 'the metaphor of the network has progressively taken responsibility for a new general representation of societies' (Boltanski and Chiapello, 2005a, p 138). It has become 'a common form that tends to define our ways of understanding the world and acting in it' and the 'tendency of this common form to emerge and exert its hegemony is what defines the period' (Hardt and Negri, 2004, p 142). Zeldin's (1994, p 488) paean to the network epitomises the celebratory mood:

> I see humanity as a family that has hardly met. I see the meeting of people, bodies, thoughts, emotions or actions as the start of most change. Each link created by a meeting is like a filament, which, if they were all visible, would make the world look as though it is covered with gossamer. Every individual is connected to others, loosely or closely, by a unique combination of filaments, which stretch across the frontiers of space and time.

Even the mundane pursuit of joined-up government is imbued with the 'almost spiritual' nature of a quest for 'connexity' or 'holism' (Pollitt, 2003, p 36), the sense that networking is a new and potentially redemptive form of sociability in a world sundered by de-traditionalisation, globalisation and the rise of the 'me generation' (Milburn, 2006). The displacement of 'government' by 'governance' in academic discourse is thoroughly enmeshed with the view that networking might 'overcome the limitations of anarchic market exchange and top-down planning in an increasingly complex and global world' (Jessop, 2003a, pp 101-2). In the most optimistic accounts, governing through networks is deemed capable of fostering a new deliberative pluralism with the potential for an equitable, trust-based consensus about the means and ends of social life. The network potentially unlocks a 'third space' between state and market, extending the public sphere, empowering communities and cultivating inclusive policy making (Deakin and Taylor, 2002, p 17).

The celebration of networks is characteristic of what is hereafter called the 'post-traditional' worldview, denoting the common ground in a diverse spectrum of thought from radical postmodernism to theories influenced by postmodernism but which reject the idea that we are approaching the postmodern condition. Pivotal to the post-traditional outlook are claims about the dispersion and disorganisation of power and institutions. Its premise is that transformation has occurred, or is occurring, where the rise of the network heralds an emerging postmodern or reflexively modern condition freed from the ossified hierarchies of the mid-20th century. Where the term 'transformation thesis' is used hereafter, it is as shorthand for these post-traditional claims.

Following Marinetto (2003a) and Marsh (2008), this volume argues that the post-traditional worldview has become a potent 'orthodoxy'. An orthodoxy may not eliminate rivals, but its influence means they lack intellectual leverage and can be caricatured, recuperated, censored or ignored by its protagonists. Orthodoxies are best understood as the unwarranted assertions and silences of dominant paradigms. Vital questions, such as the alleged move from 'government' to 'governance' are bracketed in favour of 'pragmatic', often normatively inspired questions about how to manage or democratise the emerging, taken-for-granted network society. Kenis and Oerlemans (2008, p 299), for example, note that much interorganisational research is biased towards studying the positive effects of networking, ignoring manifold negatives. Lotia and Hardy (2008, p 371) comment: 'A theme that characterises all the work discussed above is the assumption that, when it can be made to work, collaboration is clearly beneficial'. The literature is 'thoroughly functionalist', concerned with finding 'practical solutions to practical problems', underpinned by the normative bias towards networks. Instead of asking whether 'trust' really holds networks together and if so whether this is necessarily a good thing, orthodox governance theory proceeds from the question of how to cultivate trust-based networks, a problem with which social capital theory (Putnam, 2000) has been notably preoccupied.

This volume challenges the orthodoxy, asking who has an interest in network-boosterism and why? It argues that contemporary governance has little in common with the visionary regulative ideal of networks. Rather, 'networked' governance institutions look very like the 'modernist' hierarchies they were supposed to replace. Across the social sciences, the purported rise of the network is more or less directly contested by scholars arguing in different ways that it really is 'governance as usual', or worse, that we are in a hyper-bureaucratic conjuncture where the virtues associated with the networker 'connectionist' or 'combinard' (Lash, 2002, p ix), such as self-starting, creativity and trust, are overwhelmed by hierarchies, network closure and technocratic managerialism. Moreover, a brief excursion into the political science and organisational behaviour literatures of the early to mid-20th century demonstrates that there is nothing new about networking and that there is no real evidence of more governance through networks now than in 1900 or 1945. If so, to paraphrase Wolin (2000, p 20), the celebration of networks is embalmed in scholarly and governmental rhetoric equally and in proportion to its lack of substance.

Accordingly, the terms 'governance network' and 'network governance' are hereafter distinguished. 'Network governance' refers to an ideal-type, the post-traditional claim that the network is proliferating and fosters ethical virtues such as trust and empowered reflexivity, heralding a rupture with the past. The term 'governance network', by contrast, refers to recurring and/or institutionalised formal and informal resource exchanges between governmental and non-governmental actors.[1] The essence of the distinction is that while this may or may not be a period when the volume of recurring resource exchanges is increasing, it is not an era of network governance. Post-traditional theories misrecognise the alleged transformation from government to governance. A key task in rethinking governance theory is therefore to determine why 'governance networks' do not live up to the promise of 'network governance'.

Encouragement for this enterprise has recently come from two unexpected sources, leading advocates of network governance theory who now distance themselves from it. Bevir and Rhodes' latest work (2010) is a reflexive critique of 'first-wave' network analysis, which posited the decentring of state power and the rise of the network. It also distances them from what they call the 'second wave', which brought back the state as the orchestrator of 'metagovernance' (see

Chapter One). Bevir and Rhodes (2010, p 20) announce a 'third wave' and with it pronounce the 'death' of the first two waves, which they see as instances of 'modernist empiricism' (treating networks as real objects of analysis) by other means. In doing so, they reject earlier versions of network governance theory, such as the work of Rhodes (see Rhodes, 2011, p 198 for a mea culpa), because 'there is no single account or theory of contemporary governance, only the differing constructions of several traditions' (Bevir and Rhodes, 2010, p 98) and no causal pathways determining the emergence or form of governing practice. Radicalising the interpretive approach in this way means that for Bevir and Rhodes, network governance is now just one among many governance stories.

In his tribute to Rhodes' 25 years as editor of *Public Administration*, Gerry Stoker (2011, p 16) suggests very candidly that he, Rhodes and others may have sold local government 'a pup' in claiming that local authorities could lead the development of networked community governance. Stoker now doubts the strength of the shift from government to governance, suggesting that networking is a function but one with considerably reduced significance than originally claimed by Rhodes and himself. He reflects (2011, p 28):

> The first flaw in the governance thinking offered by Rhodes and Stoker is this failure to fully recognize the value of hard power. Rhodes ... thought that the skills of diplomacy, communication and bargaining would be enough in achieving co-ordination. But this overlooked the importance of hard power in terms of coercion and strong material incentives. Our second mistake was not to fully recognize the limited amounts of soft power available to local government.

These very different partings of the way suggest that the high tide of network governance theory may have passed and that the time is ripe for a rethink. The major theoretical question is why the disjuncture between the ideology, theory and practice of networks? What kind of theory is capable of explaining it and, at the same time, of offering a different approach to studying governance? Flinders (2005, p 87) put the question succinctly in asking of New Labour how it could be that a government ostensibly committed to devolving power was seen 'at the same time, as having a strong centralising and controlling approach to governing'. This question recurs again and again in the social sciences, wherever claims are made for the novelty or redemptive potential of networks. The explanation developed in Chapters Four to Six is that network governance is a form of neoliberal ideology, defined not simply as the championing of free markets but as an active project for economic and political modernisation inspired by informational capitalism, the heart of the 'connectionist' objective of fostering an entrepreneurial, reflexive and communicative sociability. The ideology of network governance can therefore be understood in Gramscian terms as part of a hegemonic project for cultivating the dispositions of the 'combinard'. As a modernisation strategy, however, it confronts intractable barriers such as the trend towards political and economic centralisation characteristic of crisis-prone capitalist modernity.

In contrast with network governance theory and inspired by Marxism, the book emphasises historical continuities in the nature of states, capitals and classes. Drawing from Gramsci's theory of the integral state, the dialectical unity of state and civil society (where 'dialectical' refers to an enduring antagonistic relationship), it argues that coercion is the immanent condition of consent inherent in capitalist modernity. As long as hegemony is partial and precarious, hierarchy can never completely retreat to the shadows. This dialectic plays out in the day-to-day politics of governance networks through the clash between connectionist ideology and roll-forward hierarchy or 'governmentalisation'. The idea of the integral state thus helps to explain why 'modernist' continuities tend to trump any incipient trends toward network governance. It seeks to resituate the institutional and organisational levels of analysis in a systemic analysis (for example Benson, 1977) obscured by the tendency for governance research to focus on meso-analysis. Changing the background assumptions in this way helps make sense of the striking tendency for actually-existing governance networks to subvert network governance. The challenge of researching governance as hegemony is therefore to explore how this dialectic operates, or not, in the routine politics of networks and other governing institutions.

It must be stated at the outset that the target of critique is not the concept of networks per se. Networks and connectedness matter in all human societies. The information age undoubtedly furnishes some people with the ability to connect more extensively with other people than before, although there is nothing inherent in technologies like the internet that preclude them being the medium of hierarchical power. The challenge is to grasp the nature, quality and purpose of connections and the power relations they embody. As Hart (2003, p 221) cautioned, we should not 'imagine that network society is necessarily non-hierarchical or open'. On the contrary, connectedness is a form of power and can be a medium of exclusion, or 'netsploitation' (Jansen, 2002, p 272). Yet, it is not sufficient merely to acknowledge that networks can reproduce power inequalities. It is also necessary to put them in their place, considering why hierarchical power remains pervasive and cannot be displaced by network power. As Thompson (2003, p 17) commented, while networks and flows matter they are a 'limited governance/coordinating device, which have to be properly placed in a wider context of other socio-organizational mechanisms of management and regulation'. The target is the post-traditional transformation thesis, which depicts the network as a virtuous mode of sociability suited to an epoch in which hierarchy is increasingly redundant.

The discussion proceeds in three steps. Chapters One and Two are an overview, respectively, of the intellectual influences on governance theory and the rise of governance networks in the world of public policy. Chapters Three and Four turn to critique: first the limits of network governance theory in explaining critical empirical observations about governance networks and then an alternative theoretical platform grounded in Marxism from which to reconsider governance as hegemony. Chapters Five and Six elaborate the Gramscian conception of 'governance as hegemony' and reflect on the research implications of a Gramscian approach.

Chapter One begins by exploring the roots of orthodox network governance theory and the variety of approaches influenced by post-traditional ideas. It then discusses the roots of post-traditional thinking in social theory, notably the theory of reflexive modernisation (Beck, 1992; Giddens, 1994, 1998). Reflexive modernisation is by no means a master-concept. However, it is a clear statement of the transformation thesis and has influenced both governance theories and policies, notably through 'The Third Way'. The latter part of the chapter examines the influence of post-traditional thought on currents in contemporary Marxism and emancipatory theory. It illustrates that the network is at the heart of a cross-disciplinary, cross-theoretical orthodoxy influencing elites and subalterns alike: the move from command to cooperation, being to becoming and fixity to flow.

Chapter Two explores the diffusion of network governance ideologies and the cultivation of governance networks globally. Using the evolution of New Labour as its paradigm case it shows how ideas like reflexive modernisation influenced political thinking through network governance policies. The question posed by Chapter Two is the extent to which, in internalising and advocating influential academic ideas governments are able to perform the 'theory effect', cultivating institutions and practices faithful to the concepts that inspire them.

Chapter Three begins developing the critique of network governance theory, exploring the avalanche of literatures suggesting that state–market–civil society networks are 'governance as usual'. Governance networks often turn out to be the same kinds of institutions as those they were meant to transcend, replicating hierarchies, exclusions and inequalities and arguably aggravating endemic distrust. The latter part of the chapter explores the strengths and weaknesses of the Foucauldian account as a critical perspective from within the post-traditional milieu itself, arguing that despite its undoubted potency, it is undermined by scepticism towards structure and the consequent failure adequately to recognise the role of capitalist state as an agent of both governmentality and coercive power.

Chapter Four takes the critique beyond post-traditional terrain, restating the case for Marxist analysis. It begins by arguing for a critical-realist conception of structure and contradiction, recognising the causal powers of both structures and agents and the contradictory nature of structures, such as capitalism. It reiterates the Marxist point that the crisis-prone nature of capitalism ultimately renders the whole social formation, the contradictory totality, unstable and open to transformation. The chapter then revisits claims that capitals, states and classes are being transformed, arguing instead that there are powerful continuities ignored by post-traditional theory. These include the concentration and centralisation of capital, the effective capture of states by the imperatives of economic and geopolitical competition, new processes of class formation and the revival of class militancy. Substituting these alternative 'background assumptions' for the post-traditional worldview casts a very different light on the purported rise of the networked polity, suggesting that it is better understood as an ideology, but in socioeconomic conditions that render it utopian.

Chapter Five develops this thinking, drawing on the work of Antonio Gramsci. In place of the transformation thesis, it proposes that the ideology of networks can be understood as a central facet of the neoliberal hegemonic project. It attributes the rise of the connectionist project to the confluence of four factors: the social, economic and political crises of the late 1960s, the defeat of the social movements of 1968 and after, the recuperation of parts of the left critique of capitalism by avant garde entrepreneurs and managers and the rise of informational capitalism. Amid the bankruptcy of Keynesianism and the struggles over who should pay for the crisis, it gradually crystallised as the agenda of incipient neoliberal regimes for the modernisation of states, markets, corporations and societies. Network governance ideology is one manifestation of that agenda. The chapter suggests that the neoliberal project may have succeeded to the extent that it fosters de-politicised governance networks and enrols new layers of civil society activists. However, as Chapter Three highlighted, it cannot transcend hierarchy, which is integral to the governance system. In other words, the explanation for why the purported rise of the network is 'governance as usual' lies in tendencies towards the centralisation of power across economy, state and society. These tendencies manifest in the day-to-day politics of governance networks, enacting the dialectics of the integral state. Hence, although local conditions may be more or less favourable, it would be very surprising indeed if authentic and sustainable network governance emerged on a significant scale in the capitalist epoch. The final part of Chapter Five considers the importance of connectionist ideology in the context of other hegemonic technologies upon which its credibility depends.

Chapter Six reflects on the research implications of the preceding arguments. It begins by linking the Gramscian approach with dialectical network analysis (Benson, 1977). It develops three heuristics to summarise the substantive theoretical and empirical claims developed in preceding chapters and inform future research. The first summarises the Gramscian perspective at the macro, meso and micro levels of analysis. The second highlights the distinctions between the Marxist-Gramscian 'strongly dialectical' approach, the 'weakly dialectical' approach associated with neo-Gramscians and the 'post-dialectical' account characteristic of approaches such as the Differentiated Polity Model (Rhodes, 1997). The third heuristic considers possible varieties of governance from the standpoint of hegemony, domination and resistance. Chapter Six then explores the dilemmas of researching network governance as hegemony, considering the role of critical researchers as would-be public intellectuals and potentially fruitful research strategies for studying governance networks comparatively. Since the ultimate purpose of Gramscian critique and inquiry is emancipatory, to challenge and transcend structures of domination, it reflects finally on the respective merits of networked and concentrated forms of resistance.

Chapter Seven concludes by revisiting the main arguments for rejecting the transformation thesis and reconsidering governance from Marxist and Gramscian perspectives.

Note

[1]Thanks to Helen Sullivan for pointing out that I needed a distinction of this kind for the sake of clarity.

ONE

The network governance milieu

Introduction

Chapter One begins by exploring core ideas in network governance theory understood as the 'orthodoxy'. It then discusses the variety of approaches that espouse post-traditional ideas about changing forms of governance. The second part of the chapter explores the intellectual roots of post-traditional thinking through the lens of the theory of reflexive modernisation, perhaps the most influential social-theoretical current in contemporary public policy. The chapter concludes by considering the influence of post-traditional thought on contemporary Marxism. It therefore demonstrates how the network is celebrated across a wide spectrum of mainstream and critical theory. Chapter Two then charts the rise of the governing network in international public policy.

The rise of network analysis

Although it only recently became fashionable, the study of networks is far from new. Exploring the history of formal network analysis, organisation theorists Borgatti et al (2009) cite the development of Moreno's 'sociometry' in the 1930s as the precursor to Social Network Analysis (SNA). Moreno famously explained a spate of truancies in terms of the position of central protagonists in a network of absconding school students. Whyte's (1943) study of 'Street Corner Society' modelled the relationship between group structure and individual performance. He found that the most successful individuals were those best connected within a network. In the 1950s, experimental studies of networks purported to show that centralised decision-making was more effective than decentralised (Borgatti et al, 2009, p 892). Borgatti et al chart how network theories thrived in anthropology during the 1960s as scholars discovered that society is not monolithic, but consists of patterned relationships. They studied networks using relational algebra and saw them as a way of explaining social outcomes, a form of structural analysis used in SNA and research on the causal power of policy networks, discussed later. In the mid-1970s, Granovetter (1973) developed his influential theory of the strength of weak ties, underpinning social capital theory and neo-institutionalism and drawing attention to the relationship between connectedness, resources and wellbeing. SNA became established in the 1980s and, with the rise of postmodernism, network theories 'radiated into a great number of fields, including physics and biology' (Borgatti et al, 2009, p 893). The basic premise of SNA, or formal network analysis, is that people, being social animals, network and that our networking affects social outcomes. SNA makes no special claims for networking as 'the good' or as the emblem of social change. It is often used to study elites and could, in theory, tell us much about the relational dimensions of an extreme hierarchy like Stalin's Politburo. Formal network analysis is adept at finding patterns in self-organising networks, which protagonists may or may not recognise as networks.

Another venerable tradition in network analysis, influential in political science, is the model of policy networks as 'a structure of resource-dependent organisations' (Rhodes, 1997, p 24). The resource dependency model draws attention to the interdependence of powerful state and non-state actors in policy arenas like British agriculture, where the network was long dominated by the Ministry of Agriculture and the National Farmers Union, and health, where it was dominated by the ministry and hospital consultants. Debate flourished about the nature of resource dependency networks and the degree to which they could explain policy outcomes (Jordan, 1990; Marsh and Rhodes, 1992; Marsh and Smith, 2000; Evans, 2001). Various heuristics were developed to classify networks, such as the 'policy community' and the 'issue network'. Policy communities are relatively stable networks, usually based on interdependence between governmental and non-governmental elites like those in agriculture and health. They are prone to path-dependency and, in times of 'normal' policy, change only incrementally. Policy making is segmented into relatively impermeable subsystems or silos comprising resource-rich actors who negotiate around common or congruent interests. In issue networks, on the other hand, power and dependency relationships are diffuse and the locus of decision making is harder to trace (Thompson, 2003, p 152). Resource-dependency theorists recognised that policy communities could fracture into issue networks, such as when the 'salmonella in eggs affair' triggered a political crisis allowing health interests to gain new leverage in agricultural policy (Smith, 1991). During crises, actors external to the network can influence the policy field. However, powerful actors typically regain the upper hand and a new process of closure reinstates the policy community, perhaps around a different interest group configuration. (Chapter Three discusses network closure in greater depth.) The resource dependency model draws attention to the importance of networks as power structures, but like formal network analysis makes no special claims about the rise of networking or the transition to a networked society.

Post-traditional network governance theory

The rise of post-traditional network governance theory marked a paradigm shift. Governments and businesses, trade unions, intellectuals and community groups all became increasingly conscious of the virtues of connectedness and seek to foster networks (Thompson, 2003, pp 28-9). We are in the era of 'newly acknowledged interdependence' (Hay, 2010, p 19). During the 1980s and early 1990s, the Gramscian conception of hegemony was widely used to explain governing strategies such as Thatcherism (for example Hall and Jacques, 1983; Jessop et al, 1988; Gamble, 1994). However, following the grave defeats suffered by the left internationally, Gramscian and neo-Gramscian research became rarer and lost influence in governance and public policy, although it remains prominent in geography and international political economy (see Chapter Two for an extended discussion of these issues). A new set of conceptual tools became popular, influenced by post-traditional thinking and dispensing with hegemony and counter-hegemony along with the much derided 'command and control' model. 'Post-hegemonic' theory (Johnson, 2007) became established as the orthodoxy.

Network governance is a good example of post-hegemonic theory. It is distinguished by the analytical and normative priority accorded to networking, depicted variously as the 'new ingredient' in governance (Lowndes, 2001, p 1962), as a virtuous form of social interaction and as symbolic of the transformation to post or second modernity. Unlike the more ebullient social theorists, few empirically minded governance theorists argue that governance networks render conflict and hierarchy obsolete. Nevertheless, there was a pronounced tendency for network-boosterism in 'first-wave' governance theory. Rhodes, among the most influential network theorists, argued that with the demise of the Westminster Model and the fragmentation of the welfare state under the New Public Management, coordination was increasingly organised through networks conceived as the dynamic or novel element in a 'mix' with hierarchies and markets. However, Rhodes also defined 'governance *as* networks', stating that they 'are the analytical heart of the notion of governance in the study of public administration' (2000a, p 60, emphasis added). Through such elisions the mix could be forgotten and 'governance' was quickly captured as a synonym for 'networks'. Even when the 'mix' was acknowledged in the abstract, hierarchy and inequality were prone to disappearing from the story. Bevir and Rhodes (2008, p 729) conceded as much in debate with Marsh (2008) when they stated that they were, of course, aware of inequalities within networks but were interested in a different research question.

Rhodes' approach is often called the 'Differentiated Polity Model' or the 'Anglo-Governance School'. It is more or less closely related to continental approaches such as the Danish 'Democratic Anchorage' School (for example Bogason, 2000; Sorensen and Torfing, 2008), and the Dutch 'Network Management' School (for example Kickert et al, 1997). These 'schools' (for example Hall et al, 2009), or traditions have different preoccupations and are influenced by different theorists. Agger et al (2008, p 36) of the Danish School, for example, are critical of the 'consensus' view of networks they associate with neo-institutionalism. They see networks as being about 'power games' and 'conflictual contestation' based on 'agonistic respect' and the mutual recognition of rights, hinging on the development of trust. They differ again from thinkers who see network governance as the potential medium of an equitable deliberative discourse (see Chapter Three for a more detailed discussion). These differences are important, but each tradition recognises that there has been a tendential move from government to governance in 'complex, fragmented and multilayered societies' (Agger et al, 2008, p 15). Accordingly, each sees the network as an increasingly important medium of political association. As Bevir and Rhodes (2010, p 83) put it: 'Social scientists typically describe network governance as consisting of something akin to a differentiated polity characterised by a hollowed-out state, a core executive fumbling to pull rubber levers of control, and, most notably, a massive proliferation of networks'. Network governance is supposed to offer flexible solutions to political problems, or so-called 'wicked issues' and, for advocates, escape the limits of the command state and market fundamentalism.

As was suggested in preceding paragraphs, part of the explanation for network-boosterism is that even when the 'mix' is taken seriously, the network is still accorded analytical and normative priority. Anglo-European governance research frequently demarks periods, suggesting a shift from the Keynesian Welfare State (hierarchy), to networked governance via market fundamentalism (neoliberalism) (for example Kickert et al, 1997, p 40; Kjaer, 2004, pp 38-40; Bevir, 2010, p 103). Scholars often temper or qualify the periodisation, but it remains part of the orthodoxy. As Newman (2004, p 71) notes:

> Governance theory starts from the proposition that we are witnessing a shift from government (through direct control) to governance (through steering, influencing, and collaborating with multiple actors in a dispersed system). The predominant focus is on the increasing significance of governance through networks as an alternative to markets and hierarchy ... The state, it is argued, can no longer assume a monopoly of expertise or resources necessary to govern, and must look to a plurality of interdependent institutions drawn from the public, private and voluntary sectors.

Stoker's influential work on networked community governance was part of this analytical trend, arguing that while 'the old has not entirely given way to a finally formed new', 'the obituaries for the old system can be written' (2004, p 9). Pierre and Stoker (2000, p 29) argued:

> Today, the role of the *government* in the process of *governance* is much more contingent. Local, regional, and national political elites alike seek to forge coalitions with private businesses, voluntary associations and other societal actors to mobilize resources across the public–private border in order to enhance their chances of guiding society towards politically defined goals.

Similar narratives on the nature of social change became common across Europe (Denters and Rose, 2005). According to Bogason (2000, p 4), as state–civil society collaboration proliferates internationally, network analysis is increasingly seen as the most effective means for understanding collective action, with network governance seen as the most effective means for organising it.

Kooiman (2000, p 138), one of the leading Dutch scholars of governance networks, argues similarly that the challenge is how to govern in a 'shared power, no-one in charge, interdependent world'. However, the new world is not so complex that it cannot be directed subtly. In their influential work on network management, Kickert et al (1997, p 39) argue that network governance is about 'directed influencing', creating conditions for collective action without prescribing ends, to achieve 'mutually beneficial solutions' and 'integrative negotiation' (1997, p 40). Networking is thus a consensus-oriented mode of coordination, encouraging the mutual adjustment of actors' behaviour. Contributing to the mood of optimism, Lowndes and Wilson (2003, p 277) observed that '[e]clecticism is an institutional design principle whose time has come and which encourages reflexivity and learning, and signals the end of modernist "grand narratives" about the "right way" to govern'. Network governance became, to borrow from Hardt and Negri (2000, p 280), 'hegemonic in qualitative terms'.

Networks based on trust

According to Rhodes (2007, p 1246), 'governance as networks' has four characteristics: 'interdependence between organizations', 'continuing interactions between network members', 'game-like interactions rooted in trust' and 'a significant degree of autonomy from the state'. Networks are 'self-organizing' and the state, now just one governance actor among many, can steer them only 'indirectly and imperfectly'. Trust therefore displaces command as the primary coordinating mechanism. As Frances et al (1991, p 15) put it, '[i]f it is price competition that is the central co-ordinating mechanism of the market and administrative orders that of hierarchy, then it is trust and co-operation that centrally articulates networks'. Network governance depends on 'co-existent attributes such as sympathy, customary reciprocity, moral norms, common experience, trust, duty, obligation and similar virtues' (Thompson, 2003, p 40). If they are to thrive, argues Thompson, 'a generalized trust, honesty, and solidarity must transcend any minor negotiating infringements'and 'a shared common overriding objective' must exist. The existence of authentic network governance therefore depends on the cultivation of these 'ethical virtues' (Thompson, 2003, p 47).

Whereas for formal network analysts elites and hierarchies can be depicted in network form, network governance is a very different mechanism, mixing with hierarchies and markets 'like oil and water' because they have a 'corrosive effect … undermining trust, reciprocity, informality and cooperation' (Rhodes, 2000a, p 82). Network governance depends on a 'value system of mutual interest, trust and reciprocity' across state, market and civil society (Stewart, 2003, p 76). As Lambright et al (2010, p 77) put it, 'trusting relationships facilitate cooperation in networks. Trust acts as the glue that holds networks together, enabling networks to function effectively even though they lack a hierarchical power structure'. The obvious implication is that if there has been an authentic transformation from hierarchical to network governance, high levels of trust must be present. The social basis of trust is the preoccupation of diverse literatures influenced, for example, by Transaction Cost Analysis, SNA (for example Bachmann and Zaheer, 2008; Kenis and Oerlemans, 2008; Thompson, 2003) and sociological institutionalism (Granovetter, 1973). For present purposes, however, it is sufficient to notice that in the post-traditional account network governance requires trust and by implication no trust means no network. (Chapter Three returns to this issue.) This, then, is the complex of ideas that Marinetto (2003a) and Marsh (2008) call the new 'orthodoxy' in contemporary governance theory. As the orthodoxy, it has a substantial reach and influences many perspectives, from neo-institutionalism to contemporary Marxism.

Neo-institutionalism

Neo-institutionalism is one of the approaches most closely associated with the rise of network governance theory (March and Olsen, 1989). Lowndes (2001, p 1958), for example, identified six assumptions distinguishing 'old' from 'new' institutionalism. The latter is based on the shift from: the study of organisations to the study of rules, a formal to an informal conception of institutions, a static to a dynamic conception, submerged values to a value-critical stance, a holistic to a disaggregated conception of institutions and from the conception of institutional independence to embeddedness or interdependence. Like the three European traditions discussed earlier, neo-institutionalism assumes a shift from fixity to flow and portrays governance as networked. As Lowndes (2001, p 1962) put it, governance networks are promoted by governments in a 'strategically selective' context that favours networking, although hierarchies and markets remain an important part of the mix. For neo-institutionalists networks are embedded through learning and developing shared norms and trust, affective relationships that constitute the 'logic of appropriateness'.

Social capital

In a different tenor, networks are also heralded as important mechanisms for developing 'social capital', defined as citizen connectivity and involvement in community affairs (Putnam, 2000). Civic traditions like community networks 'generate social connectedness and social participation, enabling participants to act together more effectively in the pursuit of shared objectives' (Thompson, 2003, pp 167-8). In other words, the more connected they are the more people cultivate trust and serve civic ends, becoming embedded in a cycle of virtuous returns. According to Francis Fukuyama, strong social capital was the means by which liberal democracy sealed its post-Cold War triumph because 'spontaneous sociability and a healthy economy go together' (cited in Thompson, 2003, p 169), a combination unavailable to the sclerotic dictatorships of Eastern Europe. Social capital is one of the virtues that neo-institutionalists believe networks can cultivate (Rothstein and Stolle, 2008).

Adaptive leadership

The influence of post-traditional ideology is also prominent in contemporary leadership studies. Grint, for example, notes that 'in the attempt to escape from the clutches of heroic leadership, we now seem enthralled by its apparent opposite – distributed leadership' (2010, p 89). Instead of being concentrated in the hands of Weberian charismatics, the tasks of leadership are depicted as increasingly distributed, 'an emergent property of the group, network or community' (2010, p 90). Distributed or adaptive leadership is another facet of the transformation thesis, deriving from the purported decline of the structures of industrial society, rising complexity and the associated need for reflexive, non-coercive leaders. According to Bentley and Wilsdon (2003, p 26), leadership is adaptive 'when it responds to changes in its environment without central direction or control, while retaining some core structure or values'. They argue in the same vernacular as network governance theorists that public services are complex adaptive systems and cannot be understood using the 'mechanistic models' that they claim dominated traditional thinking. For Hartley and Allison (2000, p 36), adaptive leadership arises in a world of 'increasing complexity and uncertainty', its task to work on tough problems – those 'wicked issues' for which there are no off-the-shelf solutions. They conclude (2000, p 39) that leadership is not about 'directing a steady state organisation where the problems and the solutions are largely known'; it 'takes place in a context of change, flux and uncertainty'. The qualities required of the adaptive leader in developing innovative solutions, are those of the combinard: affectivity, trust and reflexivity (Heifetz et al, 2009).

Urban Regime Theory

An example of a somewhat different kind is Urban Regime Theory, one of the most influential theories of urban politics over the past 20 years. Regime theory, emanating from the US, rose to prominence more or less concurrently with other theories discussed in this chapter. It too is based on the critique of structuralism. Clarence Stone (1989), its most influential theorist, asserted against his understanding of Marxism that the notion of a comprehensively rational ruling class exercising command power is implausible. He took a process-oriented approach to power, arguing that those actors endowed with the most resources are in the best position to forge alliances in informal regimes capable of pre-empting the governing agenda and denying others access to it. The key actors are corporate leaders and local government elites because ownership of productive assets rests in the hands of business, whereas the machinery of government is subject to popular control through elections and other public inputs. Systemic power is the relationship between public and private power at the macro level, negotiated and enacted at the city scale through regime politics. However, business control over production tends to give it a privileged voice. Urban regimes are founded on the need for city managers to raise revenue by securing the consent of corporations to purchasing city bonds and levying taxes, which they do only if they favour the policies of the authority in question. These fiscal strictures create an environment where businesses and city governments find congruent interests and construct governing alliances around them.

Regime theory is therefore influenced by Lindblom's (1977) neo-pluralist proposition that in market societies governments are generally predisposed to indulge the preferences of business leaders. However, successful governance occurs only when the key actors manage to form an alliance and pre-empt the governing agenda. This does not always happen – inertia or non-governance is a significant risk. Stone's (1989) classic case study of Atlanta is the paradigmatic example of a business regime, an enduring relationship between local state and down-town corporate elites in pursuit of economic development that coopted the emerging Black middle class, marginalised lower-class interests and survived some 40 years.

This account may appear to bring back Marxism through the back door, but Stone saw it as a decisive break because of the inherent contingency in the governing arrangements (see Chapter Four for a critique of Stone's position on capital and class). Regimes are hard to build and depend on resource-rich actors recognising congruent interests and forming coalitions around them. Stone was influenced, among others, by Charles Tilly (for example Tilly, 1984, 2001), who started life as a structuralist but later developed a relational ontology emphasising social embeddedness over both structure and rational choice. Relational sociology focuses on process rather than object and the nature of the connections that create embedded institutions. Neo-institutionalism has a Tillyan flavour.

Stone adapted the Tillyan perspective to argue that the different spheres of society – state, market and civil society – are loosely coupled and that consequently there is relatively low structural coherence between them. This underlying position is sceptical towards theories of totality, explaining why regime building and maintenance must be done actively and why in some policy fields, like education, there is purportedly greater potential for progressive regime politics than in economic development, closely tied to business control of production, distribution and exchange. Albeit by a somewhat different route, then, Urban Regime Theory reflects elements of the post-traditional critique. An important difference is that Stone (2009, pp 266-7) rejects any notion of a transition from 'government' to 'governance', is profoundly concerned with inequality and, like other resource dependency theorists, sees collaboration between governmental and non-governmental actors as the always-existing historical condition of political action. Regime theory works with a decentred conception of power, but rejects the transformation thesis.

Regulation Theory

In contrast, Regulation Theory remains grounded in neo-Marxist political economy and crisis-theory. Again, however, it imports aspects of the transformation thesis, discovering a shift from hierarchical to networked modes of social regulation. The Regulation School (for example Boyer, 1990) noted the emergent crisis of Fordism – the era of mass production and mass consumption – after the late 1960s, itself arising from crisis tendencies in the accumulation process. The regulation approach is diverse and, depending on perspective, asserts that we have moved to an era of disorganised capitalism (Offe and Keane, 1985), post-Fordism (Amin, 1994) or, more cautiously, the 'search for a fix' based on post-Fordist principles of flexible accumulation, part-time employment, the reform of the welfare state, the decline of trade union solidarity and the rise of network governance (James, 2009). While many of the conditions for post-Fordism were enacted by the New Right, there were also more or less progressive variants, depending on the nature of the political regime through which it was mediated.

Alongside urban regime theory, and sometimes in synthesis with it (Lauria, 1997), the regulation approach was much used in the study of urban governance during the 1990s. With the upward aggregation of power at the supranational scale and the devolution of some responsibilities for economic development, it argued that the nation-state was squeezed in a global–local dialectic (Harding, 1994). This interpretation drew attention away from the national to the supranational and subnational scales and, with the latter, towards phenomena such as the network governance of economic development in 'entrepreneurial cities'. Although it is no longer as influential as in the 1990s, one of its most distinguished practitioners, Bob Jessop, still posits the shift from the Keynesian Welfare National State (KWNS) to the Schumpeterian Workfare Post-national Regime (SWPR) in quasi-Regulationist terms including, among other features, the rise of networks. As Chapters Four to Six highlight, the regulation approach overlaps closely with neo-Gramscian and 'weakly-dialectical' analyses of contemporary political economy. For Jessop (2007a, p 187), the evolution from Fordism to post-Fordism was marked by:

> ... its emphasis on mobilizing social as well as economic sources of flexibility and entrepreneurialism and ... general attempts to penetrate micro-social relations in the interests of valorization. It is reflected in the emphasis now given to building social capital, trust, and communities of learning as well as to the competitive role of entrepreneurial cities, enterprise culture, and enterprising subjects.

Jessop (2007a, p 21), however, does not celebrate the tendential development of the SWPR and, though using 'post-national' language, rejects the view that it represents the demise of the nation state. If SWPR trends include the hollowing out of the state, the de-statification of politics and the globalisation of policy regimes, noted Jessop, counter-trends include increased scope for state influence over inter-scalar articulations, the contestation and implementation of international or global policy regimes and the state-led orchestration of metagovernance (the governance of governance).

Metagovernance

Bevir and Rhodes (2010) describe metagovernance theory as a 'second wave' in governance research following the 'first-wave' Anglo-Governance School. While accepting elements of the 'first-wave' idea of a shift from hierarchies to markets and networks, metagovernance theorists are sceptical of claims that the role of the state has diminished. Metagovernance brings the state back in as the coordinator of myriad self-regulating governance mechanisms and, in the case of governance failure, as accountable body of last resort (Jessop, 2000). As Somerville (2004, p 139) argued, metagovernance requires the state to act strategically. However, its strategic role differs from that of the command state in that while it must still be capable of exercising command power, its role today is much more reflexive, that of coordinator in chief (including coordinating its own decentred activities), inter-scalar mediator, bricoleur, medium of democratic accountability and legitimacy and institutional entrepreneur (Crouch, 2005). To this extent, metagovernance theory is also about transformation, but influenced by the regulation approach and from a perspective that brings back the state in a manner rejected by Bevir and Rhodes (2010, p 88) as 'modernist empiricism' by other means. It too shares common ground with neo-Gramscian approaches.

The theory of reflexive modernisation

Bang (2008) observes that political science has 'grown deaf to macro-models', arguing that it should acknowledge new meta-theories such as the hugely influential 'network society' (Castells, 1996) and 'theory of reflexive modernisation' (Beck, 1992; Giddens, 1994). As he points out, these theories differ on the precise nature of transformation and its implications for political organisation. However, as Chapter Two highlights, the theory of reflexive modernisation has arguably been more influential in contemporary public policy than other 'grand narrative' theories of transformation, notably through the auspices of Giddens' (1998) *The Third Way*. Wetherly (2000, pp 71-2) argues that reflexive modernisation represents a much wider current in mainstream sociology, reflected to a greater or lesser degree in political science, public policy and contemporary governance scholarship. It is the intellectual touchstone of the transformation thesis and worth discussing in some depth.

The theory of reflexive modernisation was founded by Ulrich Beck and has been elaborated in different ways by, among others, Bauman, Giddens and Lash (see Beck et al, 1994, for a debate). The core claims pertain to the decline of tradition, the rise of the individual, the rise of the 'risk society' and the dawn of an age of reflexive modernisation in which the structures of industrial society are dissolving, replaced by fluid networked relationships among reflexive individuals.

Beck's ground-breaking analysis of 'the risk society' posits the rise of risk as the unintended consequence of 'industrial society', a concept he disaggregates from capitalism but which often appears (like neoliberalism) as a euphemism for it. His paradigm example is the environmental hazard generated by industry (the Bhopal disaster occurred shortly before he published *Risk Society* in German in 1986) and the pervasiveness of invisible toxins in the atmosphere, water and food supplies. Beck argued that industrial society has generated novel risks that, unlike economic inequality, have global and universal effects

(1992, p 13). Big business is certainly a major producer of environmental risk, but unlike poverty it produces a boomerang effect. When risk manifests in injury or illness, it strikes back at the risk producers, who are themselves unwitting consumers of the toxins they unleash. Hence, Beck's famous aphorism 'poverty is hierarchic, smog is democratic' (1992, p 36). These manufactured risks pose a greater threat to all than class-based economic inequalities do to specific social groups, persistent though these may be. The emergence of the risk society therefore begins, tendentially, to trump class cleavages with a universal challenge, one of the pre-conditions for 'inclusive' network governance.

For Beck, science became the 'secular religion of modernity' through its claims to objective knowledge and omnipotence (1992, p 214). In its industrial form it is responsible for both the proliferation of risks that escape immediate detection and are thus ignored until they become disasters and the hubristic assumption that risk is calculable (1992, p 83). The challenge of reflexive modernisation is to develop a reflexive science that concedes the boundedness of human knowledge, the uncertainties and complexities arising from human action, the interpenetration of the social and the natural worlds and the inherently sociological dimensions of technological risk (1992, p 5). Science cannot determine risk with any precision and meaningful estimates must depend on the testimonies of those exposed to it. Beck therefore heralds the rise of the environmental movement as the sign of an emergent critical, reflexive subjectivity of risk awareness, challenging the cult of experts and subjecting risk production to public scrutiny (1992, p 155); a distributed and networked mode of social critique.

One of Beck's most important claims (2007) is that with the rise of an '*objective community*' of global risk class decays into a 'zombie category' (1992, p 46, original emphasis), and 'members of divergent classes, parties, occupational groups and age groups organize into citizens' movements' (1992, p 47). Whereas in first modernity the struggle for the reproduction of being determined consciousness, in the risk society risk-consciousness determines being (1992, p 23). Translated into *The Third Way* (Giddens, 1998), risk management becomes a raison d'être of contemporary politics, a process of practical problem solving by active, responsible citizens unfettered by traditional cleavages.

In both Beck's and Giddens' accounts, the potential for risk reflexivity hinges on conquering scarcity. Plenitude undermines the imperative for continued expansion of the means of production as material needs are satisfied and enables our attention to be drawn to the risks arising from production. Reflexive modernisation therefore presages post-materialism, where quality of life issues supersede day-to-day struggles for economic survival (Giddens, 1998, p 19; Beck and Beck-Gernsheim, 2002, p 212). Post-scarcity by no means signals universal abundance, but rather weakens 'the drive to continuous accumulation' among the prosperous (Beck et al, 1994, p 195). In other words, saturation consumption decentres the accumulation imperative, frees us from the realm of necessity and creates time for new preoccupations.

The second fundamental concept of reflexive modernisation is individualisation. Beck acknowledges that there have been several waves of individualisation, including the demise of chattel slavery and the emancipation of the peasantry, cast off the land and into the capitalist labour market by the enclosures movement (Beck and Beck-Gernsheim, 2002, p 202). Here, he endorses Marx's account of capitalism as a system continually uprooting communities and giving birth to the class of deracinated wage labourers, freed from feudal ties but with nothing to sell but their labour power in a one-on-one contract with the capitalist. However, new traditions evolved or persisted alongside earlier waves of individualisation, not least through the class consciousness forged, Beck argues, in common experiences of immiseration and also through national identities emerging alongside the national organisation of capitalist production and, much later, the welfare state (Beck, 1992, p 95).

The present epoch of individualisation is distinguished by the fact that old traditions are eroding without new ones arising in their place. According to the theory of reflexive modernisation, the rise of the Western European welfare state created the conditions for class consciousness but ultimately undermined it by creating an educated, relatively prosperous citizenry capable of thinking and acting for itself. Vast inequalities still exist, but these are confronted by disembedded individuals – the socially excluded – rather than organised class interests. Gender-based traditions and divisions of labour within the nuclear family are similarly undermined by increased female control over fertility, the feminisation of the workforce and the legal and cultural legitimacy of divorce. The nuclear family is therefore on the way to becoming another 'zombie category' (Beck, 1992, p 112). The Westphalian notion of nationhood (and other traditional forms of spatial community such as city and neighbourhood) is also crumbling as the globalisation of risk production and the information revolution annihilate space and uproot traditional identities. Nation (and hence methodological nationalism) is another emerging zombie category because the state is too small to deal with global problems and too large to deal with local ones (Beck et al, 1994, p 192). Hence, the development of suprastate institutions like the European Union, which

Beck sees as a form of networked polity (Beck and Grande, 2007, p 69). A fourth source of individualisation is the changing nature of work, with the decline of the 'old hulks' of mass production (Beck, 1992, p 215) and the rise of flexible, high-technology enterprises in the knowledge economy. Informational capitalism requires that the individualised worker demonstrates uniqueness, as the added value he/she brings resides in intellectual creativity, or immaterial labour, rather than repetitive physical labour (1992, p 94). However, the flexibility of informational capitalism also undermines stable employment, creating meaningful choices for privileged workers, but precariousness and underemployment for millions of others (Giddens, 2007, pp 84-5), most strikingly in the barrios, townships and favelas of the developing world.

Thus, all the foundations of class, space, nation, family, profession, science, progress and democracy 'begin to crumble and disintegrate in the reflexivity of modernization' (Beck, 1992, p 14). Beck leaves open the question of whether individualisation might unite individuals as subjects self-conscious of their own affairs, or sweep away the 'last bastions of social and political action' leading to 'insidious forms of a modernized barbarism' (1992, p 101). This uncertainty is reflected in the changing emphasis he gives to key terms. For example, depending on the mood of the text, 'reflexivity' can refer to the knee-jerk or anomic reaction to a world in which we are deracinated and compelled to be free, or to empowered critical reflection and conscious action on the risk environment. Bauman (2002, p xvi) notes the distinction in Beck between individuality as fate and as self-assertion. In the former case, the term individualisation usually applies. 'Individuation' refers to the optimistic account of individualisation as self-realisation asserted notably by Giddens in *The Third Way*. Limerick et al (1993, p 121) describe the archetypal combinard as someone 'emancipated by discontinuity, empowered by knowledge and driven by values. They collaborate with others because they agree with their values and the joint mission, and not because of their commitment to the organization'.

Risk and individualisation are more menacing in Beck's account than in Giddens'. The individual of second modernity bears little resemblance to the rational calculating subject of classical economics, often cutting a lonely, fretful path through life, ill-equipped to manage the risks he/she must confront. Individualisation 'means market dependency in all dimensions of living' (Beck, 1992, p 132) and is juxtaposed with the increasing standardisation of markets, money and education. Thus, the individual lacks the haven of tradition, but is subjected to an '*institution-dependent control structure*' (1992, p 131, original emphasis). Risks and contradictions are still 'socially produced', 'it is just the duty and the necessity to cope with them that is being individualized' (Bauman, 2002, p xvi). The deracinated individual has no choice but to make decisions and actively construct a biography that would previously have been inscribed by tradition. As Bauman (2002, p xv) put it, individualisation transforms identity from 'a "given" into a "task"' performed by individuals, endowing them with *de jure* but not *de facto* autonomy. Reflexive modernisation is 'forcing men and women to be constantly on the move and promising no rest and no satisfaction on "arrival", no comfort on reaching the destination where one can disarm, relax and stop worrying'. Bauman (2002, p xvi) concludes that 'individualization is a fate, not a choice'. Or, in Giddens' terms (1994, p 7), 'clever people' are today confronted by a world saturated with information previously confined to experts. Post-traditionality compels them to interpret and act upon it 'if they are to survive'. As Beck put it, he, Bauman and Giddens all agree that individualisation is imposed by the institutions of modernity themselves (Beck, 2007, p 681).

Giddens is generally more optimistic about the prospects for empowered individualisation than Beck. He argues (1994, p 192) that the goal of politics must be to foster the 'autotelic self', the 'inner confidence which comes from self-respect, and ... where a sense of ontological security, originating in basic trust, allows for the positive appreciation of difference', a disposition essential for network governance. The autotelic personality is reflexive on risk, capable of translating 'potential threats into rewarding challenges' and 'entropy into a consistent flow of experience'. It does not 'seek to neutralize risk or to suppose that "someone else will take care of the problem"; risk is confronted as the active challenge which generates self-actualization'.

As Beck's example of environmentalism suggested, one harbinger of reflexive socialisation is that confronting risk management encourages people from diverse backgrounds to build networks, forming and dissolving as issues rise and fall in political salience. Beck (1992, p 101) argued that it is 'possible to cheerfully embrace seemingly contradictory causes, for example, to join forces with local residents in protest against noise pollution, to belong to the Metalworkers' Union' and, at the same time, to 'vote conservative'. Moral pluralism is therefore another harbinger of reflexive modernisation and, together with the capacity to respect difference, forms part of the justification for the politics of 'the Third Way' (Bentley and Halpern, 2003, p 88).

Thus understood, reflexive modernisation has inescapable implications for political action. De-traditionalisation, individualisation and the rise of the risk society render government by expert obsolete, recasting politics as collective learning and creative action. 'In tandem *with* the democratization, networks of agreement and participation, negotiation, reinterpretation and possible resistance come into being *across* the formal horizontal and vertical structure of authorizations and jurisdictions' (Beck, 1992, p 192, original emphasis). The command state will not meekly depart the stage, but it is confronting the globalisation of risk and information flows, phenomena that escape the clutches of hierarchical power (Giddens, 1998, p 72). Beck therefore observes approvingly that the old, means-ends model of politics

> … has begun to crumble. It is being displaced by theories that emphasize consultation, interaction, negotiation, network: in short, the *interdependency and process character* in the context of the responsible, affected and interested agencies and actors from the formulation of programmes through the choice of measures to the forms of their enforcement. (Beck, 1992, p 199, original emphasis)

Politics is now 'the collaboration of different agents even *contrary* to formal hierarchies and *across* fixed responsibilities' (Beck, 1992, p 199, original emphasis). During reflexive modernisation, the principles of centralisation and bureaucratisation come into conflict with the principles of flexibility. Flexibility gains priority in situations of risk and uncertainty and gives rise to 'as yet unforeseeable, forms of *externally monitored self-coordination* of subsystems and decentralized units of action' (Beck, 1992, p 231, original emphasis). Giddens concurs that it is a mistake to conflate post-scarcity individualisation with a selfish 'me generation'. New solidarities 'can be very intense and perhaps durable'. However, these relationships are neither *Gemeinschaft* (traditional communities), nor *Gesellschaft* (rational individuals linked by instrumental, impersonal ties). They require agency; the energetic creation of 'active trust' and the active production of new communities by autonomous, responsible individuals (Giddens in Beck et al, 1994, pp 186-7). These are the good combinards of second modernity.

Like Beck and Giddens, Lash and Wynne (1992, p 3) deny that reflexive modernisation is an example of postmodernist theory, arguing that it rejects the 'rampant subjectivism' of postmodernism. The notion of a transition from one phase of modernity to another is certainly a grand narrative that radical postmodernists reject. Nevertheless, the *zeitgeist* of uncertainty, unknowablity, fluidity and ambivalence resonates with postmodernist themes (Beck et al, 1994, p 297). As Lash commented (2002, p vii), if first modernity was based on a 'logic of structures', second modernity is based on the 'logic of flows'. 'Becoming' (change) has epistemological priority over 'being' (continuity), performance over representation (for example Latour, 2005). Where being allegedly had a certain fixity and predictability in the era of first modernity, it is now much more fluid and unpredictable. Thompson paraphrases: 'We now live in a complex world, a kind of open system where the future is unpredictable and unknowable and this undermines the possibility of constructing such models let alone the desirability of doing so' (Thompson, 2003, p 227).

Reflexive modernisation thus poses the question of what institutions, if any, might be suited to the governance of flows. Lash (2002, pp xi-xii) contends that they should be based on constitutive rather than regulative rules, the kind that 'let us play the game'. Giddens notes trends towards replacing bureaucratic hierarchies 'with more flexible and decentralized systems of authority', although he cautions that a 'wholesale shift from hierarchy to flexibility may very well be quite unrealistic' (Beck et al, 1994, p 193). For Giddens, active trust depends on building open, reflexive institutions (1994, p 187). Lash (2002, p ix) argued that the 'non-linear individual … puts together networks, constructs alliances, makes deals. He must live, is forced to live in an atmosphere of risk in which knowledge and life-changes are precarious'. In the world of network governance theory, Rhodes' conception of governance networks as game-like interactions rooted in trust, and Stoker's (1998, p 22) notion of networks as 'games about rules' rather than 'games under rules' have clear affinities with the principles of reflexive modernisation.

Yet, why should the deracinated individual necessarily become a combinard? Part of the answer is that the individual is reflexive and compelled to engage and, in the post-scarcity world, possesses sufficient ontological security to respect rather than fear 'difference'. Connectedness is also advantageous. Given the futility of both command and calculative rationality in the age of flows, connections between nodes in a network are the conduit for sharing knowledge, learning and innovation that add value and contribute to the emergence of trust and, eventually, embedded network practices. As networks are flexible, nodes can form, dissolve and reform, connect and reconnect in the manner of synapses (Urry, 2003, p 51). Network analysis is perceived to have the same advantages. Thompson (2003, p 227) notes that it is 'thought to offer an almost unique methodological opportunity to dispense with static forms of analysis and to embark on a genuine journey of self-organization and self-generation ... even "self-realization"'.

In summary, then, the age of reflexive modernisation is the age of the network, the 'dominant metaphor for global times' (Urry, 2003, p 51). There is a lengthy theoretical continuum between Beck's and Giddens' meta-theoretical conception of second modernity and the extreme subjectivism of radical postmodernism. Depending on its locus on this continuum, networking may be more or less fluid or embedded. However, the common theme is that being is increasingly decentred. Flux and flow render command power obsolete and require the reinvention of institutions for a new epoch or post-epochal condition; institutions that are flexible, revisable, fluid and reflexive on the reflexive individuals that construct them. Networks are necessary and advantageous because societies today are less governable than they were and there are no undisputed values against which governments can benchmark policy. In the most celebratory accounts, the impulse to network is fundamental to being, liberated from the realms of necessity and tradition. These are the macro-parameters of the transformation thesis, embedded to a greater or lesser degree in network governance theories at the meso-level.

Marxism and the network society

The theory of reflexive modernisation and related concepts in network governance theory comprehensively reject Marxism (for example Giddens, 1998, p 3). Giddens announced in *The Third Way* that the far left was exhausted and that 'no-one any longer has any alternatives to capitalism' (1998, p 43). As Callinicos put it (2000, p 117), he invited Marxists to 'meekly depart the historical stage, leaving progressive politics to those who will, in a spirit of "democratic pragmatism", devote themselves to "problem solving"'. In contrast, some contemporary Marxists concede a lot of ground to post-traditional theory, albeit that their objective is still to move beyond capitalism to socialism. They too chart the decline of the working class and the rising heterarchy of social movements and other forms of networked resistance (discussed further in Chapters Two, Four and Six). In these accounts, the network is an emancipatory medium rather than a governance mechanism or control technology.

Hobsbawm famously elaborated post-proletarian Marxism in his paper 'The forward march of labour halted?' published by *Marxism Today* in 1978. He argued that structural change meant the working class was losing its central role as the agent of socialist transformation. Consequently, socialists must engage with a wider layer of interests including proponents of identity politics and the progressive middle classes to construct a broad-based counter-hegemonic bloc. These were the politics of Eurocommunism, discussed further in Chapter Two.

A different tradition, Open Marxism (Holloway, 2005), also rejects proletarian revolution for the politics of refusal; the 'scream' against capitalism. Holloway argues that the experience of Soviet totalitarianism demonstrates the folly of attempting to construct a proletarian state and he rejects statism tout court. His work is close to the autonomist tradition, of which Hardt and Negri have become by far the most influential practitioners following the publication of *Empire* (2000) and its sequel *Multitude* (2004).

Like other Marxists who believe that the structural integrity of the proletariat has been fundamentally undermined, Hardt and Negri's goal is to preserve an emancipatory politics capable of escaping capitalism amidst the ruins of modernity. Network power is central to their project. They contend that economic globalisation and the rise of informational capitalism, or immaterial labour, render both Marx's theory of value and the nation state redundant. 'Empire' refers to the tendential universalisation of knowledge-based capitalism, progressively 'united under a single logic of rule' (2000, p xii). All is subsumed by the capitalist network. However, just as organised capitalism gives rise to its proletarian grave-digger in classical Marxism, so Empire finds its nemesis in the Multitude. Multitude, a heterogeneous social force, arises from the tendentially hegemonic character of immaterial labour in the age of informational capitalism; labour that is inherently communicative, affective and networked. It is the 'always already existing' emancipatory force. While Hardt and Negri maintain that the theory has no immediate empirical reference point, their book *Multitude* was undoubtedly inspired by the no-global movement, celebrated for its diffuse, fluid and flexible approach to networked resistance. Networking is the modus-operandi of both Empire and Multitude. Today, 'we see networks everywhere we look – military organizations, social movements, business formations, migration patterns, communications systems, physiological structures, linguistic relations, neutral transmitters and even personal relationships' (Hardt and Negri, 2004, p 142). Hardt and Negri continue by stating that although networks obviously pre-existed Empire and Multitude and today coexist with increasingly impotent command systems, they define the epoch as the 'the form of organization of the cooperative and communicative relationships dictated by the immaterial paradigm of production' (2004, pp 142-3). Networking is thus the organising principle of the new spirit of resistance. It is based on much more than mere trust, what Callinicos (2006, p 120) calls 'The Generosity of Being' at the heart of Negri's work.

If the affinities between Empire/Multitude and reflexive modernisation are plain, so are the differences. As was noted earlier, there is no question of moving beyond capitalism or of collective emancipation for Beck and Giddens. There is only the possibility of the empowered combinard engaging with others in problem solving. Emancipation is precisely the idea that Hardt and Negri are trying to rescue in the face of what they see, in effect, as the postmodern condition. The network is thus claimed and contested alike by pro-capitalist proponents of 'the Third Way' and the anti-capitalist opposition (Callinicos, 2006, p 63). From the standpoint of the issues addressed later in this volume, the question is whether Hardt and Negri and other loosely affiliated Marxists and neo-Marxists are right to posit the rise to hegemony of the network, or whether, in contrast, hegemony is today organised, in part, through the ideology and institutionalisation of networks. Chapters Four and Five return to this question.

Summary

It is interesting that thinkers such as Bang (2008) still see post-traditional theory and practice as the critical position arraigned against modernism. The primary goal of Chapter One has been to demonstrate that, on the contrary, it constitutes a powerful orthodoxy. The wide-ranging body of claims underpinning this orthodoxy, with which the remainder of the book takes issue, are inter alia that:

- The risk society and individualisation have caused the breakdown of old traditions and cleavages, creating the need and potential for a new reflexive mode of active, responsible citizenship enacted in trust-based networks.
- Internationalisation and globalisation have undermined the nation state system, making it more difficult for individual states to exercise command power. They have to work with the grain of market forces and learn to steer through international and local networks.
- The revolution in information systems and technology and the rise of immaterial labour has led to unprecedented information flows that cannot be subordinated to command power. Economic and political power is increasingly multi-polar, or everywhere and nowhere. It is affective, communicative and networked.
- As societies evolve they have become more complex, chaotic and less amenable to control, since governments can never account for all relevant variables. Social systems are capricious, making command power ineffective. Metagovernance (the network governance of

network governance) is the least-worst, necessarily imperfect, governmental solution to social complexity.
- Finally, public management reforms, including out-sourcing to market providers, have fragmented governmental capacity creating the need for joined-up government, entailing intra- and intergovernmental networking and cross-sector state, market and civil society collaboration.

However, it is not only in the intellectual domain that network governance theory is the orthodoxy. During the 1990s and 2000s, a positive feedback loop emerged between the theoretical and the political fields (Pierson, 2000, p 252), encompassing intellectuals celebrating networks and their political counterparts attempting to cultivate them. Chapter Two now explores how network governance theory influences global politics and policy, particularly the UK, which is arguably the paradigm case of network governance theory in action.

TWO

Network governance policy

Introduction

This chapter begins by briefly exploring the relationship between academic theory and public policy. It then explains how network governance became the orthodoxy in global public policy. It thirdly explores a paradigm case, the UK, and the socioeconomic conditions and ideas that made building governance networks a cardinal governing principle under New Labour. In doing so, it highlights the political claims for network governance subjected to critique in Chapter Three. The chapter concludes that in contrast with ideologues in the theoretical and political domains, even sympathetic empirical researchers rarely offer unqualified support to the network governance project.

The theory effect

To what extent is the transformation thesis a case of theory influencing politics and policy? Alternatively, to what extent are theories responsive to changes in governance? How do different fields influence one another? Governance and social theorists seek to understand and influence social development. Equally, governments can hardly avoid drawing more or less selectively from scientific and other academic paradigms. Bourdieu (1998, p 11) defined the 'theory effect' as remaking society in the image of ideas about it. One indicator of the theory effect is the extent to which it crystallises from a programme of knowledge into a programme of action, such as the move from recognising a social class to mobilising it (Callinicos, 1999, p 89). Borgatti et al (2009, p 895) argue that the concept of the network society circulates widely in society, influencing the way we think and act. Their example is the rise of the social network, an immediate product of technological innovation, and the possibility that it has profound implications for the way people think, act and organise their relationships. Another way of thinking about this relationship is the 'double hermeneutic' (Giddens, 1984), describing the interpenetration of scientific knowledge and the non-scientific world.

Others question the extent to which theory and practice can interpenetrate meaningfully. Rasche and Behnam (2009) draw on Luhmann's systems-theoretical work in their discussion of 'research relevance'. They argue that academic knowledge has no a priori relevance and only becomes useful in the medium of its application. Treating knowledge creation and governing as self-referential systems, they maintain that knowledge produced in one system is invariably modified when it enters another. In acting 'as if' knowledge is relevant, the recipient system generates 'fictions'. Research is 'relevant' if the fictions generated enable the recipient system to develop practices it deems helpful (Rasche and Behnam, 2009, p 252). Rasche and Behnam highlight the question of how far governmental applications of political and social theory copy, adapt, recuperate or otherwise transform the knowledge claims on which they are based.

Another way of posing the question is to ask in what conditions and to what extent ideas about transformation can remake the world. Hay (1999a, p 37), for example, argues that in propagating the ideology of globalisation, neoliberal governments author the very processes they claim they cannot control. Here, the ideational remakes the material world. Conversely, New Labour falsely claimed that its variant of 'the Third Way' could end boom and bust, ignoring that they are essential features of capitalism. From a Marxist perspective, the knowledge claims of mainstream economic theory organise and transform economies and societies in many different ways, but they cannot prevent accumulation crises without transcending capitalism. In cases like this, material conditions will thwart erroneous ideas about them, notwithstanding the inventiveness of agents.

In social science, the question might be stated as follows: in what conditions do theories and practices in different fields reinforce one another? With respect to network governance theory, how far are actually-existing networks faithful to the theories that espouse them? If the resemblance is often tenuous, as Chapter Three argues, why might this be? Could it be different? Or, does the tenuous, perhaps dialectical, relationship between theory and practice invalidate or falsify the theory? Chapters Four and Five argue that the emergence of authentic network governance is incompatible with contemporary political economy.

The universe of governance networks

One immediate challenge facing scholars of network governance is to define the object. Geddes (2008) identifies an extraordinarily wide range of governance networks, spanning public–public, public–private, public–citizen, public–private–citizen and private–citizen collaborations. Many are established voluntarily in response to programmes, others have a statutory footing. Some are project-focused and time limited, others have a 'strategic' function and are multi-dimensional, what Geddes (2008, p 208) calls the classic 'partnership' function.

The impossible challenge of systematically evaluating the vast literatures on this topic is further complicated by the variety of labels given to governance networks. Terms such as advisory board, partnership, tri-sector partnership, interactive governance, joined-up governance, interactive policy making, community governance, participatory governance, participatory management, collaborative governance, collaborative management, stakeholder governance, urban regime, policy community, issue network, the new public governance, the new public service and new social partnerships often describe similar practices but can also disguise important differences. For Dryzek (2010, p 121), governance networks 'abound' across the policy domains including criminal justice, energy policy, urban governance, finance and economics, water resources, environmental policy and 'regulation of all kinds'. Beck and Grande (2007, pp 69-70) conceive the European Union (EU) itself as a post-national 'networked polity' and form of 'network power'. In contrast with the centre-periphery relations characteristic of the old empire, they argue, command power is transformed into negotiating power and hierarchy into asymmetric 'network power'.

Ansell and Gash (2008, p 544) settle on a tight definition of collaborative governance for the purposes of their systematic literature review as: '[a] governing arrangement where one or more public agencies directly engage non-governmental actors in a collective decision-making process that is formal, consensus-oriented, and deliberative and that aims to make or implement public policy or manage public programs or assets' (2008, p 544). This definition focuses attention on the state-organised variety of governance network. However, for current purposes it is too narrow, closing down important questions about what kinds of networks define and fulfil particular social purposes. A wider conception is required for the exploration of hegemony, focusing on the state–market–civil society interface and, thus, collaborative mechanisms that seek to mobilise 'active citizens'. This conception includes formal 'invited spaces' and informal networks where civil society organisations play a prominent role. It also includes donor-backed, NGO-led institutions that do not directly involve governmental actors at all, yet fulfil a similar purpose (for example Cooke and Kothari, 2001). It includes looser forms of networking associated with exercises like participatory planning and participatory budgeting. Elite or exclusive networks comprising only state and/or market actors, such as policy communities, growth machines and urban regimes, are not the immediate focus of the discussion. However, they are revisited in Chapter Six, which develops a broad framework for reconsidering governance as hegemony, encompassing a larger universe of networks.

Conceived as the variety of mechanisms for engaging citizens in collaboration with states and market actors, the governance network has been cultivated by governmental and non-governmental elites alike. According to Abrahamson (2003, p 13):

> More than ever partnership is being promoted as the development approach of our time. Social development and social cohesion are no longer seen as the sole responsibility of governments; increasingly actors from the business community and civil society are becoming actively involved as well. Partnership is now part of global-level policy making.

Geddes' account of interorganisational relations at the local and regional scales provides a helpful menu of European initiatives promoting collaboration (see **Table 2.1**). He shows that establishing a partnership is often the pre-condition for government funding and that funding streams, which require partnership, drive the diffusion and proliferation of governance networks involving citizens, governments and corporations. Geddes points out that the network governance ideologies driving the cultivation of partnerships have been adopted faster in some countries than others, those retaining social democratic commitments adapting later than those that turned to neoliberalism sooner. However, he argues (2008, p 207) that despite their 'variable geometry, it is clear that local and regional partnership is becoming hegemonic across the whole of the EU'.

Table 2.1: Examples of different forms of local and regional development partnerships

Name	Remit	Location	Source of resources	Scale	Partners
	Economic				
Territorial Employment Pacts	Employment development	EU member states	EU	Regional	State agencies, employers, trade unions
Initiative for Employment partnerships	Labour market and employment policy	Germany	Private and public	Regional	Businesses and business associations, trade unions, public agencies
Greater Halifax Partnership	Economic development	Canada	Public and private sectors	City	Public and private sectors
Regional growth agreements	Economic competitiveness	Sweden	Public and private	Regional	Public and private sectors
Marlborough Regional Partnership	Economic competitiveness	New Zealand	National and local government	Regional	Public and private sectors
EQUAL partnerships	Employment discrimination based on gender, racial or ethnic origin, religion, disability, age, sexual orientation	EU member states	EU	Varies	Public, private sectors, trade unions, voluntary organisations
Workforce development partnerships	Workforce/local economic development	USA	Public sector	Urban	State and other public bodies; businesses, training bodies.
	Social				
Social Inclusion Partnerships	Social inclusion	Slovakia	National government, EU	Municipality	Public sector, NGOs, business, community leaders
Poverty 3 partnerships	Poverty	EU member states	EU	Neighbourhoods	Public, private, voluntary and community sectors

Table 2.1: continued

Name	Remit	Location	Source of resources	Scale	Partners
	Multi-dimensional				
Community Renewal partnerships	Disadvantage	Queensland, Australia	Federal government	Neighbourhoods	Federal and local government, local community, private sector
LEADER partnerships	Rural development	EU member states	EU	Rural areas	Public, private, voluntary and community sectors
New Deal for Communities	Regeneration of poor neighbourhoods	England	National government	Neighbourhood	Public, private, voluntary and community sectors
Empowerment Zones	Urban regeneration	USA	Federal government	Urban districts	Public agencies, community organisations, business
	Social group				
Pavee Point Partnership	Social justice and socio-economic development for traveller communities	Ireland	EU, other public sector, trusts	Traveller communities	Travellers and settled people
Hiuumaa Initiative	Jobs for disabled young people	Estonia	Estonian public sector, Danish government	Municipality	Public sector, employers, voluntary organisations
Informal economy in Durban	Informal economy women traders	South Africa	Durban municipality	Municipality	Local government, businesses (formal and informal), trade unions.
Ry Partnership	Socio-economic integration of refugees	Denmark	National and municipal government	Municipality	Public sector, businesses, voluntary organisations

Source: Reproduced from Geddes (2008, pp 211-12)

In a report sponsored by the Danish Government, for example, Nelson and Zadek (2000, p 5) described the emergence of partnerships between government, business, unions and civil society organisations as 'one of the most important trends emerging throughout Europe as we enter the 21st century ... for meeting the dual challenges of social cohesion and economic competitiveness'. The report, celebrating and encouraging collaboration, is a classic example of post-traditional thinking about networks, claiming that

> [t]raditional power hierarchies are being replaced by a more complex, multi-relational balance of power, where citizens and companies are playing an active role in shaping socioeconomic change and addressing problems that were previously the sole responsibility of government. (2000, p 7)

Policy transfer is one important mechanism by which governance networks spread around the world – indeed elite governance networks are themselves a medium of policy transfer (Evans and Davies, 1999). This may occur at the interstate level, like the ongoing transfer of ideas and initiatives between the US and the UK, where the Urban Development Grant, Enterprise and Empowerment Zones, and Sure Start are good examples (Geddes, 2008). Transnational institutions like the EU, OECD, United Nations and World Bank are also vehicles for the diffusion of network governance policy. According to the World Bank:

> The growth of civil society has been one of the most significant trends in international development. Partnerships between governments, businesses and civil society organizations (CSOs) are now one of the most effective ways to raise standards of living and achieve sustainable development. Civil society organizations (CSOs) play a critical role in helping to amplify the voices of the poor in the decisions that affect their lives. The World Bank recognizes the important role that CSOs play in meeting the challenges of development and welcomes the opportunity to work with civil society. (http://go.worldbank.org/2FWQUGY580)

The Business Partnerships for Development initiative (BPD, 2002) exemplifies the World Bank approach. It established the BPD in 1998 to promote 'tri-sector' partnerships between business, government and civil society. It states its mission in the familiar language of network governance theory:

> The roles and responsibilities of business, civil society and government have changed dramatically since the World Bank charter was drafted, and perhaps most dramatically in the past ten years. With the advent of globalisation, the reduction in cost of telecommunications, expansion of market economies throughout the world, and the endurance of democracy, the roles of the three sectors have become increasingly interdependent. We have moved from a world where the state had sole responsibility for the public good and business maximised profits independent of the interests of society at large, to a world where success depends on the close synergy of interests among business, civil society and government. (www.bpdweb.com/overview.htm)

The BPD established four 'clusters' designed to 'achieve development and business results'. Each cluster was tasked with developing grass-roots 'focus projects', including interventions in areas such as sanitation, environment, education and infrastructure development. Focus projects were intended to work with and within local communities, engaging a variety of governmental and non-governmental 'stakeholders'. The BPD report highlights examples including the BOTT (Build, Operate, Train and Transfer) sanitation project in South Africa, where community involvement was considered crucial for long-term sustainability. According to the BPD (2002, p 11), stakeholder engagement at the community level typically took the form of involvement in a steering committee, including project monitoring and evaluation, which it hoped would evolve 'into a water committee that bears the primary responsibility for operating and maintaining the system', including the training of 'water bailiffs and revenue collection officers'.

This project took place in a policy context favourable to building governance networks, with the South African government enthusiastically promoting the idea of a state–civil society partnership. Harrison (2006), for example, noted the resemblance between South African integrated development planning structures and community planning in the UK, from where South Africa draws inspiration for much of its public policy and management repertoire.[1] The South African Municipal Systems Act obliged municipalities to supplement the formal system of representative government with participatory mechanisms involving citizens in, amongst other things, the preparation of the city-based Integrated Development Plan, the review of municipal performance, the preparation of the budget and strategic decisions about service delivery, while fostering the 'capacity' of communities to participate. Most of these processes remain underdeveloped in South Africa, where governmental agencies still have limited capacity to deliver them, particularly in the most impoverished township communities (Habib, 2005). Credible or not, the intention to cultivate governance networks is clear.

Mexico is another good example of a developing country where governance networks have proliferated influenced by global ideology, global governance institutions and policy emulation, including cross-border policy transfer between American and Mexican cities (Flores, 2005, p 174). Walker et al (2008) show in their study of Oaxaca in rural southern Mexico, how technical assistance operates as a powerful lever for mobilising networks of donors (in this case the Inter-American Development Bank), NGOs and local communities. The principles they describe are similar to the BDP, with the private donor encouraging collaboration. At the same time, Guarneros-Meza's (2008) study of state–civil society collaboration in Mexico explored the international diffusion of the concept of network governance popularised by Rhodes. She found a proliferation of state-led participatory mechanisms at the local and neighbourhood scales, such as advisory councils. Her study of historic centre regeneration partnerships in the cities of San Luis Potosi and Querétaro showed that the creation of governance networks oriented towards consensus was indeed influenced by network governance theory.

Participatory budgeting is a more radical 'indigenous' example from Latin America. This is one case where the UK and European countries have sought to emulate a developing country. Participatory budgeting was introduced in Porto Alegre in 1989, involving some 50,000 people out of a population of 1.5 million each year. The procedure begins with area-based meetings to elect delegates, which all residents are eligible to attend. These delegates represent their areas in negotiations with other areas and city officials and also deliberate on the needs of the city as a whole. From this larger grouping of delegates, a smaller number is then elected to the 'Municipal Council of the Budget' where citizen-delegates work with officials to reconcile district-based demands with available resources and approve an agreed budget (Osmani, 2008, pp 22-3). This process is among the most radical experiments in citizen-centred governance and has been heralded as the most effective known synthesis of participatory and representative democratic processes, also having positive outcomes for citizens living in deprived areas and cultivating high levels of civic vitality.

Participatory budgeting has found favour with international organisations, with the EU, IMF, OECD, World Bank and the United Nations all endorsing it as a positive medium for citizen inclusion and civil renewal. In the UK, New Labour began piloting participatory budgeting schemes in 2007 with a view to all authorities 'mainstreaming' it by 2012, anticipating that it would enhance the democratic process, nurture social capital/cohesion, enhance resident understandings of public finance and increase civic pride. The place of participatory budgeting in the post-New Labour 'big society' remains unclear. However, its enthusiasm for neighbourhood-based action, reflected in the 2010 coalition agreement between the Tories and the Liberal Democrats, suggests that it will continue in some form (Cabinet Office, 2010). Activists, aware of its limitations, nevertheless give it a cautious welcome as a medium of community engagement.

Even the Chinese government appears to be embarking tentatively on the path to a form of networked local governance. Having selectively adopted New Public Management (NPM) reforms in the 1990s, it is moving towards developing participatory structures and even tolerating limited social movement mobilisation, such as Gay Pride. Bray (2006) argues that with increasing concerns about the impact of market forces on social cohesion, it is adapting western ideas about community building and partnership to Chinese circumstances, reconfiguring the urban bureaucracy in an attempt to foster cohesion through restricted self-governance. Bray (2006, p 533) found that Chinese policy has been influenced by international debates, combining aspects of both 'New Communitarian and Third Way programmes'. He concludes (2006, pp 545-6) that 'urban China presents a hybrid combination of strategies for community governance; it combines some fairly direct modes of governmental intervention, with a well-developed system of voluntary service and a commitment to the efficacy of community as an agent for moral improvement'.

As in other developing nations, international agencies and NGOs have been active in promoting Chinese-style governance networks. Plummer (2004, p 4) highlights how the United Nations Development Programme, Oxfam, the Ford Foundation, the World Bank, the Asian Development Bank and the UK's Department for International Development all fostered collaborative institutions with the consent, if not at the behest of, the State of China. Taylor (2004, pp 33-4) cautions that such processes remain fragile in a country where the Communist Party continues to exercise monopoly power (with considerable public support). However, it is prepared to countenance a limited move towards participatory governance in order to meet social needs that fall beyond the reach of state institutions, provided that 'voice' does not morph into political dissidence (Taylor, 2004, p 29). To this extent, it too is open to the philosophy of network governance theory in hybrid form.

Network governance policy in the UK

The convergence of international policy around the goal of involving civil society organisations in network governance is striking. Variants of the mission are to be found across large swathes of the globe in countries with very different political traditions and socioeconomic challenges. The discussion now turns to the emergence of network governance theory as government ideology and policy in the UK. The UK is an important exemplar, partly because myriad studies of governance networks have been conducted there, partly because other countries promoting network governance seek to emulate it and partly because, under New Labour, it was perhaps more ambitious in creating networks than either predecessors or comparators (Hunt, 2005). In the UK's towns and cities governance networks are ubiquitous, their structures labyrinthine.

The Conservatives and the partnership turn

During the mid-1980s, a major confrontation occurred between the trade unions and Margaret Thatcher's second Conservative government. At the same time, there was a significant clash between central government and prominent Labour local authorities (Boddy and Fudge, 1984). By 1986 both movements had been comprehensively defeated and left-wing local authorities, like the Greater London Council, were marked for abolition. During the remainder of Mrs Thatcher's premiership, local government was marginalised from decisions about development and regeneration, as central government sought to foster market-led growth and local entrepreneurship. Part of a global trend, these practices were captured by the term 'new urban politics' (Cox, 1993).

However, by the time Mrs Thatcher was removed from office in 1990, the Tory government was calling for a 'spirit of co-operation, of partnership between all of those involved in central and local government, including local business' (Lawless, 1994, p 1304). The Tory coup against Mrs Thatcher and her replacement as PM by John Major in November 1990 lent impetus to the new policy direction.

It did not come out of the blue, but built on political developments in the late 1980s after the major struggles of the decade had been resolved. Once serious resistance was subdued, the government turned to building a new consensus. In 1987, Mrs Thatcher made perhaps her most notorious comment:

> ... you know, there is no such thing as society. There are individual men and women, and there are families. And no government can do anything except through people, and people must look to themselves first. It's our duty to look after ourselves and then, also to look after our neighbour. People have got the entitlements too much in mind, without the obligations. There's no such thing as entitlement, unless someone has first met an obligation. (See http://briandeer.com/social/thatcher-society.htm)

Davies (2011) argues that in the furore over the beginning, it is forgotten that the rest of the passage presages the New Labour formulation 'no rights without responsibilities'. According to Gilbert (2004, p 32), as nationalists, leading Conservatives 'instantly regretted' the opening sentences and the latter part was arguably a far more accurate representation of Thatcherite philosophy. This was a tacit theory of citizenship, further elaborated by leading minsters who began talking about 'active citizenship as a way of overcoming the lack of a sense of community, lawlessness and overdependence on the state' (Douglas Hurd, cited in Oliver, 1991, p 157). Accordingly, the foundations of an ideological turn towards network governance can be traced to the late 1980s, including the emergence of a 'speech genre of partnership' (Collins, 1999, pp 76-7).

Kearns (1995, p 158) argued that once the unions and municipal socialists were beaten, the turn to active citizenship marked a logical step from confrontation to consensus-building. In 1991, the Major government introduced City Challenge, a regeneration programme encouraging local actors to form partnerships to bid for funding. State-sponsored collaboration gathered momentum during the mid-1990s through programmes such as the Single Regeneration Budget, gradually extending the city-business approach to include the voluntary and community sectors. Kearns (1995, p 160) interpreted the Conservative's partnership turn as part of a reconciliationist strategy to discourage further protest, a central theme for New Labour (Fairclough, 2000, p viii).

New Labour, 'new realism' and 'New Times'

As a party historically of the left, Labour was committed, nominally at least, to reducing substantive inequalities by reforming or, for some, even abolishing capitalism. The New Labour turn from tripartite corporatism involving state, unions and employers towards consensual network governance represented a break with this historical commitment. However, what became the Blairite faction was always present in the Labour Party. In the early 1990s, this 'bourgeois radical' faction triumphed over the 'social reformist' wing (Coates, 2001). However, in the early stages of 'modernisation' in the mid-1980s Labour intellectuals drew inspiration from a different tradition, Eurocommunism.

The crisis of Marxism began to intensify in the 1970s. Marxists previously wedded to structuralism, like Castells (1977), were among those leading the journey away from class politics towards social movements and popular fronts (Rabrenovic, 2009). Eurocommunism was one revisionist trend emerging from the crisis. It was anti-insurrectionary, committed to constitutional methods and downplayed the role of the working class on the road to socialism. The key players in the movement were the French, Italian and Spanish Communist parties, whose leaders declared the 'new way' in 1977 (Laclau and Mouffe, 2001).

Eurocommunism was influenced by Nicos Poulantzas's (2000) argument that the modern state is not fundamentally subordinate to the capitalist mode of production, but is rather a heterodox assemblage reflecting the condensation of the relations of class forces (see Chapter Four for a discussion of Marxist state theory). This conception underpinned the claim that a progressive counter-hegemonic movement could seize the apparatus of power and use it for emancipatory means. At the same time, the Eurocommunist tradition espoused a controversial rereading of Gramsci's 'war of manoeuvre' and 'war of position'. The war of manoeuvre is the insurrectionary moment, occurring when communists achieve hegemony within a mature counter-hegemonic movement. The war of position is waged when the movement is engaged in the gradual and painstaking struggle for ideological hegemony. Armed also with the Poulantzian rereading of Marxist state theory (for example Jessop, 2007a), and in light of the perceived decline of the working class highlighted by Hobsbawm and others, the Eurocommunists rejected insurrectionary politics for the long war of position. They nevertheless asserted fidelity to Gramsci on the grounds that although he was undoubtedly a revolutionary in the tradition of Lenin and Trotsky, his political thought evolved towards dissolving the distinction between reform and revolution (Laclau and Mouffe, 2001, p 90 ff).

The Italian Communist Party (PCI), the most influential Eurocommunist Party in the 1970s, built a powerful base. It took a lead in implementing the new strategy, forming the so-called 'historic compromise' with the Christian Democrats. The rationale was to stabilise Italian politics at a time of crisis and provide a democratic bulwark against the perceived threat of the far right (Goldsborough, 1977). The PCI and its descendants, despite regular vacillations leftward and rightward, has pursued similar politics ever since. In the UK, the Eurocommunist current in the Communist Party of Great Britain achieved some intellectual influence on the mainstream left despite its marginality in electoral politics. It argued for a cross-class alliance against Thatcherism, notably through the auspices of the now defunct magazine *Marxism Today*. A variety of thinkers more or less closely associated with *Marxism Today*, including Hobsbawm, Laclau, Mouffe, Hall and Jacques (the magazine's editor), began developing a politics for so-called 'New Times' drawing on Eurocommunist theory. They posited an emerging post-Fordist economy based on the shift from mass production to flexible production in the nascent knowledge economy. Thatcherite de-industrialisation added an unwelcome neoliberal twist to these trends. *Marxism Today* saw developments such as globalisation, financialisation, the rise of consumerism, the associated preoccupation with lifestyle and taste and the feminisation of the workforce as fundamentally undermining the proletariat of Marx's time. In the cultural sphere, it noted increasing identity pluralism, reflecting the changing economic structure. As Hall and Jacques (1983, p 11) put it:

> ... the world has changed, not just incrementally but qualitatively ... Britain and other advanced capitalist societies are increasingly characterised by diversity, differentiation, and fragmentation, rather than homogeneity, standardisation and the economics and organisations of scale which characterised modern mass society.

In the wake of Thatcherism, much of the left rallied to the banners of identity, difference and the need for broad-based counter-hegemonic politics. A viable counter-hegemonic strategy, argued Hall (1988, pp 275-82), must recognise that the new 'disorganised' capitalism tends to fragment the working class. These developments required that classical Marxism be jettisoned and a new conceptualisation of socialism developed as the 'struggle for popular identities'. In a world where consumerism and identity politics were perceived to be supplanting class, it was to claims for 'citizenship' that Hall and others looked for a theme around which popular identities could coalesce in a broad anti-Conservative alliance. Thus understood, the strategy was to mobilise a progressive coalition including the trade unions, social movements, churches and groups asserting their identity rights, challenging and pursuing state power through networked forms of organisation. As Laclau and Mouffe (2001, p xv) noted, this political current was congruent with much of what Beck and Giddens were arguing in sociology, chiming with the goal of forging a 'radical and plural democracy'.

From 'New Times' to 'the Third Way'

However, Laclau and Mouffe also noted important differences. The *Marxism Today* tradition aspired to socialism-of-a-kind through the organisation of a counter-hegemonic bloc, a struggle for political power (2001, p xv). For theorists of reflexive modernisation, the idea of a counter-hegemonic bloc is a 'zombie category'. In fact, Giddens (2000, pp 27-8) criticised Hall for failing to confront the political implications of 'New Times', which for him meant abandoning the traditional socialist commitment to collective goods as a means of countering 'the inequalities and instabilities produced by markets'. However, during the 1980s the forerunner of 'the Third Way', Neil Kinnock's 'new realism', was influenced by *Marxism Today*. Eric Hobsbawm achieved the dubious honour of being branded 'Kinnock's favourite Marxist', after Kinnock, Labour leader from 1983 to 1992, reportedly called him 'the most sagacious living Marxist' (Carlin and Birchall, 1983). *Marxism Today* won a platform in the political mainstream and its leading thinkers were published in centre-left media like *The Guardian* (Pimlott, 2005).

Following Labour's fourth successive general election defeat in 1992, the new leadership (first the late John Smith and then the Blair–Brown partnership) joined forces with a very different set of intellectuals, of whom Giddens became the most influential. Chapter One explained how the theory of reflexive modernisation dismisses traditional political cleavages as 'zombie categories', claiming that developments like the universal challenge of risk management create the conditions for network governance. Hence, rather than seeking to marshal the forces of the left in a progressive counter-hegemonic bloc, Giddens (1998) conceived 'the Third Way' in terms 'beyond left and right'. He sought not to reverse the Thatcherite settlement, but to build a new communitarianism on free-market foundations. This position represented a decisive break with counter-hegemony and a move onto the terrain of 'post-hegemonic' politics (Johnson, 2007) based on the idea of a common interest spanning the whole of society. The Eurocommunists felt betrayed. In a retrospective, Martin Jacques conceded that *Marxism Today* 'begat' New Labour. However, it had had a very different project in mind for a new left, 'an utterly transformed world'. Jacques saw the Blair project as 'acquiescence in the Thatcherite agenda and a denial of the very notion of the left', what Laclau and Mouffe (2001, p xv) called the 'sacralisation of consensus'.[2]

The actions of New Labour in government certainly cannot be read directly from the work of Beck, Giddens, *Marxism Today* or any other intellectual current. Nevertheless, it had more than an elective affinity with Giddens' interpretation of reflexive modernisation. At the 2005 Labour Party conference, in the aftermath of New Labour's historic third election victory, Tony Blair (2005) stated:

> I hear people say we have to stop and debate globalisation. You might as well debate whether autumn should follow summer. ... The character of this changing world is indifferent to tradition. Unforgiving of frailty. No respecter of past reputations. It has no custom and practice. It is replete with opportunities, but they only go to those swift to adapt, slow to complain, open, willing and able to change. Unless we 'own' the future, unless our values are matched by a completely honest understanding of the reality now upon us and the next about to hit us, we will fail. And then the values we believe in become idle sentiments ripe for disillusion and disappointment. In the era of rapid globalisation, there is no mystery about what works: an open, liberal economy, prepared constantly to change to remain competitive.

It is hard to imagine a better synthesis of post-traditional and neoliberal ideology. Ironically, given his own predilections, Blair went on in the same speech to state: 'Policy becomes ideology, sometimes theology. To challenge it, is heresy'. As subsequent chapters argue, it is now the theology of network governance theory that needs challenging. Mr Blair's idea of a cross-societal, one-nation coalition was central to New Labour's 'rhetoric of reconciliation' (Fairclough, 2000, p viii). According to him:

> The creation of an economy where we are inventing and producing goods and services of quality needs the

> engagement of the whole country. It must be a matter of national purpose and national pride ... One-nation politics is not some expression of sentiment, or even of justifiable concern for the less well off. It is an active politics – the bringing of the country together, a sharing of the possibility of power, wealth and opportunity. (Tony Blair, cited in Fairclough, 2000, p 87)

Much of the centre-left went along with this idea and the underlying theory of change. After nearly 20 years of Tory rule, the battered trade union movement, the Labour Party and radical local authorities surrendered to the 'new realism' and took shelter in New Labour's 'big tent'. These processes gained momentum with the collapse of the Soviet bloc in 1989–90. If western socialist politics were badly weakened by endogenous factors during the 1970s and 1980s, exogenous developments delivered the coup de grace. Some socialist currents celebrated the death of Stalinism, but it caused profound demoralisation on much of the left, which had thought that authoritarian state 'planning' represented progress of a kind towards socialism. It heralded the global capitalist renaissance (Marquand, 2004, p 35), the announcement of 'the end of history' as a struggle between competing grand-narratives and the dawn of post-hegemonic politics (Lash, 2007; Thoburn, 2007). Surveying these ruins, *Marxism Today* folded in 1991, returning only in a one-off special issue in 1998 to launch a bitter critique of New Labour.

In a conjuncture where counter-hegemonic politics could be depicted as futile, it is not hard to understand why the promise of network governance might appeal. As New Labour coalesced in the early 1990s, many citizen-activists in the new generation of governance networks shared painful memories of defeat and marginalisation and saw the 'big tent', though imperfect, as progressive compared with Thatcherism (Davies, 2004). Over time, what was first understood as a necessity became a virtue, reflected in the partnership ethos of citizen-activists who might previously have looked to struggle for solutions (Davies, 2009, p 88). Cooperation and trust replaced solidarity and resistance as symbols of the new realism. In the UK, the disappearance of class from the political lexicon meant that the trade unions found themselves outside the 'big tent'. The ideology of network governance substituted the worker of the tripartite corporatist bargaining structure for the déclassé volunteer, or community activist. Like network governance theories, governing networks treat class as a 'zombie category'.

Governance networks and the 'Third Way'

One way that New Labour's approach differed from Beck's vision of reflexive modernisation was its optimism about the productive relationship between economic globalisation and social wellbeing. Its enthusiasm contrasted with downbeat perspectives on individualisation, chiming with the optimism of Giddens, whose best-seller, *The Third Way*, Callinicos (1999, p 81) aptly described as a 'relentless flow of uplifting verbiage'. For Third Way thinkers, the work of the modern left with respect to individualisation was not mourning but celebration. The great success of post-war social democracy, they claimed, was to free the majority from brute deprivation and the daily struggle for survival (Bentley and Halpern, 2003, p 79). However, in doing so, social democracy abolished the conditions that gave birth to it, softening the capital accumulation imperative and rendering the socialist project obsolete (Giddens, 1998, pp 2-3). Freed from the subsistence imperative, 'post-materialist' individuals, the cosmopolitan 'me generation' discussed in Chapter One, were recast as authors of their personal biographies for the first time and, thus, as history-makers. Freedom from the realm of necessity promised by communism had been achieved by capitalism, with the socialists of yesteryear heroic but now redundant midwives to the new society. In this celebratory account, market-led development is faithful to the new spirit of the individuated citizenry, embedded in a vibrant global knowledge economy.

For Third Way theorists and New Labour leaders alike, this view of individualisation as progressive provided a potent explanation for why Thatcher was able to defeat the miners and why they could not go back to post-war egalitarianism and state ownership, even if they wanted to. Thus, argued Giddens (2000, p 39), 'established leftist doctrines have lost their purchase on the world'. There is an obvious homology between the liberal ontological claim that 'we are individuals' and the Third Way claim that 'we are individualised', the latter a significant ideological concession to the former. Leggett (2009, pp 151-4) rightly comments that political orientation cannot be read from individualisation, just as it cannot be read from post-Fordism. Nevertheless, the homology is important in explaining the juxtaposition of individualism, free market economics and the celebration of networks in New Labour politics. Liberalisation, marketisation and personalisation were faithful to the new spirit of the individuated citizenry and its penchant for networking in the global knowledge economy (see Chapters Four and Five for a more detailed discussion).

According to Tony Blair, the information revolution and the emerging knowledge economy signalled the 'greatest economic, technical and social upheaval' since the industrial revolution (cited in Callinicos, 2001, p 29). In the words of New Labour intellectual Charles Leadbeater (2000, p 167), informational capitalism held out the promise of a society 'both open and innovative, and yet inclusive and cooperative'. Thus inspired, New Labour was rapturous: '... the world has moved on apace. The pace of change, often driven by global forces can be startling' (DCLG, 2006, p 154). With the knowledgeable, prosperous, reflexive individual embedded in a connected economy and increasingly connected polity, globalisation could be embraced as an opportunity. The network society became the good society, liberating mind from materiality, dissolving structural antagonisms and opening the door to an all-embracing trust-based consensus grounded in the new capitalism. Leadbeater went so far as to suggest that we might be witnessing the birth-pangs of 'post-capitalism' (2000, p 228). Chapter Five explains how this ideology of informational capitalism, and its promise of a vibrant and inclusive new economy, became integral to the neoliberal hegemonic project.

New Labour's view of the emerging post-traditional world was that it represented progress, but not a final triumph. It perceived a variety of structural and cultural impediments to grasping the opportunities afforded by globalisation, contributing to the rationale for 'partnership'. For example, it acknowledged the social anomie engendered by the uprooting of community under neoliberalism (Retort, 2004), and so sought to reinvent citizenship. Neoliberalisation and its attendant inequalities, argued Retort, have led to declining levels of participation in public life. This matters to neoliberals because social fragmentation tends to undermine both national competitiveness and patriotism (2004, pp 9-10). For New Labour, the challenge posed by the causal relationship between individualisation and weak citizenship was how to revitalise community while maintaining the spirit of competitive entrepreneurialism unleashed by the flowering of individuality. It was conceived in a number of ways.

First, it recognised that de-traditionalisation, while emancipatory, also posed a problem. As former Foreign Secretary David Miliband (2006) put it, people talked about 'a sense of powerlessness, despite being better off, about which they are pleased'. New Labour was acutely aware of what Devine et al (2007) call the 'social recession' or 'feel-bad Britain'. According to former minister Alan Milburn (2006), 'a less deferential, more democratic world is threatening a crisis of legitimacy for the active politics that is the hallmark of the left'. Thus, the 'me generation' yearned, we were told, not for old class solidarities but a 'new mutualism' compatible with cosmopolitan, post-materialist aspirations (for example Birchall, 2001). Networked community governance (Stoker, 2004) was one obvious solution to this challenge, tapping the desire for mutualism without traditional bonds.

Second, it recognised that not everyone had shared in rising prosperity. Following Beck and Giddens, the idea of inclusion and exclusion displaced the notion that society is divided into classes. The problem of social exclusion was reinterpreted as that of 'non-membership' (Gray, 2000) and inclusion as the means by which the deracinated minority could be reintegrated with the 'mainstream'. The 'community cohesion' narrative is a variation on this theme, focusing on the assimilation of minority and immigrant communities and de-prioritising institutional racism (Beebeejaun, 2010). Again, mechanisms to create partnerships connecting state, citizen, corporation and voluntary sector were a logical response to this integrationist imperative.

The preceding challenges were those of rebuilding, or remaking. A third was to break the remaining 'forces of conservatism'. Hay and Rosamond (2002, pp 152-7) argued that New Labour discourse was Janus-faced. Representing capitalist globalisation as non-negotiable, it simultaneously saw it as fragile and to be defended from recidivists. Despite the apparent contradiction, globalisation might be both non-negotiable and fragile if backward-looking forces undermine it, but with no viable alternative. This is one reason why, according to Stoker, despite its enthusiasm for globalisation and individualisation, the New Labour elite was also paranoid and fatalistic (Stoker, 2002, p 432). The message was that the 'forces of conservatism' subvert the new realities at their and our peril. To invert Rosa Luxemburg's famous prophesy that we must choose between socialism and barbarism, New Labour confronted us with Hobson's choice: capitalism or barbarism.

It was partly to address these challenges that it appropriated the Conservative active citizenship agenda, seeking to forge collaboration between state, business and déclassé citizens through the medium of governance networks. As a corollary of expunging the 'working class' from mainstream political discourse, we saw the 'rise and rise of civil society' (Edwards, 2009, p 11). For New Labour, the task of civil renewal had three elements: 'active citizens who contribute to the common good'; 'strengthened communities in which people work together to find solutions to problems'; and 'partnership in meeting public needs, with government and agencies giving appropriate support and encouraging people to take part in democracy and influence decisions about their communities' (www.ippr.org; also Bevir and O'Brien,

2001, p 537). These were the tasks of the citizen-combinard in the new wave of governance networks established the length and breadth of the country after 1997.

During 13 years in office at the vanguard of the global network governance movement, New Labour established a vast array of new collaborative mechanisms. These included everything from statutory Crime and Disorder Reduction Partnerships, Children's Partnerships and Local Strategic Partnerships in every town and city to targeted regeneration programmes such as New Deal for Communities (NDC). Many of these institutions involved CSOs and citizen-activists as well as business leaders. At the time of writing, it is unclear whether this dense network of governing networks will be ignored, conceived by the new government as a 'local quango state' to be vigorously pruned or heralded as the 'big society' in action, particularly where volunteers and activists have a prominent role as neighbourhood leaders. Chapter Three explores the limits of these institutions as the medium of authentically networked governance.

The case for network governance

The purpose of this volume is to develop a critical understanding of network governance theory and governance networks in practice, but it is important to acknowledge research that views governance networks in a positive light. There are many purported benefits of networking, including better informed and more joined-up policy, the cultivation of trust through deliberation and discourse and enhancing democracy by opening up governmental decision making to a wider variety of interest groups – the claim of associative democrats (Meredith and Catney, 2007). Optimists about network governance theory see it as an alternative normative framework through which genuine collaboration or co-governance can be built (Vigoda, 2002). According to Skelcher et al (2005, p 580), the perceived virtue of 'partnership' is that it has:

> the potential to open up the local policy making system to those interests that do not find effective expression through the normal representative democratic system ... The participatory discourse is couched in terms of the value of inclusivity reinforced by a notion that partnerships implies equality of standing and power between the actors involved.

However, the 'network-boosterism' characteristic of both post-traditional theory and governance policy, while often shared by public officials and civil society activists (see Chapter Five), is not usually replicated in empirical research. There is little that celebrates networking without qualification, even among those who see it as progressive in principle. One relatively unambiguous celebration is Gilchrist's (2009) monograph on networked community development. Gilchrist reports cross-national research, constructing what she calls 'phronetic knowledge' (2009, p vii) based on the experience of those involved in networking. She recognises that empowerment is often achieved through struggle, but accords normative priority to the network, concluding (2009, p 175):

> In a world characterized by uncertainty and diversity, the networking approach enables people to make links, to share resources and to learn from each other without the costs and constraints of formal organizational structures. Empowerment is a collective process, achieved through compassion, communication and connections. This book is a contribution to the discussion on how community development uses networking to develop 'community' and to promote 'strength through diversity'.

Gilchrist's Third Way philosophy downplays struggle in favour of 'connexity' (Mulgan, 1998). The problem is that, like Rhodes in the passage cited on pp 11-12, she recognises the 'mix' of networks and traditional power structures, but still treats the network as 'the basis for an optimally functioning social system' (Gilchrist, 2009, p 171). Power asymmetries are perceived not as structural constraints requiring the reorganisation of society, but as a problem for reflexive citizens and professionals to solve. For example, Gilchrist never mentions neoliberalism, let alone recognising that it might be a constraint on democratic community development.

Another example of optimism about networks is the international collection on empowered participation edited by Hickey and Mohan (2004). Hickey and Mohan seek out the positive experience of participatory governance, affirming the transformative potential of purposive human action. In the same collection, Gaventa (2004, p 39) argues that 'widespread engagement with issues of participation and local governance creates enormous opportunities for redefining and deepening meanings of democracy, for linking civil society and government reforms in new ways, for extending the rights of inclusive citizenship'. However, he and other contributors emphasise that the potential of network governance has yet, for the most part, to be realised. Like many other commentators before and since, they are sensitive to the limits imposed by asymmetric power and inequality. Pearce's (2010) international collection on participation spans a wide continuum of views from anti-capitalism and radical democracy to mainstream pro-participation perspectives. Here, all the contributors take a value-critical anti-neoliberal stance, recognising 'the need to seriously tackle inequality, poverty, exploitation and violence' if participatory mechanisms are to be credible and sustainable (2010, p 2). Pearce develops an analytical distinction between 'participatory governance' and 'participatory democracy', the former a control technology, the latter a form of popular control (2010, pp 13-16). Pearce sees the practice of participatory institutions as a battle between the two rationales. Like Hickey and Mohan, she concludes by affirming the 'transforming power' of reflexive human agents (2010, pp 252-3).

In addition, many researchers pragmatically explore the barriers to collaboration and the conditions in which it is most likely to succeed (for example Ansell and Gash, 2008; Cropper et al, 2008). This literature is also cautious about the achievements of collaboration, even where 'trust' has been established. Panelli and Larner's (2010) study in Australia and New Zealand shows that collaboration can succeed in transcending adversarial conceptions of 'state' and 'activist' but risks reconstituting activism as 'social capital'; in other words, it risks recuperating 'voice' as a governmental 'resource'. Based on findings from their systematic literature review, Ansell and Gash (2008, p 561) conclude that collaboration is most likely to become embedded when it delivers 'small wins', 'encouraging a virtuous cycle of trust building and commitment'.

Summary

A key question arising from this discussion is how far the roll-out of governance networks advances the project for network governance, from which it draws inspiration. None of the studies discussed above, including those normatively inclined towards network governance, reveal much about whether the connectionist disposition is becoming 'hegemonic in qualitative terms' (Hardt and Negri, 2000, p 280), or whether day-to-day governance practices support the claims of transformation theorists. It is impossible to answer this question definitively based on existing social theory, or the empirical evidence base in the governance field. However, it is clear, following the earlier discussion of the 'theory effect', that the political zeal for cultivating networks cannot be interpreted straightforwardly as a medium of reflexive modernisation. Chapter Three draws on a range of critical literatures in arguing that network governance is probably rare and highly vulnerable to being swamped by the hierarchical, inequitable and instrumental practices it was meant to transcend. Chapters Four and Five develop a Marxist and Gramscian explanation of why this should be.

Notes

[1] According to a senior South African civil servant, speaking under Chatham House rules, South Africa copies most of its policy and management frameworks from the UK.

[2] See www.amielandmelburn.org.uk/collections/mt/index_frame.htm

THREE

The limits of network governance

Introduction

Chapter Two suggested that there is little direct empirical evidence pointing to the emergence of authentic connectionist practices. On the contrary, much of the literature highlights barriers to this outcome. This chapter explores key themes in the critical literatures, highlighting the empirical basis for a critique of network governance theory: that it misreads both past and present, that governance networks are prone to resolving into hierarchies and incremental closure, that they reproduce inequalities, and that distrust is common. Consequently, there is a pronounced tendency for governance networks to re-enact the practices they are meant to complement or displace. The final part of the chapter considers a theoretical critique of network governance from within the post-traditional worldview, the Foucauldian view of networking as fostering neoliberal governmentalities. The chapter concludes that Foucauldian research shines a powerful lens on the limits of post-hegemonic theory but that it needs resituating in the political economy of network governance, which is developed in Chapters Four and Five.

Governance networks in the 20th century

Nickel (2009, p 383) observes that 'celebrations of transformation abound' in public administration. One immediate problem with the transformation thesis is the way it celebrates the novelty of the present by distorting the past (Lynn, 2001). Interdependence between governmental and non-governmental actors is axiomatic to governing systems, however remote and hierarchical they may appear to be. More specifically, the kinds of governance institution heralded today as transformative have been woven into the fabric of state–citizen relations at least since the rise of universal suffrage. Certainly, the preoccupations of scholars writing near the beginning of the 20th century are familiar.

Fairlie (1926), for example, explored the emergence and proliferation of the Public Advisory Committee in British public administration at the end of the 19th century and particularly after the First World War. He argued that such committees should reflect the different interests affected and be consulted on matters of policy, although they ought not to supersede ministerial decision-making. At the end of the Second World War, White (1945, p 142) noted that 'the inclusion of so-called public representatives is an old custom', arguing that civil servants should be sensitive to the voice of public service users to 'humanize the bureaucracy'. He discussed examples from the UK and the US showing how state–citizen collaboration was routine, finding 97 different kinds of national and local advisory committees attached to various Whitehall departments and myriad place-based examples of each (1945, p 145). White also found that 60% of the membership of statutory borough health insurance committees comprised insured members of the public (1945, p 144). He argued that the citizen 'needs a place in administrative organization from which he can defend himself from bureaucracy and assert his right to self government'. Without such a voice, the state could 'exercise a terrific social-economic tyranny over the citizen' (1945, p 141). Much like supporters of 'the Third Way', White thought that advisory committees could provide a 'release of the great reservoir of human talents and energies to aid in the administration of a program for the conservation of human resources' (1945, p 146).

If governance networks are nothing new, neither is governmental control-freakery. Fisher's (1977) account of community organising and citizen participation in New York explored the relationship between voluntary organisations, citizens and public officials in the 1910s. His account of one organisation, the People's Institute, explained that it was meant to mobilise resident energy and commitment 'from the bottom up instead of the top-down'. Yet, he found that the programme gradually became more bureaucratic, centralised and professionalised with increasingly tokenistic citizen participation (1977, p 186). Riedel's (1972, p 219) insight that 'talking of community-control groups as if the government were about to surrender anything more than nominal ... power is to entertain a dangerously false expectation' reminds us that 20th century history is littered with claims and counter-claims about the authenticity of participatory governance mechanisms (see also Arnstein, 1969).

The historical ubiquity of governance networks itself says nothing about the power relations they embody, hierarchical or otherwise, their authenticity as vehicles for democratic inclusion or their changing form and function over time. Developing a comprehensive taxonomy of networks since the dawn of universal suffrage would be an impossible task, albeit one that could better put the governance network in its historical place. Thus, with appropriate regard for historical specificity it seems reasonable to posit that 'governance' arises alongside 'government' as a means of 'breaking administrative measures on the back of the public' (Fairlie, 1926, p 821), certainly in democracies and almost certainly in other kinds of political system. Governance networks are old-hat.

If so, the distinction between epochs of 'government' and 'governance' should be abandoned for a perspective that looks instead at different historical and geographical configurations of the 'mix', recognising that networking is as routine and unexceptional as command (for example Stone, 2009, pp 266-7). For example, Crouch's (2005) exploration of models of capitalism represents networking as always operating in a fluid mix alongside market and hierarchy. Governance modes are complementary and may be deployed strategically or coexist in 'coincidental diversity' in organisations or systems that readily gravitate from one to the other (2005, p 52). Crouch makes no heroic assumptions about the rise of the network. His account begs the question addressed in Chapters Four to Six of what kinds of societies favour particular modes of coordination and juxtapositions thereof.

What is new?

If governance networks are old-hat, then the rise of network governance ideology is significant mainly because it makes a virtue of everyday practice. Interdependence is 'newly acknowledged' (Hay, 2010, p 19) and, we might add, newly proselytised. According to Boltanski and Chiapello, the current epoch is distinguished by the fact that the 'art of connecting' is increasingly valued in and of itself, not merely as the means to an end (2005b, pp 168-9). Post-traditional ideology repackages tried and tested ideas in the language of 'innovation', making it difficult to know whether there has been a real increase in the frequency and intensity of networking, or not. In their critique of the Differentiated Polity Model, Marsh et al (2003, p 314) allow that governance involves 'a wider series of exchange relations than in the past', albeit that these relations are asymmetric, reflecting structural power differentials – their 'Asymmetric Power Model'. The promotion of networks and development of communications technologies such as the internet suggest that the volume of governance exchange relations might well be increasing and dramatically so. However, it is not self-evidently the case, and the matter cannot be settled without meaningful historical benchmarking that admits earlier practices to the category of 'governance networks'. Even if there has been a huge increase in exchange relationships, such as the explosion of virtual networking that lent impetus to the 'network ideology' (Flichy, 2005), this tells us nothing about the power relations therein. In surveying the governing landscape, scepticism towards network-boosterism and a-historical claims about transformation, what Moran (2010, p 42) calls 'epochalism', is a prudent starting point. Klijn (2008, p 119) too observes that predictions about change in the underlying nature of society 'remain very hard to prove'. However, he suggests that 'the growing attention (at least rhetorical) to forms of co-governance and public-private partnerships ... indicate that they should be taken seriously'. Klijn is right, but taking governance networks seriously does not entail accepting the transformation thesis. There is strong evidence, past and present, that they are organised hierarchically and do not require high levels of trust to operate. The following sections selectively discuss the large body of research suggesting that the world of networks is a case of 'governance as usual'.

The governmentalisation of governance networks

As the ideology of network governance spread, so did scepticism about the degree to which the apparent surge in networking marked an epochal rupture. From the perspective of the shift from Fordism to post-Fordism, for example, cautious commentators recognised that attempts to bring about a flexible networked economy represented no more than the 'search for a fix'. Mayer (1994, p 329), something of a network enthusiast, questioned whether 'social and political conflict will allow the actual establishment of these new institutional arrangements'. And, as Pierre and Stoker (2000, p 43) put it: 'It is not clear that most of those involved in government have the capacity – or, indeed, even the desire – to behave in tune with a governance "mission statement" and governing style'. This distinction between aspiration and practice is important and a significant element of the analytical challenge addressed in the current volume.

Many international studies suggest that organised networks fail to live up to the governance mission. In a study of partnership in Rotterdam, for example, Teisman and Klijn (2002, p 204) noted that despite repeated calls for network governance 'as the public answer to the rise of the network society', traditional practices prevailed. State agencies were unable to achieve their own collaborative goals, with policy still based on 'self-referential organizational decisions' (2002, p 197). Kokx and van Kempen (2009) found that governance networks in the Dutch city of Breda were vehicles for achieving national government goals and that other 'social partners' were excluded from the dominant state and market alliance. A similar theme can be detected in the literature on the social democratic heartlands of Scandinavia. Reviewing the Scandinavian literature, for example, Hall et al (2009, p 527) found that Swedish 'governance networks seem to perpetuate, rather than replace, older political and social power structures'.

The same trends are evident in developing countries trying to create the system of governance networks proselytised by the West. In Mexico, Guarneros-Meza (2008) found that governance networks institutionalise elite governance and, at the same time that the governmentalisation of these exclusionary mechanisms makes Rhodes' 'premise of self-governing irrelevant' (2008, p 1032). In South Africa, the Panos Institute (2000) noted the gradual centralisation of power under the ANC despite its devolutionary and partnership rhetoric. In its first term, it argued, the ANC was open to creative ideas. Emerging partnerships were 'based on equality and efforts to explore problems together'. However, in its second term, 'partnership' gradually came to mean 'people's organisations co-operating in government processes, programmes or practices rather than meaningful alliances based on equality' (Panos, 2000, p 30; see also De Jager, 2006).

If, as Chapter Two suggested, the UK is a paradigm case of network governance theory in public policy, it is also a paradigm case of its limits. The literature is replete with critical voices. Early on, the findings of the ESRC Local Governance Programme (1992–97) (Stoker, 1999, 2000a) seemed to contest the claim by Rhodes (1999, 2000b) in his forewords to the two volumes that the conception of governance as self-organising, autonomous networks was the 'centrepiece' of the programme (Rhodes, 1999, p xvii). Much of the research suggested that hierarchy was still the norm (see Davies, 2000 for a review). Morgan et al (1999, p 196) memorably concluded their study of local economic development networks in Wales by arguing that the notion of 'governing without government' was a 'fatal conceit'. Certainly, the reported findings of the programme lent little support to Rhodes' claim that networking was 'pervasive'. If it was, this was overlooked by most of the scholars participating in the programme.

Little changed after 1997. Chandler (2001, p 10) observed of New Labour's first term that every 'paean to local involvement and active communities ends with a rider that brings the state back in and institutionalises government regulation at an even greater level than before'. Coruscating criticisms of governmental control-freakery in governance networks became the norm during its 13 years in office. The flagship community regeneration programme, New Deal for Communities (NDC), came in for particularly sharp criticism, perhaps because it held out the greatest promise. Most NDC partnerships elected their boards and were nominally the most 'democratic' and 'inclusionary' of governance networks. However, according to Perrons and Skyer (2003), relations between officials and citizens in one London partnership were bitter and resentful. Centrally imposed performance management made 'the task of adequately representing the community difficult – "virtually impossible"' (2003, p 278). Later, Wright et al (2006, p 347) observed: 'if NDC is a community-led programme, it is community led in the sense that government decides how the community will be involved, why they will be involved, what they will do and how they will do it'. Marinetto (2003a, p 600) concluded that any detailed examination of the central architecture of the British state demonstrated 'further centralisation rather than the haemorrhaging of power and authority' from the state. Or, as Davies (2002, p 315, original emphasis) put it, the proliferation of governance networks symbolised not democratisation but the attempt to 'purchase wider *effective* control' of the political process.

At the European level, Magnette (2003, p 144) found, in contrast to Beck and Grande (2007), that participatory structures across the continent 'are extensions of existing practices, and underpinned by the same elitist and functionalist philosophy' as before. More recently, Bell and Hindmoor's 'state-centric relational approach' (2009, p 10) concludes that network governance is a control strategy and that 'states have not been hollowed out'. Rather, 'the exercise of state authority remains central to most government strategies' (2009, pp 1-2). Thompson (2003, p 187) went far as to argue that networks have been squeezed in a 'pincer movement' between roll-forward hierarchies and markets, perhaps even 'heralding the demise of the policy network paradigm ... not only in the United Kingdom but also throughout Europe and the United States of America where similar pressures and moves have been felt over recent years'.

It is important to record that reference to hierarchical coordination does not imply that command systems deliver effective control any more than market transactions necessarily deliver choice or horizontal connections entail strict reciprocity. With this qualification, however, there is little evidence of governments either devolving significant political power to governance networks or substituting harder control technologies with softer ones.

Bevir (2010, p 119) calls this 'top-down and elitist' approach 'system governance'. He suggests that the (futile) attempt to build networks from the top down derives from the influence of institutionalism within governments, although evidently not the reflexive institutionalism advocated by Lowndes (2001) and others. He further comments (2010, p 271) that 'local networks cease to be local networks if they are directed from the centre'. Yet this is surely the problem that requires our attention. If governance networks inspired by network governance theory are excluded simply because they do not live up to the governance 'mission statement' (Pierre and Stoker, 2000, p 43), it is unclear what remains of it. Excluding cases of 'system governance' from the discussion, furthermore, leaves us with no explanation for why states continue to direct governance networks in the face of their ideological commitments to network governance.

Network closure and creeping managerialism

Related literatures suggest that where there is some openness and plurality at the outset, a trend towards 'network closure' often reduces policy development from a debate about core values to one about service delivery (for example Lawless, 2004; Davies, 2007; Skelcher et al, 2005). The impetus, or direction of travel, is important since the transformation thesis predicts network governance displacing, or at least becoming more prominent alongside, hierarchy. If, by contrast, the trend is towards governmentalisation and network closure, then it challenges the notion that networks are transforming the governance landscape, even if only gradually and in the face of resistance.

The literature provides good reason for thinking there might be a trend towards network closure. Taylor (2007, p 306), for example, suggests that city strategic partnerships in the UK increasingly exclude voluntary and community sector representatives if they lack the financial resources to warrant a leading position on the partnership, a finding echoed by Davies and Pill's (2012) study of governance in Baltimore and Bristol. Describing the NDC programme as a potentially 'volatile political cauldron' (2004, p 399), Lawless argued that 'the original assumption that partnerships should be given a strong degree of local flexibility and freedoms has been steadily eroded' (2004, p 383).

Ironically, closure around the congruent interests of powerful groups may be a precondition of sustainable networking, as the literature on policy communities and urban regimes attests. Stone (2004, p 3) observed that 'political differences enlarge as one moves from general proposition to the handling of a concrete course of action'. If so, action-focused institutions require fairly detailed agreements ruling some goods in and others out. If consent cannot be achieved, one solution is for powerful interest groups with common or congruent interests to oust or otherwise exclude dissenting voices. Another solution, a governmentality manoeuvre, is to create a collaborative culture that encourages participants to restrict themselves to problem solving (Skelcher et al, 2005). 'Creeping managerialism' (Davies, 2007) makes even token collaboration difficult in some arenas. In social work, for example, Jordan (2001) found that the professional is increasingly forced to withdraw from community outreach work and is, instead, locked into legalistic, formal and office-bound arms-length practices meaning that social workers lose touch with communities. In South Africa, Heller (2001, pp 146-7) found 'technocratic creep' where the imposition of contract relationships disempowers non-governmental organisations, forcing them to mimic the corporate and professional style. The recuperation of civil society organisations (CSOs) is an oft-reported example of creeping managerialism, where instrumental rationalities overwhelm any deliberative impulse and create inhospitable conditions for authentic network governance.

If it is the norm historically for governments to try and close down political debate and make their own positions seem common sense, it is arguable that neoliberalisation has compounded this tendency. Du Gay (2003) drew attention to the struggle within the British state, led by the Tories and continuing under New Labour, to change the disposition of the public servant from that of impartial adviser to that of policy partisan or 'enthusiast'. The transformation from ideal-typical studied neutrality would only add to pressures limiting policy deliberation to matters of delivery and measurement. Newman (2005), for example, found that state managers use discursive strategies both to advance the perspective of government and recuperate critics. Or, as Geddes (2008, p 223) put it, collaborative governance demands the 'reorientation of the traditional roles of state bureaucrats to function as change agents and social entrepreneurs'. Skelcher et al (2005, pp 590-1) provide a vivid illustration of the 'responsive' disposition, finding that when questioned about the public accountability of partnerships, network managers displayed 'puzzlement' because they saw their role as securing efficient 'delivery'. Du Gay's critique of the new partisanship provides important insights into the means by which hegemony is contested and secured within the state. It may be somewhat rose-tinted with respect to the Mandarinate of old, but shines a powerful light on the imperatives driving administrators, today charged with building and managing governance networks.

Institutionalising inequality

One of the optimistic claims for network governance is that it has the potential to enhance democratic inclusion and equality. Accordingly, there is a vibrant literature on the rules and conventions of networking from the standpoint of democracy, the 'democratic anchorage' debate. Led by leading European scholars including Bogason (2000), Skelcher (2005) and Sorensen and Torfing (2008), this debate explores the challenge posed by networks for jurisdictional integrity, the accountability of networks to citizens and the rules governing the conduct of network discourse. The key actors in this debate are often critics of actually existing governance networks, who nonetheless see potential in them for democratic renewal.

One important element in this debate is the nature and quality of democratic discourse within networks. Should it be adversarial and agonistic in the style of bargaining or negotiation? Might it, alternatively, rely on cultivating Habermasian practices among committed network democrats, where deliberation itself leads to 'anthropological transformations' and protagonists become ethical interlocutors thus generating equitable discourse power (Baccaro and Papadakis, 2009, p 5)? Alternatively, should it invoke non-discursive rules and regulations to level the playing field among actors with different material and cultural resources as the pre-condition of more equitable discourse, such as by state managers conceding veto power to their CSO counterparts (Skelcher, 2005)?

Questions about how to do network democracy are complicated by the problem of whether governance networks are fit for purpose. To the extent they are prone to closure and resolving into hierarchies, the challenge is compounded. The present author (Davies, 2007) addressed this issue in a study of governing networks in Dundee (Scotland) and Hull (England). Like others, Davies found evidence of creeping managerialism and network closure. However, the study also revealed that community activists and public managers drew on competing values in defining the purpose of partnership, centred respectively on social democratic rights (to resources and a voice) and neoliberal responsibilities (to collaborate and contribute). These value conflicts were sublimated and closed to conscious deliberation. To explain this finding, Davies drew on Bourdieu's concept of habitus, the unconscious dispositions acquired in daily life (1990a, p 9). Highlighting how cultural and linguistic resources shape power relations, Bourdieu's insights explained why partners from diverse backgrounds failed to understand each other, displaying 'mutual incomprehension' despite sharing a common vocabulary. They were working towards different goals but the de-politicised and consensual culture of the partnerships meant these differences were not surfaced, let alone debated. As Marxist theorist of language, Voloshinov, argued in the 1920s:

> The rub is that different groups with radically different points of view share a single language. Yet, when they speak, their characteristic evaluations can produce quite different meanings within the same words. The result is that the singular nature of the language can serve to mask the multiple and conflicting meanings which different groups realise when they speak. Powerful groups will seek to reinforce this masking of diversity and conflict by seeking to extinguish or drive inward the struggle between social value judgements in language. (Voloshinov, 1986, p 23, cited in Collins, 1999, p 76)

Or, as Crossley (2004, p 109) put it, when 'social distance reduces the level of comprehension achieved in a communicative encounter, "symbolic power" determines which party is attributed the blame'. In Davies' study (2007), mildly dissenting citizen-activists were cast as trouble-makers by network managers, showing how institutions promising 'democratic empowerment' can do symbolic violence to subaltern groups long before any face-to-face discourse takes place. These outcomes are found even in seemingly authentic democratic encounters. Fung and Wright (2001, p 34) identified five mechanisms through which the wealthy and otherwise powerful dominate, wittingly or not: they are more inclined to participate; they have greater resources to participate; they are liable to seek control of the agenda; they can disarm activists by demanding 'responsible' behaviour, discouraging radicalism and militancy; and where deliberative discourse poses a serious political challenge, they ignore it or, as in Dundee and Hull, 'restructure' it to externalise the problem.

To this list we can add a sixth mechanism. Bourdieu reminds us that class cultural capital precludes interlocutors engaging in a truly equitable discourse, try as they might. If so, in unequal societies mechanisms intended to enhance inclusion and equality, even where all interlocutors are sincerely committed to doing so, will be liable to reproduce the inequalities they seek to overcome. As Wälti et al (2004, p 94) put it in a study of governance networks in Switzerland, collaboration can actually reduce the democratic legitimacy of public decisions 'by fostering a technocratic and secluded style of decision making, which operates according to tacit and informal rules unfamiliar to outsiders'. Where this occurs, the democratic voice is undermined by the very processes designed to enrich it. Such processes form part of the explanation for Wolin's (2000, p 20) conclusion that 'democracy is embalmed in public rhetoric precisely to memorialize its loss of substance'.

According to Fraser (1990, p 60), generating an equitable democratic consensus in a radically unequal society requires 'counterfactual' space where real-world 'status distinctions are bracketed and neutralized'. Habermas maintained that this space exists in the rules internal to discourse. He argued: '[o]ur first sentence expresses unequivocally the intention of universal and unconstrained consensus' (1971, p 314). Consensual aspirations are the 'telos' of any authentic communicative encounter (1984, p 247). From this principle Habermas derived the claim that communicative reason, the disposition to engage in unrestricted, uncoerced deliberation inherent in the speech-act, is the pre-condition of a discourse where participants overcome subjective bias 'in favour of a rationally motivated agreement' (1987, p 315), a form of anthropological transformation. For Habermas, deliberation flourishes in the 'informal and unmarketized' areas of social life he calls 'lifeworld'. In theory, lifeworld is a realm of freedom in civil society where open deliberation can occur between unequal actors on equitable terms.

However, Habermas also found that modernity encroaches on and undermines lifeworld. The increasing complexity of modern societies disembeds state and market institutions from the social bases in which they were originally rooted. As they become more remote and disconnected, governments and corporations act ever more strategically and instrumentally. Instrumentally rational action encroaches on lifeworld in a 'parasitic' relationship eroding the communicative space (Finlayson, 2005, p 47). Habermas calls this process 'the colonization of the lifeworld'. He therefore argues for 'restraining barriers' to protect lifeworld against the encroachments of modernity on communicative reason. Lifeworld must 'assert itself against' the state and market systems if democracy is to survive and thrive (Habermas, 1987, pp 363-4). In other words, Habermasian advice to CSOs might be that they should minimise their interactions with the state to maintain their democratic vitality. The theory of colonization is a telling warning that governance networks binding state, corporation and citizens together may erode rather than extend the public sphere (see Chapter Six for further reflections on this issue).

The Bourdieusian idea that power is inscribed in language (Hayward, 2004) lends further support to the notion that the democratic potential of network governance is exaggerated. At the same time, colonization is a counterweight to the transformation thesis because it depicts the roll-forward of processes that Beck dismisses as 'zombie categories'. From a Beckian perspective Habermasian theory remains grounded in the 'utopic evolutionism' of first modernity and is the work of an earlier epoch rendered obsolete by reflexive modernisation (Lash and Wynne, 1992, pp 1-2). Yet, if knowledge about actually-existing practice is relevant in determining the matter, the colonization thesis seems more compelling than the transformation thesis. The latter is not disproven by these observations, but in highlighting the roll-forward of processes it declares obsolete, they pose a challenge that post-traditionalists ought, at least, to take seriously.

Networks based on distrust

As Chapter One explained, the main distinction between hierarchies, markets and networks in post-traditional thought is that networks are based on 'trust' rather than coercion or contract. Trust is founded in intersubjective processes such as deliberation, through which actors develop shared norms and values (affective trust), or, in the case of firms, repeated mutually advantageous transactions where opportunities for free-riding are forsworn in anticipation of further collaborative advantage (instrumental trust). For Giddens (1994), the conditions for affective trust emerge from the ontological security born of prosperity. In neo-institutionalist theory, trust is a 'weak tie' that constitutes and sustains social capital and governance networks (Granovetter, 1973; Lowndes, 2001). The propagation of affective trust in a burgeoning system of governance networks would be a powerful affirmation of the transformation thesis.

However, the notion that networking based on trust is on the increase seems highly counterintuitive, when levels of trust in political systems as a whole are at historic lows (Newman, 2004, p 77; Devine et al, 2007). As Cook et al (2007, p 1) put it, interpersonal trust is an important social bond but 'cannot carry the weight of making complex societies function productively and effectively'. Strikingly, they find that 'societies are essentially evolving away from trust relationships towards externally regulated behaviour' (2007, p 196). Or, as Bockmeyer (2000, p 2437) observed in a study of the Empowerment Zone programme in Detroit, 'external enforcement is the counter-balance for distrust'. Consequently, trust must be treated as 'an endemic problem for the reproduction of networks' (Thompson, 2003, p 9) and the question of whether 'trust' exists at the beginning of a network, for example in 'recognition of a mutual purpose for which we work together and in which we all benefit' (Blair, 1996, p 292), is very important. If it is not then networks must generate it, meaning that there have to be other reasons for starting to cooperate such as resource interdependency, calculation of interests, collaborative governmentalities, asymmetric power or coercion. Stoker (1998, pp 22-3) distinguished three kinds of relationship between governmental and non-governmental actors: the contract, the bureaucratic partnership and the self-governing network, which he saw as the 'ultimate' collaborative activity. Here, the journey to self-governing networks is contingent and mediated by state-organised partnerships, which depend on motives other than trust, such as financial incentives. The problem this perspective poses for governance theory is that instead of superseding them, networks appear to be rooted in hierarchies and contracts.

Accordingly, many studies of governance networks are sceptical about trust. Stoker (2000b, p 106) commented, for example, that the 'trust on which governance arrangements often rely may prove too weak to carry the burden placed on it'. For Guarneros-Meza (2008, p 1029), governance networks in two Mexican cities generated 'no trust'. Ansell and Gash's (2008) review of the international literature on collaborative governance found that networks thrive with low levels of trust, provided there are resource interdependencies between actors. As Geddes (2008, pp 216-19) argued, there are many motivations and dispositions driving collaboration and it is entirely feasible for horizontal exchanges based on low levels of trust to work effectively. He commented: 'If trust-based partnership remains an ideal, making partnership work in a context of limited trust may be a pragmatic necessity in many cases' (2008, p 217).

Davies' (2007, 2009) study of partnership, discussed earlier, found that one source of distrust between citizens and state managers was the different political meanings accorded to signifiers, such as 'social inclusion' and 'partnership'. Here, distrust was begotten of misrecognition and the misalignment of the respective habitus of community activists and network managers. Misrecognition does not preclude trust, particularly in collaborative institutions where politicised discourse is taboo. However, trust based on conflict avoidance and failure to grasp the perspective of other protagonists would arguably be based on a false premise, that of naive trust. When it is based on misrecognition, trust between asymmetrically powerful actors is a form of domination or thraldom. From the standpoint of emancipatory politics, where overcoming power inequalities depends on struggle, distrust is a prerequisite (Cook et al, 2007, p 2) and a 'very healthy fact of our condition' (2007, p 60).

The notion that governance networks are based on trust depends, at least tacitly, on the idea that 'traditional' antagonisms are dissolving to the extent that we all confront 'risk' togetheras autotelic personalities. But, if levels of trust are commonly low, it follows that approaches claiming that networks are based on trust cannot be the most fruitful lens through which to study them. Where trust exists, conversely, we need to ask who has an interest in maintaining it, to what ends is it oriented and whether it is based on shared meanings or misrecognition. Today, there are grounds for scepticism towards the view that governance networks are commonly built on authentic and mutually enriching experiences of affective trust among unequal interlocutors.

Recuperating post-traditionality?

The pervasiveness of hierarchy, network closure, inequality and distrust all suggest that post-traditional ideology is vulnerable to recuperation by the very practices it declares obsolete and seeks to transcend. The avalanche of scepticism about the rise of network governance certainly requires explanation by its celebrants. However, it does not in itself falsify the transformation thesis. Post-traditionalists might challenge sceptics in various ways. One riposte might be to concede that state- or market-organised networks tend to resolve into closed hierarchies because managers respond to the challenges of reflexive modernisation with the tools of primary modernisation, acting 'as if' they still possessed rational decision making power. Beck alluded to this response when he and Beck-Gernsheim (2002, p 209) coruscated the communitarian turn in European public policy as 'reactionary in its attempt to recuperate the old values of family, neighbourhood, religion and social identity, which are just not pictures of reality anymore'. By extension, the attempt to manufacture governance networks could be seen as 'reactionary' because it attempts to address the challenges of reflexive modernisation with the clunky bureaucratic tools of industrial modernisation – using the 'logic of structures' to establish the 'logic of flows' (Lash, 2002, p vii). Observations challenging the transformation thesis can then be depicted merely as recording the death throes of an old order. Steen and Wayenberg's (2003, p 266) finding that Belgium's citizen advisory boards lack legitimacy because they are composed of groups whose social influence is declining hints at this kind of explanation in governance research. Yet, if the persistence of old practices is immediately dismissed in the language of 'zombie categories', it is difficult to see how the transformation thesis can be falsified at all, raising suspicions that this defence is a conventional stratagem. The critique behoves us to at least question whether governmentalisation, closure, inequality and distrust are less the fading echoes of obsolete modernism than they are central to the current mode of development. Moreover, as suggested earlier, dismissing governmentalisation as 'reactionary' evades the question of why governments wedded to post-traditional ideology and committed to reflexive practice should be incapable of cultivating the network governance institutions that they aspire to. Chapters Four and Five reflect on this question.

Some post-traditional thinkers in public administration also concede that the field remains enthralled by and mired in modernism (Catlaw, 2007; Bevir and Rhodes, 2010). As Frederickson intuited (2005, p 290), the subtext of governance theory is still the search for 'order'. More radical post-traditionalists seek to escape the analytical coordinates and categories of modernism such as 'state', 'market' and 'civil society' and, in the case of Bevir and Rhodes, to decentre 'network governance' itself. However, the failure to escape the strictures of modernism might reflect not the limits of the imagination but its excesses in a society mired in the actually-existing condition of modernity. Chapter Four develops this perspective.

Another riposte might be that the critique misrepresents post-traditional analysis. Some accounts qualify themselves by depicting the emergence of network governance as partial or contingent, with traditional practices persisting alongside new forms (Bogason, 2000). Thus, networks may be the 'new ingredient' but it is the 'mix that matters'. However, as Chapter One highlighted, such concessions to contingency often appear tokenistic, gesturing to the 'mix' but nevertheless conflating 'governance' with 'network' (Rhodes, 2000a, p 60). The theory of reflexive modernisation arguably does the same thing. Beck elaborates the theory, recognises contingency (1992, p 115) but proceeds to dismiss class, family and the welfare state as 'zombie categories' (2007).

Realists and more moderate constructivists, by contrast, might find cause in these critical perspectives to ask whether the ideology of network governance has been recuperated and if so, why? Chapters Four and Five take the discussion further, arguing that the roll-forward of modernist practices is not merely a narrative, an accident, or a wrinkle in the transition to a brave new world. It is rather integral to contemporary political economy and very unlikely to be reversed in the capitalist epoch.

Foucauldian network governance

The remainder of this chapter considers the Foucauldian concept of governmentality, itself a post-traditional approach influential in critical governance theory, highlighting the downside of networking as a medium of social control. Like other great social theorists, Foucault was prone to inconsistencies and his legacy is contested. There is no settled view, for example, about his attitudes to Marxism and dialectics, the state, the relationship between disciplinary power (coercion) and self-regulation (governmentality), or whether struggle can be transformative or is condemned to reproduce 'subjection and rule' in an unending 'sequence of struggles for power' (Wilson, 2008). One point of clarity, however, is, as Newman (2004, p 81) observes, that the Foucauldian self-governing subject is the 'obverse of the Giddensian reflexive subject whose emergence onto the historical stage produces a need for new forms of collaborative governance'. Whereas for Giddens networks are comprised of autotelic personalities or empowered individuals, for Foucauldians the network is a medium of social control in which individuals are trapped. The Foucauldian account therefore challenges reflexive modernisation from within a critical post-traditional framework originally marshalled, by Foucault, against Structuralism and Stalinism.

Foucauldian research on neoliberal governmentalities is a welcome riposte to the celebration of networks. It provides powerful insights into the enrolment and regulation of subjectivities (for example Marinetto, 2003b) and a power-laden account of behaviour rejected by radical interpretivists, for whom individual beliefs and desires are the only legitimate reference points in constructing any 'social'. Foucauldian research stresses the role of networks in producing informal rules for the 'conduct of conduct', which Foucault called 'governmentality'. Lotia and Hardy (2008, p 378), exploring interorganisational relations from a Foucauldian perspective, suggest that once a discourse of collaboration takes hold it becomes harder for interlocutors to resist, more likely that governments and other agencies will invest in collaborative programmes and more likely that grant-seeking researchers will reflexively adapt their programmes to the official collaborative ethos.

Foucauldian research therefore highlights how governmentalities make actors complicit in their own subjection to rules, norms and practices. Swyngedouw, for example, sees network governance as a 'a particular rationality of governing ... combined with new technologies, instruments and tactics of conducting the process of collective rule-setting, implementation and often including policing as well' (2005, p 1992) and part of a general shift from formal to informal means of governing (2005, p 1997). Governmentality heralds the age of 'soft power'. Neoliberalism is possibly its most mature expression hitherto, promoting 'government at a distance' through the world of agencies, targets, choices, responsive post-Weberian bureaucrats and 'nudge' policies, all of which seek to cultivate neoliberal rationalities. In Foucauldian theory, neoliberalism exemplifies a shift from disciplinary power to biopolitical power or self-regulation (Bang and Esmark, 2009, p 26), promoting the dispositions of the 'combinard' and making adversarialism taboo.

The power of Foucauldian analysis is evident in many empirical accounts of governance networks as the medium of new political rationalities (see Newman, 2005). For example, in their study of community development through technical assistance in Mexico, Walker et al (2008) consider the Fundación Comunitaria de Oaxaca, an NGO administering funds from sources including the Inter-American Development Bank (mentioned in Chapter Two at p 39). They found that targeted communities were 'normatively structured' by the programme as learners and entrepreneurs (2008, p 534) and that technical assistance operated at the grass roots as a 'major vehicle for cleansing "civil society" of its oppositional political possibilities, rescripting it as the social realm in which communities are improved through human capital acquisition' (2008, p 539). Their study symbolises the archetypal neoliberal governmentality, although they also emphasise that it is contested by 'beneficiary' communities. The strength of the Foucauldian account is that it distinguishes between domination crushing the power to act and an art of government that is reflexive on the actions of the governed (Rose, 1999, p 27). Power in the form of governmentality 'continually seeks to give itself a form of truth … offering an ethical basis for its actions', mobilising the capacities of those governed for its own objectives (Rose, 1999, p 7).

These insights contribute much towards understanding 'governance as hegemony'. As Nickel comments:

> With Gramsci we use the term hegemony, with Lukács ... we use the term reification, with Marcuse we use the term one-dimensionality, and with Foucault we discuss governmentality; in all cases we are discussing oppression through ontology and the politics of knowledge. (Nickel, 2007, p 215)

However, there are significant differences between Foucauldian and Gramscian perspectives. The challenge is not to refute Foucauldian insights into biopolitical regulation, but to draw attention to their limits for explaining observations such as the presence or absence of neoliberal governmentalities and the governmentalisation of governance networks discussed earlier in this chapter.

Unlike Gramsci, Foucault rejected general theories of structure and 'the state' as 'mythical abstractions', instead focusing on the micro-physics and 'swarming' of power. In the governance system, all actors are subject to the power effects of discourse, a 'prevailing web of power/knowledge relations which resides in every perception, judgement and act, and from which the prospects of escape are limited for dominant and subordinate groups alike' (Lotia and Hardy, 2008, p 376). Foucauldians see this decentring of power as a helpful corrective to essentialism, but critics argue that Foucault re-admits structure by the back door (Wilson, 2008). He has also been criticised for defining power as a process without a subject (Jessop, 2007a, p 146). Foucauldian theory neglects 'governmentalisation', the prevalence of strategic and tactical state interventions to produce and correct failures of governmentality – such as metagovernance. McKee (2009, p 474), for example, argues that governmentality fails to explain why the 'governable subject ... fails to turn up in practice' and why disciplinary power coexists with, facilitates or substitutes for self-regulation. From the standpoint of the critical observations discussed earlier in this chapter, mistrust, network closure and the roll-forward of hierarchy all suggest that effective biopolitical regulation is limited. Towards the end of his life, Foucault recognised that 'power relations have been progressively governmentalized, that is to say, elaborated, rationalized, and centralized in the form of, or under the auspices of, state institutions' (Foucault, 1982, p 793). He thus drew attention back to 'the state' as an emergent actor in which power is codified and condensed (Jessop, 2007a, p 146). This is one area where Jessop sees him moving towards a 'tactical alliance' with Marxism, opposing it at the level of discourse while the underlying analysis converged (Jessop, 2007a, p 142).

Arguably, however, recognising the 'governmentalisation' of power erodes the distinctiveness of the Foucauldian approach. Foucault-influenced accounts of governing networks are prone to citing 'the state' or 'the market' as agents of biopolitical regulation without the requisite theoretical adjustment. Atkinson (1999, p 67), for example, argued that within partnerships governmental guidance played a vital role by incorporating stakeholders into the 'linguistic market and products which dominate urban regeneration, creating an appreciation of what is appropriate and likely to be valued'. Edwards et al (2001) make the same point about 'social inclusion', arguing that to be 'included' is 'to be harnessed to the project of the centre' that seeks to 'govern their souls' (2001, p 425). Similarly, Taylor (2003, p 190) sees network governance as a 'new arena for social control' where 'the rules of the game [are] still very much dictated by government'. She is influenced by Foucault, but recognises the need to bring the state back in, suggesting metagovernance theory as a fruitful complement (see also Taylor, 2007). Thus, Foucault-influenced accounts are unquestionably insightful, but invoking the state as an actor requires us to consider how and why disciplinary and biopolitical power are entwined. As Joseph (2010a, p 21) argues, governmentality implies stateless power in cases where the state is, in fact, the primary agent.

Foucault himself was plainly aware that power is a repertoire of techniques including coercion. Yet he did not theorise the relationship between different forms of power, and, in emphasising the biopolitical, Foucauldian governance research often leaves social structures lurking half-noticed in the background. It cannot then adequately conceptualise the relationship between the 'art of government', crises and coercive power. Roy's account of the attempt to construct governmentalities in Beirut and Mumbai makes the point powerfully:

> The question that must now be answered is whether [the strategy of fostering a civil governmentality] can outsmart the "bourgeois environmentalism" … and brutal primitive violence that is unfolding in Indian cities. Can the civility of civic governmentality survive and tackle this war?' (Roy, 2009, p 177)

Foucauldian insights need reinforcing with theory that brings back the state as a strategic-coercive actor, better juxtaposing governmentality, coercion and resistance.

Foucault was also resolute in his hostility to dialectics, although Grant (2010) argues that he was complicit in 'dialectical thought' about the relationship between power and resistance. If so, there are further grounds for rapprochement with Marxism. The central focus of Marxist dialectics is the structural crisis tendencies of ageing capitalism. It is allied to a conception of human agency that allows for the possibility of emancipatory collective consciousness and action. This is the basis of socialist optimism about transcending oppressive power structures of both the coercive and biopolitical kinds. It is where Gramscian theory has added value. As McClary argues (1991, p 29), Gramscian (and Bakhtinian) political criticism is an empowering corrective to Foucauldian pessimism because it focuses on 'cultural contestation, counternarratives, and carnivalesque celebrations of the marginalized'. Gramsci's optimism about the potential for escaping subjection and rule lay in his fidelity to the Marxist theory of crisis and the tendency in Bourdieusian terms for the individual and group habitus to be forced out of alignment with its social field during crises. Chapter Four considers these tendencies in greater depth. The Gramscian analysis developed in Chapter Five then reconsiders the limits of the governance network as a medium of soft or hegemonic power.

Summary

The central point of Chapter Three is that critical analyses of governing networks are both compelling and insightful but, thus far, limited in their capacity to explain significant observations to which they draw attention. Moreover, in not challenging the transformation thesis directly, the critique is vulnerable to capture. Mathur et al (2003, pp 24-5) note that dominant coalitions often succeed in recuperating the critical elements of rival positions into their own 'argumentative structure' but without incorporating the values or practices associated with them. The participatory turn is one mechanism by which neoliberal thinkers in institutions, like the World Bank have sought to recuperate the 'no-global' critique of the late 1990s. Cooke and Kothari (2001, pp 5-6) see its 'self critical epistemological awareness' and mirroring of radical democratic discourse as a powerful means of closing down the critique of participatory methodologies. In other words, there is an important distinction between critique from within the orthodoxy and critique of the orthodoxy with a view to overturning it. Chapter Four develops the more fundamental kind of critique, challenging the underlying assumptions of network governance theory and advancing an alternative perspective grounded in Marxist political economy. It argues that what post-traditionalists depict as obsolete remains integral to late modernity.

FOUR

Beyond the transformation thesis

Introduction

This chapter takes a detour from the core subject matter of governance theory. It argues that to understand why authentic network governance does not seem to be emerging we need first to challenge underlying assumptions encapsulated in the idea that we are moving from the logic of structures to the logic of flows. The chapter argues that, on the contrary, there are powerful historical continuities in the social structure that make network governance highly improbable. The discussion draws on Marxist social theory and political economy, marginalised by mainstream governance, public policy and political science scholarship for decades (Hay, 2010, p 18) but now enjoying something of a renaissance in the face of a disastrous accumulation crisis and the widespread revival of class resistance to austerity. The chapter begins by discussing the Marxist approach to structure and agency and proceeds to explain why Marxism rejects post-traditional claims about epochal change in the nature of capitalism, states and classes. This exposition of alternative background assumptions provides the platform for developing in Chapter Five a Gramscian conception of network governance as part of the struggle for hegemony.

Structure and agency

Giddens' conception of structure and agency is based on the notion of reciprocal causation, the idea that two or more terms in a relationship are interdependent and influence each other. Post-traditional governance theorists such as Bogason (2000, p. 95) find structuration appealing as a non-determinist conception of the relationship between structure and agency. The Third Way rests on this perspective, liberating Giddens and like-thinking politicians from any crisis-theoretical critique of capitalism and enabling them to substitute their vision of the individualised citizen living a connectionist lifestyle, free from historical constraint. Structuration theory is influential, particularly in neo-institutionalist accounts of network governance (Bogason, 2000; Bachmann and Zaheer, 2008, pp 543-51), where the relationship between institutional rules and norms and the actors engaging them is iterative and reflexive. From a critical-realist perspective, it tends to conflate structure with agency by failing to take the causal powers of either term sufficiently seriously and, furthermore, understating the contradictory or dialectical nature of the relationship between structures, within structures, and between structures and agents discussed later in the chapter (Callinicos, 2006, p 185).

Another influential strand in the governance literature, interpretivism, takes a more radical stance against structure. Spearheaded by Bevir and Rhodes (2006, 2010), it challenges critical realists in the following terms: if social structures are causal mechanisms, how do they differ from practices comprising 'multiple individuals acting on changing webs of beliefs rooted in overlapping traditions' (Bevir and Rhodes, 2010, p 82), or determine individual actions without passing through consciousness? If structure emerges from action and all the relevant people change their actions, surely they will stop producing that structure? If so, structures simply consist of what people do and the intended and unintended consequences of their actions. 'Governance is not', they argue, 'any given set of characteristics. It is the stories people use to construct, convey, and explain traditions, dilemmas, beliefs and practices' (Bevir and Rhodes, 2010, p 94).

One obvious problem with this account is that it declines to specify how and why some traditions are constructed, maintained and transmitted and others are not. This is an important omission when considering a phenomenon like the financial crisis. This could certainly be decentred, researched ethnographically and redescribed fruitfully in the vernacular of stories. For example, the manner in which the British political class recuperated the meaning of the crisis and narrated it as a crisis of public spending would be a fascinating subject for research on the production and contestation of hegemonic ideas. Yet it is hard to see how such a sudden development as the crisis can be explained solely in terms of the dominant traditions and beliefs immediately preceding it, as these were largely insensible to the possibility of system failure. The question for interpretivists is how could the narratives and practices of crisis appear out of thin air? Or, did they appear in response to systemic economic pathologies occurring independently of beliefs and prior to the stories later told about them?

Another problem with interpretivist accounts is that they are prone to 'epistemological slippage'. Rhodes (2007), for example, summarising the development of the network governance approach in the preceding years, described it in unambiguously positivistic terms: 'I do not dispute the British executive can act decisively. Obviously, the centre coordinates and implements policies as intended at least part of the time' (2007, p 1258). This statement unproblematically conflates reality and representation and is surely inadmissible if governance is only stories. Rhodes himself recently recognised this problem (2011, p 198) and it is why Bevir and Rhodes (2010) consign first-wave governance theory to the category 'modernist empiricism'. Archer (2000, p 470) argues that interpretivism 'effectively capitulates' when its scholars generalise in this way. Yet the alternative would seem to be solipsism and the obligatory qualification of all statements, including statements about traditions, stories and narratives about those stories as theory-laden, cognitively mediated and unreliable representations of reality.

Critical realism has a powerful riposte to Bevir and Rhodes' question of why structures differ from the interpretivist conception of practices and why agents cannot simply change their actions and the structures in which they are embedded. This is that, given the requisite alignment of intentions, capabilities and resources, of course they can, and do. However, social structures are legacies of human action that endow individual actors with some capacities while denying them others (McAnulla, 2006). Archer (2000) argues, in contrast with structurationists and interpretivists, for a temporal-analytical distinction between structure and agency where social structures are treated as real effects of social practices. Simultaneously the legacy of past action and the condition of present action structures exercise causal powers. They are emergent configurations of social relations conferring resources on actors who can then choose to use them in various ways, or not, depending on their beliefs, capabilities and actions. As a simple example, Archer cites literacy rates and assumes the universal desire to eradicate illiteracy. However, the capacity to do so depends not only on beliefs and desires but also on the initial distribution of literacy and literacy teaching skills in the population. This spatiotemporal distribution, the structural precondition of universal literacy, *determines* how quickly it can be achieved. The larger the literate population and the more teachers there are to start with, located in the right places, the quicker it will be. Thus, Archer argues 'more than knowledge plus desire is needed to explain change, its magnitude and speed' (2000, p 466). In attempting to transform a structural condition, agents work with and against it. Desire plus knowledge might eventually achieve universal literacy, but interpretivists are compelled to ignore the impact of structure on the temporal and spatial distribution of change and to assume that nothing other than changing webs of beliefs can prevent it. A society desiring universal literacy, but with no literacy teachers, would have the beliefs but lack the resources required to achieve it.

Archer further argues that some interpretivists concede that their position – 'if all the relevant people change their actions, they will stop producing that structure' – is an untenable 'stop-the-world-while-we-get-off-and-change-it' condition (2000, p 468). Put differently, when interpretivists argue that structures can be changed if everyone changes their belief, they ignore that belief systems are part of the structural condition we inherit. Thus, structures can be transformed *only if* the requisite numbers of people change their beliefs and then *only if* the change-agents have the requisite resources to enact the transformation. Hence, the resources conferred on literacy programmes by the social structure (A webs of beliefs and desires + B illiterate people + C literacy teachers + D resources for teaching and learning + E distribution of A, B, C and D in space-time) are the ineluctable conditions of universal literacy.

This account draws attention to the problem with considering governance networks from the standpoint of embeddedness or the relations between nodes – the 'weak ties' between actors – characteristic of neo-institutionalism. A critical realist approach argues that the causal power embodied in the organisation or node is not dissolved or weakened by acknowledging its interdependence with other nodes. Rather, interdependence is the precondition of enacting causal power. Harvey (2003a, p 239) helpfully distinguishes 'thing-like structures' from processes, the relative fixity of a sociospatial formation like a city that arises cumulatively from historical development and exercises causal power in the present. The analogy applies to governments, public agencies and organisations too. The challenge is not, therefore, to show how fixity is displaced by flow or being by becoming, but to understand the relationship between the terms. Bevir and Rhodes are right that we tend to mystify social structures, like capitalism. However, human actions have cumulative effects that require resources other than beliefs to transform them.

Consequently, while individuals may endeavour to transform and/or escape structures, sometimes successfully, it is unrealistic to suggest that they do not develop beliefs and desires in light of tacit and strategic consideration of the opportunities and constraints they inherit with their positions in the social structure. If we accept that the natural world and the legacies of past human action are 'largely independent of the mental', then theories, beliefs and traditions are best thought of as 'revisable proxies for truth' that change in light of experience, in other words as the interface between the mental and the non-mental unfolds (Callinicos, 2009, p 179). Anti-foundationalists reject any correspondence between the world and our assertions about it, arguing instead that beliefs and traditions change when they fall out of alignment with perceptions. However, they do not say why, in a closed mental circuit, perceptions should ever fall out of alignment with beliefs.

Capitalism

If we accept that structures and agents exercise causal powers, how is this idea applied concretely? What is the nature of the social structure today? Callinicos (2006) bases his account of structure and contradiction on Archer's analytical-temporal dualism, focusing on the dialectics of social development under capitalism. Callinicos argues that the structures of modernity are both internally contradictory and situated in a dialectical relationship with one another. Classical Marxism posits a 'strong dialectic' based on Marx's laws of motion of capital and their tendency to cause crises of increasing scope and severity. This means that capitalism is an ageing system, not strictly a cyclical one. Where elements of the social structure are situated in a strongly dialectical relationship, the relationship is prone to eventual collapse or transformation (Callinicos, 2006, p 197).

Marxist political economy is a vibrant field with many controversies about the sources of crisis and system-ageing. To be a Marxist is basically to agree that the 'existence of bourgeois society itself' is at the heart of the crisis, constituted in the 'fatal schism' between 'profit-seekers ... and wage earners' (Kunkel, 2011, p 9). The schism is fatal because it becomes progressively harder for profit-seekers to generate a return on investment, upon which future rounds of investment, growth and profitability depend. The explanation for why returns tend to diminish is at the heart of the controversies within Marxism. Some see the problem as fundamentally that of under-consumption, where the totality of commodity prices must exceed the totality of wages paid to the labourer if the capitalist is to realise surplus value. This means that supply is always prone to exceeding demand, and maintaining consumption depends on debt-financing. Others focus on the Tendency of the Rate of Profit to Fall as competitive pressures force individual capitalists to increase the proportion of investment allocated to infrastructure and technology and decrease the proportion allocated to labour. This strategy makes sense for individual capitalists, but tends to drive down returns on investment at the systemic scale because labour, not machinery or infrastructure, is ultimately the source of profit. Put simply, the spiralling cost of competition between capitalists tends to drive down returns on investment (Harman, 2009). Harvey (2010) takes the discussion in another direction, exploring the dialectics of fixed and mobile capital, the unstable relationship between thing-like structures such as cities, and finance, suggesting that finance capital becomes increasingly mobile at the same time as the 'forces of geographical inertia' increase. This disjunction between the mobility of money and sclerotic fixed investments causes increasingly dramatic and destructive 'switching crises', now operating on an intercontinental scale as finance capital moves from moribund western economies to (for now) more profitable counterparts in the East in search of better returns. Today, arguably, the 'poly-crisis' of ecology, climate change and resource depletion to which capital itself gave rise imposes additional limits on expansion (Bellamy Foster, 2000). This possibility begs the question of whether the exogenous limits of capital are becoming more pressing than the endogenous ones, or whether the spatiotemporal confluence of endogenous and exogenous pathologies merely makes the case for transcending capitalism that much more urgent.

Which Marxist account of crisis should be accorded priority does not matter for current purposes. Each supports a strongly dialectical account of development. The essence of the Marxist position is that the cycle of crises is liable to intensification, culminating sooner or later with transformation or system collapse – socialism or barbarism. Theories of capital accumulation that see crises as necessary but cyclical in the manner of an endless series of booms and slumps, which skilful states can mitigate and navigate, are hereafter described as 'weakly dialectical'.

As a social structure, the capitalist system is tendentially 'totalising' in the sense that as capitalists seek higher returns on investment, they also try to subordinate ever-greater swathes of society and space to the accumulation imperative. While the struggle to subsume everything is by no means complete, and it is hard to imagine a world in which every interstice of space, time, body and mind is commodified, classical Marxism maintains that there is no sustainable way of practising capitalism that escapes this totalising system impetus. There is no prohibition on transforming capitalism into something else, such as socialism, but more than beliefs and desires are needed to accomplish the transformation. The ability to win control of the means of economic production, distribution and exchange (and the means of destruction) is among the prerequisites, as is the practical viability of any post-capitalist system.

The 'strong' theory of contradiction and crisis is important, because it distinguishes the approach developed in this volume from other Marx-influenced governance thinkers, such as Jessop (2007a). Jessop's account is 'weakly dialectical' in that he assumes greater contingency in the couplings between social structures and between structures and agents than classical Marxism, allowing greater autonomy for the heterogeneous assemblages of the state. In the radicalised post-traditional account, dispensing with the burden of crisis altogether further liberates us from the 'realm of necessity' and accords primacy to the ideational, discursive and intentional realms (for example Laclau and Mouffe, 2001).

Creaven (2000, p 281) rightly argues that these matters cannot be determined by theoretical fiat, they have to be grounded empirically. Insofar as governance theory is concerned, the case for understanding the network governance movement from the standpoint of the struggle for hegemony derives from the claim that a strong conception of structure and contradiction makes better sense of the day-to-day politics of governance networks than 'weak dialectical' or 'post-dialectical' accounts. If contemporary political economy is as much characterised by the crises of capitalism as the mid-19th century, when Marx was writing *Das Kapital*, then the conditions for affective networking posited by post-traditionalists – the dissolution of traditional cleavages, the trumping of capital by the universalising challenge of risk-management and the era of post-scarcity – appear to be wishful thinking. They were born of over-exuberance amidst the collapse of Stalinism and the political renaissance of western capitalism (Marquand, 2004, p 35). The remainder of this chapter considers claims about the changing nature of contemporary capitalism, states and societies, which lie at the heart of post-traditional governance theory.

Capitalism today

Perhaps Gordon Brown's biggest gaffe was claiming to have ended boom and bust. Theorists cannot always be held responsible for the actions of like-minded politicians, but the authors of Third Way political economy bear much of the responsibility for such hubris. In his haste to pronounce the death of 'socialism', Giddens chose to ignore the central claim of Marxism that capitalism tends to cause wider and deeper crises. In *The Third Way* he jettisoned crisis theory altogether. Like Beck, Giddens (1995, p 13) argued that ecology has superseded capitalism as the central risk-management problem of late modernity, overlooking the conspicuous possibility that there is a causal relationship (Bellamy Foster, 2000). Giddens did worry about excessive market exuberance and argued for stronger regulation of financial markets long before the crisis (1998, p 149). However, he continues to reject crisis-theoretical accounts, insisting that 'progressive' politics must observe limits imposed by globalised capital accumulation (2010, p 37). Moreover, he states that the crisis was 'foreseen by very few if anyone' (2010, p 36), a claim rightly described by Žižek (2009, p 9) as a 'sustained effort of wilful ignorance'. Harman (2007) commented presciently:

> ... the US recovery has been based upon massive government deficits, on balance of payments deficits covered by inflows of lending from abroad, and on consumers borrowing to cover their living costs as the share of employee incomes in US GDP has fallen from 49 percent to 46 percent. This is the background to the upsurge of speculative ventures such as hedge funds, derivatives markets, the housing bubble and, now, massive borrowing for private equity takeovers of very big corporations ... Against such a background, corporate profits will be being puffed up until they lose touch with reality, and things will seem to be going very well until overnight it is discovered they are going badly.

Arguably 'surprise' at the onset of crisis among Third Way intellectuals, mainstream politicians and capitalists alike arose partly from their wilful ignorance and partly their excitement about the promise of networked capitalism. Boltanski and Chiapello (2005a, p 97) highlighted the tendency since the late 1960s for corporate managers to describe the system in the language of networks. Connectionist capitalism relies on 'autonomy, spontaneity, rhizomorphous capacity ... multi-tasking, conviviality, openness to others and novelty, availability, creativity, visionary intuition, sensitivity to differences, listening to lived experience and receptiveness to a whole range of experiences, being attracted to informality and the search for interpersonal contacts'.[1] They describe how corporate managers embraced connectionism and began heralding the ability to network as the mark of the 'great man'. In other words, avant-garde capitalist firms adopted postmodernist growth strategies, celebrating the creative, reflexive and rootless knowledge worker and (much later) professing their commitment to 'corporate social responsibility'. Postmodern capital was feted as weightless, colourful and infinitely creative, organisationally supple, diverse and environmentally friendly. It nourishes individuality and sometimes mild, ironic dissidence among shrewd consumers, FCUK style. It is flexible, benign, decentred and hip: 'cool capitalism' (McGuigan, 2009). As Chapter Two described, governments including New Labour assumed this ideology as part of their vision for economic modernisation (see Chapter Five for a discussion of informational capitalism and hegemony).[2] Even critics who reject 'post-capitalist' idealism maintain that the information age profoundly alters the nature of the economy and economic relations. It not only makes the connectionist the 'great man', it also transcends conventional theories of crisis.

However, there is growing scepticism about the distinctiveness of networked capitalism. Critical thinkers who believed that global capitalism was in 'good health' at the height of neoliberal triumphalism (for example Boltanski and Chiapello, 2005a, p xxxviii) ignored continuing low growth, investment and profitability. They overlooked structural imbalances, such as the corporate savings glut – the failure of businesses to invest in anticipation of low returns – that caused the financial bubble in the first place (Marx described 'growth' through asset-price inflation as 'fictitious capital'), and the way burgeoning personal debt supported growth and sustained illusions of 'prosperity' (Crouch, 2008). Doogan (2009, p 206) accuses credulous commentators of ignoring tensions between the fervent discourses of 'networked capitalism' and the structural limits of the neoliberal accumulation regime, evident to anyone who chose not to avert their gaze.

Apart from the eruption of crisis itself, other economic realities continue to challenge the idea that networked capitalism is qualitatively different. Most obviously they include vicious competition, predation, exploitation, monopolisation and centralisation (Harvey, 2006, p 45). It appears that the concentration and centralisation of capital have continued apace under neoliberalism, patterns evident in the highly inequitable allocation of inward investment, still concentrated in the core regions of the capitalist economy (notwithstanding the rise of China), rising income inequality and the huge, predatory multinational corporations that routinely swallow competitors and partners alike (Doogan, 2009, p 68). The crisis seems only to have aggravated these trends as smaller capitals fail and bigger ones (including those 'too big to fail') capture new assets and markets, leading to the further concentration and centralisation of economic power, as has happened in the banking sector. This is not to deny the relations of 'interdependence' between capitals, some more durable than others, but to assert a critical conception of interdependence, recognising that firms are imprisoned by competitive structures from which they cannot escape short of quitting the game.

Debate about the nature and potency of economic pathology, contradiction and crisis will continue unabated (for example Hay, 2010). Yet the state of global political economy today provides good cause, at the very least, to doubt the Giddensian conceit 'that the end of capitalism is less conceivable than the literal end of the world'. It points to the real possibility that we are now in 'a new phase of the protracted long downturn of late capitalism' (Balakrishnan, 2010, p 53). The central point, for current purposes, is that considering contemporary capitalism in Marxist terms poses a powerful challenge to post-traditional governance theories that hinge on the dissolution of structures, the abolition of scarcity and the liberation of the subject. The theory of governance as hegemony developed in Chapter Five explains how the ideologies of neoliberalism confront the structural limits of neoliberal capitalism, limits which manifest in the day-to-day politics of governance networks and make 'authentic' network governance utopian.

The state(s)

One convention of globalisation theory is that nation states are now too small to deal with global problems like environmental risk and too large to deal with local problems (Beck et al, 1994, p 192), becoming if not 'zombie categories' then shadows of their mighty Westphalian ancestors. Thompson (2010, p 132) summarises the thesis: states lost control over increasingly unfettered capital flows with the extension of international trade and the integration of production processes across borders, forcing them to pursue investment-friendly policies. At the same time, seen through the prism of post-traditional theory, questions arose about the extent to which they were any longer touchstones for political identities and loyalties with ideas such as cosmopolitanism, neo-medievalism, regionalism and urbanism becoming influential (Thompson, 2010, p 135). First- and second-wave network governance theories articulated this worldview, citing the fragmentation and increasing contingency of state power, the consequent need for states to mobilise the resources of other actors as metagovernors, and calling for a decentred perspective on interactions between state departments and agencies and between state and non-state actors. Government was now understood simply as one actor in the governance system, part of the multi-scalar aggregate of interdependent governmental and non-governmental actors. As the network is the chosen 'brand' of contemporary capitalism, so contemporary political and administrative elites describe states in the language of interdependence, decentralisation, ensembles, networks and flows (explored in more detail in Chapter Five). State power, state violence and coercive interstate struggles are typically understated or declared obsolete. Again, strands of contemporary Marxist and neo-Marxist theory embrace elements of this perspective (Hardt and Negri, 2000).

Changing forms of political community, the rise of global competition, the global institutions and economic connectivity are undoubtedly significant. During the post-war boom, coinciding with the Cold War, capitals and states became partially disaggregated (Callinicos, 2007a, p 546). They were partially re-aggregated into supranational blocs, as individual nations perceived (or were compelled to perceive) greater strategic advantage in military and economic cooperation than outright conflict. Cross-border capital flows increased, predominantly within the European, American and Asian blocs. However, interstate competition did not become obsolete and the post-traditional claim that such developments signified the dawn of a post-national epoch further exaggerates limited, precarious and contested trends. The degree and durability of suprastate agreements and the decoupling of capitals from states certainly cannot be taken for granted, as became clear with the onset of the crisis. Nation states were forced centre-stage, once more, as the saviours of global capitalism (Thompson, 2010, p 130). Moran perceptively recognised affinities between claims for the virtue of 'light touch' regulation in network governance theory and neoliberal 'free market' economics. As he put it:

> The rhetoric of light-touch control ... was not, it is now plain, the product of some functional response to the complexities of control but, rather, of the way power in financial markets lay with interests within the markets. (Moran, 2010, p 34)

One task of critique is therefore, as Jessop (2007a, p 244) recognised, to adopt a sceptical stance towards the ideologies of complexity and dispersion.

The primary locus of bailout, stimulus, sovereign debt crisis and retrenchment since 2008 has not been any multiplicity of interdependent agencies 'jostling for position' on the governance stage (Blair, 1998, p 10), but nation states and increasingly precarious alliances of nation states imposing swingeing cuts. Again, historical discontinuities can be exaggerated by talking down the state in the present and talking it up in the past. Whereas Keynesians and some neo-Marxists influenced by regulation theory did claim that nation states could mitigate or steer capitalism around crises, orthodox Marxists maintained that wider and deeper crises cannot be deferred in the long run. Conversely, globalisation theory understates the degree to which the liberation of capital flows rests on the power and interests of states. For Rosenberg (2005), capitalist globalisation is inconceivable without an international system of asymmetrically powerful nation states. It is a medium by which strong states discipline weaker ones, mine their resources and prise open their markets. Thomas L. Friedman's affirmation of capitalist globalisation brilliantly describes the relationship between states and capitals in the global era. Friedman argued that globalisation is in the 'national interest' of the US and can only be sustained by a 'stable power structure':

> The hidden hand of the market will never work without a hidden fist. Markets function and flourish only when property rights are secured and can be enforced, which, in turn, requires a political framework protected and backed by military power ... Indeed McDonald's cannot flourish without McDonnell Douglas, the designer of the US Air Force F-15. And the hidden fist that keeps the world safe for Silicon Valley's technologies to flourish is called the US Army, Air Force, Navy and Marine Corps. (Friedman, 2000, p 464)

Friedman's is a form of the 'free economy–strong state' thesis (Gamble, 1994) underpinning the Gramscian concept of the 'integral state' discussed in Chapter Five. Polanyi (1957) maintained that the idea of a self-regulating market was a 'utopian chimera', pointing to a central contradiction in would-be laissez-faire capitalism:

> Thus even those who wished most ardently to free the state from all unnecessary duties, and whose whole philosophy demanded the restriction of state activities, could not but entrust the self-same state with the new powers, organs, and instruments required for the establishment of laissez-faire. (Polanyi, 1957, p 140)

If freedom for capital depends on the coercive power of states, then the idea that the global capitalist renaissance led to the diminution of nation states is profoundly misguided. This is not to say that particular capitals always depend on particular states, but that productive capital, the ultimate source of profit, depends on a state or states providing the resources, regulatory frameworks and coercive powers for it to operate. However profound the differences might otherwise be, this remains as true for the largest multi-national as for the smallest corner shop.

In the above-cited quotation, Friedman represents the US as the global hegemon in a tendentially unipolar state system. However, Callinicos

(2007a, p 545) argues that the tendency towards unipolarity has also been exaggerated, as 'the centrifugal pulls generated by the inherently geographically uneven distribution of resources under capitalism play an irreducible role in keeping the state system plural'. The EU was heralded by post-traditionalists as the harbinger of the post-national epoch (Beck and Grande, 2007). But, instead of highlighting the increasing power and stability of supranational governance, the ongoing crisis draws attention to its weakness as states continue to fight over who should bear the brunt of the costs for maintaining the Euro, predominantly 'decentred' to the poorer Eurozone countries of Greece, Ireland, Portugal and Spain. With national and subregional schisms re-emerging and the realities of uneven development manifest, the European project looks very vulnerable. The sovereign debt crisis and the threat it poses to the Franco-German alliance was unimaginable in 2008, and today there is serious speculation about the viability of the single currency, particularly for the southern European states. The partial pooling of sovereignty in the post-war era did not eradicate national conflicts of interest in the heartlands of Western Europe, let alone across Europe or the world as a whole. The rise of China and India, the partial revival of Russia and the decline of the US, now coming face-to-face with its own debt crisis, can all be exaggerated, but they highlight further trends towards multi-polarity, a process likely to be reinforced by the scarcity of investment in debt-burdened, capital-starved states (see Panitch and Gindin, 2006, for an alternative Marxist interpretation). The relationship between the national and the supranational is therefore best understood as a dialectical one, to which both terms are integral.

Capitalism and the capitalist state

The preceding paragraphs argue that capital accumulation still relies on the exercise of state power domestically and internationally and that any account of governance must take the power embodied in nation states within a conflictual international system seriously. But, how and why are capitals able to depend on states? This is another area where there is a very rich and diverse Marxist literature. Space precludes an in-depth discussion but the following paragraphs briefly summarise key positions within Marxism and the approach informing the Gramscian account in Chapter Five.

The now largely discredited theory of 'state monopoly capitalism' (StaMoKap) asserted that state and monopoly capital are increasingly fused into a single power bloc, where policy is governed by the demands of monopoly capitalists at the expense of both other fractions of capital and other social interests. This notion of fusion between the economic and extra-economic spheres influenced 'instrumentalist' approaches, such as Ralph Miliband's (2009) theory of the state as the instrument of class rule, where capital is able to monopolise control of the state apparatus through shared sociocultural norms with political and civil service elites, cultivated through institutions such as schools, universities and clubs.

Insightful as it was about the web of interdependencies between state and capitalist elites, graphically highlighted in the UK's phone-hacking scandal, Miliband's instrumentalist approach did not satisfy theorists seeking a structural account of the relationship, or those arguing that monopoly capital is not a unitary interest. Contributors to the 'state derivation debate' argued that the distinction between 'state' and 'capital' introduces a spurious dualism. They posed questions such as: What is the political form of capitalism? What is specific about states in capitalist societies? And why does class domination under capitalism take the form of a public power such as the democratic state (Gerstenberger, 2010, p 63)? The 'derivation' debate was so-called because the position was 'derived' from rereading Marx as theorist not only of the capitalist economy, but also of the totality of capitalist social relations. One conclusion, closely associated with the Open Marxism tradition (Bonefeld and Holloway, 1995), was that the categories of economy, politics and ideology combine in different ways across all dimensions of capitalist social relations. The category 'state' could be interpreted as a form of the capital relation, or as a 'concentration of bourgeois society' (Tsolakis, 2010, p 402). The derivationists therefore inferred the existence of the capitalist state from their conception of capitalist societies as the contradictory totality of economic and non-economic relations. Derivationist scholarship was much criticised for its excessive abstraction and a-historicity – for inferring that which needs demonstrating empirically (Gerstenberger, 2010, p 65). It was also criticised for functionalism, the assertion that the state fulfilled certain duties because these were the prerequisites of capital accumulation.

One of the most influential offshoots of the derivation debate was Poulantzas's (2000) theory of the state as the condensate of the outcome of class struggles. Poulantzas began with the functionalist assumption that the state fulfils the needs of the society of which it is part. In capitalist society, therefore, it is a capitalist state. But since capitalist society is the totality of social relations, the state is also the condensate or sum of the struggle between classes, meaning that it is responsive to organised class demands and not wholly subordinate to the accumulation imperative. If class struggles tip the balance of forces against capital, then the state will reflect that. Poulantzas therefore asserted the 'relative autonomy' of the state discussed in Chapter Two on pp 43-4.

Post-Poulantzian scholarship is arguably more influential in critical governance theory today than the orthodox derivation perspectives associated with Holloway and others. Jessop, for example, cites Poulantzas as a major influence, but seeks a complete break with structural-functionalism, redefining the relationship between states and capitals in system-theoretical terms. He argues (Jessop, 2007a, p 26) that systems are 'autopoetic', materially interdependent but operationally autonomous. A system, like capitalism, can dominate the overall development of a 'self-organizing ecology of self-organizing systems' because it causes 'more problems for other systems than they can cause for it', making it 'ecologically dominant', but not determinant of state form and practice. Jessop (2007a, p 34) further argues that multiple capital logics compete within the circuit of capital meaning that the system itself is internally heterogeneous. Why, then, might capitalism cause more problems for other systems than they do for it? Marxism highlights that just as capital is ecologically dominant within an ecology of self-organising systems, so competition and accumulation and their ineluctable pathologies dominate the ecology of capitalism and create major spill-over effects. The crisis tendencies discovered by Marx have no immediate counterpart in politics. This is not to say that political or ideational crises do not occur independently of the economic field, or that political crises cannot themselves cause economic problems. It is rather that there is nothing inherent in politics that undermines the political or the economic fields, whereas capitalism is undermined by its own 'fatal schism'. As the internally contradictory element it tends to perturb other ecologies more than they perturb it (Jessop, 2007a, p 26). As Jessop (2007b, p 79) put it, 'it is the system with the highest tendency to fail with the most significant consequences for other systems that will gain primacy': the stronger the tendency to fail, the greater the consequences.

This is an important insight, but Jessop's approach remains 'weakly dialectical' in that the structural coupling he posits between the autopoetic systems of state and capital is sufficiently loose for states subject to organised political pressure to be able to deliver progressive reforms in the face of corporate opposition (2007a, pp 25, 27). In a debate with Joseph (2003) on Gramsci, Jessop (2003b, pp 138-9) commented:

> ... I question the feasibility of totalization practices and argue that they can succeed only relatively, precariously, and temporarily within specific socially constituted spatio-temporal fixes that displace and defer many contradictions, crisis-tendencies, and conflicts to marginalized places and spaces within and beyond the boundaries of this fix and/or into the future.

As Jessop intimates, orthodox Marxism is distinguished from his approach by the claim that different domains of the social world (for example states, markets, civil societies) constitute a dialectical or contradictory totality (Callinicos, 2007a) and that crises cannot be forever deferred or outsourced. Underpinning this view, discussed earlier in the chapter, is the claim that capitalism is 'totalising', tending to subsume ever-greater swathes of space-time to the accumulation imperative. As Jessop elsewhere recognises (2007b, p 82), citing Meszaros, capitalism is 'inexorably all-engulfing', blindly 'subjecting to the same imperatives health care no less than commerce, education no less than agriculture, art no less than manufacturing industry'. Accepting the notion of capitalist society as an emergent, emerging, contradictory totality suggests that its elements are both materially and operationally interdependent and therefore more weakly autopoetic than Jessop's theory allows.

If so, it is necessary to think again about the relationship between states and capitals. The approach developed by Harvey (2003b) and Callinicos (2007a) rejects functionalism, instrumentalism and relative autonomy, instead conceiving of capitalist states as situated in a relationship of structural interdependence with capitals. The important point, neglected by the state derivation debate, is that ithere are many states and many capitals. As Barker put it (1991, p 189), the global ruling class meets as 'hostile brothers' in the 'IMF vaults' and the 'United Nations soup queue' alike. Hence, the capitalist state operates simultaneously as 'an apparatus of class domination' and 'an apparatus of competition between segments of the bourgeoisie' (Barker, 1991, p 182). In other words: 'the socially uneven worldwide spread of capitalism is embedded within the *combined* geopolitical circumstances of the modern states-system' (Bieler et al, 2010, p 27, original emphasis).

This standpoint is distinguished by the claim that being structurally interdependent, states and capitals are governed by distinct but congruent and 'homologous imperatives', respectively the pursuit of territorial power and economic profits (Harvey, 2003b). The territorial and profit imperatives can clearly conflict, for example when imperialist adventures go wrong or when profit-seeking capitalists undermine the reproduction of the social order. Moreover, strategic territorial goals may be contested and subject to struggle within the state system. Nevertheless, because capitalism is defined by uneven spatial development, territorial competition remains fierce and closely entwined with economic competition. What Harvey (2005, p 31) calls the inherent asymmetry of 'spatial exchange relations' means that geopolitical competition, including competition of the military and imperialistic kinds, remains central to contemporary political economy. States and capitals need each other to compete successfully: capital needs access to territory to make a profit, the state need revenues to maintain social order and pursue territorial advantage.

Unlike capitalists, politicians and state managers face a variety of pressures, not least on the electoral front. However, they can respond effectively and sustainably to public pressure only if system maintenance is first secured, an immediate and increasingly pressing challenge at a time of crisis and austerity. Thus, state managers tend to behave like 'collective capitalists' not primarily because they are part of the capitalist class, are compelled by the capitalist class or are otherwise culturally inclined (although they may well be), but because it makes practical sense to them given the daily tasks of system reproduction and maintenance in which they are employed. Each group of actors tends to seek strategic alliances with the other to fulfil their own goals, but the goals themselves are also homologous. The crisis in Greece, where the capitalist state is arraigned against a vast, cosmopolitan majority, is a stark example. This account supports the notion that the social system constitutes an emergent, emerging and contradictory totality rather than a precariously coupled ecology of autopoetic systems, but in a way that neither conflates nor creates a dualism between the terms in the relationship.

The primary purpose of elaborating this Marxist conception of the state–capital relation is to challenge the post-traditional account of the heterodox, post-coercive state inhabiting an increasingly benign post-national order, a world unencumbered by the conflictual imperatives of old. It is to maintain that states and statism are inescapable features of contemporary political economy and deeply embedded in the structures of geopolitical and economic competition. If the imperative to compete encompasses both capitals and states, then it is difficult to see how governments can successfully or sustainably foster connectionist politics. This is not to deny the importance of changes in the organisation of states, but to avoid conflating institutional changes, such as marketisation or the celebration and cultivation of governance networks, with fundamental changes in the social structure. As Chapter Five argues, the essential role of capitalist states in economic and geopolitical competition is crucial in explaining why 'governmentalisation' tends to trump any impulse towards post-traditional network governance.

Classes

As Chapter One highlighted in discussing Beck and Giddens, the case against class is that the epoch is 'simply too fluid, too transient and too awash with turbulent global scapes, mobilities or networks to be comprehended with the static and clunky ontological categories of the past' (Atkinson, 2007, p 363, paraphrasing Beck). We must therefore liberate ourselves from 'old theoretical schemes' and start again from scratch with networks (Urry, 2003, p 95). The journey from capital and class to dispersion and networks occurred in the context of the unquestionably debilitating defeats suffered by the international working class during the neoliberal offensive, particularly in countries like Chile, the UK and the US (Harvey, 2005). With a few notable exceptions, trade union struggles in countries like the UK and the US have not delivered decisive victories for three decades (although the picture is very different elsewhere in Europe). However, the post-traditional theory of class dispersion is both replete with contradictions and ignores contemporary class formation, reformation and revitalisation.

Class and inequality

Atkinson (2007, p 356) rightly notes that the persistence of class-based inequality does not falsify the theory of reflexive modernisation. Beck works, at least tacitly, with the Marxist distinction between 'a class in itself' and 'a class for itself'. He does not suggest that the class relation between wage labourers and capitalists is disappearing, rather that the conscious manifestation of class in collective action is becoming untenable. Reflexive modernisation dissolves 'classes for themselves' so that individuals look to 'biographical solutions for systemic contradictions' (Beck, 2007, p 686). However, this distinction arguably rests on the dubious claim that classes achieved sustained levels of consciousness 'for themselves' in first modernity. In fact, the influence of 'traditions' such as sectionalism, nationalism, welfarism and attachment to mass social democratic parties, seen by Beck as the conditions of class loyalty, is often held up as the reason why working-class unity against capitalism could not be achieved (Elliott, 1993). In other words, the decline of the working class cannot be inferred from a-historical claims about past class consciousness any more than the rise of the network society can be inferred from the notion that we were once governed by a monarchical state machine.

The same is true of the ruling class, discussed by Clarence Stone in explaining the differences between regime-theoretical and Marxist accounts of urban politics. Like Beck, Stone does not deny the presence of class effects in the distribution of goods, but asserts that they occur contingently and in ways requiring no ruling elite or command forms of domination (1980, p 979). On the contrary, he claims that public officials exhibit a level of discretion, which Marxism cannot explain. But, as was argued in the preceding section, a non-functionalist Marxism does not require that one group obeys the instructions of the other or even knows its wishes instinctively. It rather maintains that the structurally interdependent and homologous interests of capitalists and state managers tend to draw them into strategic alliances in pursuit of their own goals. The other founding father of urban regime theory, Stephen Elkin, argued that Marxism requires the ruling class to exercise an 'implausible' degree of rationality and planning (1985, p 184). However, no serious Marxist today argues that the ruling class of 'hostile brothers' is homogenous, except in seeking to extract profits. Read as the conscious action of an undifferentiated elite, class domination is clearly implausible. But, to predicate the existence of any class on its consciousness is wholly at odds with Marxist analysis. Conscious working-class unity is the objective of socialist strategy, not its premise.

However, defending Marxist analysis in this way does not tell us whether social class today is a 'zombie category'. For Beck, 'the risk society' dissolves class and underpins the shift towards networks. He notes that certain risks continue to be distributed along class lines and the fact that wealth accumulates at the top of society, risk at the bottom, can 'seem to strengthen, not to abolish, the class society' (1992, p 35). He accepts that the wealthy are able to purchase safety or insurance against certain risks. They can eat organic foodstuffs, or better manage their diets to avoid toxins. However, he still maintains that the globalisation of risk pluralises societies, breaks down borders and barriers and gives rise to new social formations trumping class. Risk cannot be contained by old categories because private escape routes shrink and 'class-specific barriers fall before the air we breathe' (1992, p 36). Risk produces a 'social boomerang effect', meaning that it catches up, sooner or later, with those who profit from it.

The most compelling argument in favour of this position is the global sustainability crisis caused by resource depletion, mass extinctions and human-influenced climate change. These crises might be explained by the frenzied pursuit of profit in the first instance, and the associated risks might be distributed along class lines. Nevertheless, Beck argues that they pose a universal threat, which is why poverty is hierarchic and smog is democratic. Yet this beguiling aphorism is misleading. Beck himself recognises that smog plainly is not democratic as 'the proletariat of the global risk society settles beneath the smokestacks ...' (1992, p 41). Here, the levelling effects of risk might be conceived as unrealised tendencies – toxins will catch up with the rich in due course. However, it is difficult to conceive of any catastrophe short of the instant annihilation of all humanity that would not be mediated, in the first instance, through class and other traditional power asymmetries. The history of catastrophes from which few were immune, such as the great depression and two world wars, does not suggest that they affected different social groups equally. Rather, they had class effects (Rose, 2003).

Nor is it clear how Beck draws the boundary between different kinds of risk – why traditional risks, such as economic crisis, aggravate class divisions whereas contemporary ones do not (Wetherly, 2000). Take, for example, the Marxist view that the crisis-prone nature of capitalism threatens the 'common ruination of the contending classes'. From the perspective of the risk society, the prospect of common ruination (the universalising 'toxin' at the heart of the economic system) ought to trump the fatal schism between capital and labour. Yet, although the current crisis has produced some 'social boomerang' effects such as hostility towards bankers, the costs have been distributed unambiguously along class lines. The theory of risk as class leveller exaggerates the distinction between different kinds of risk and understates the unequal abilities of class actors to *defer* and *redistribute* the consequences of risk gone wrong. 'Risks to all' in the abstract have concrete asymmetric effects along class lines and indeed other 'traditional' lines such as nation, race and gender.

The limits of individualisation theory

Individualisation theory claims that although 'objective' class relations persist, people are forced to confront them as individuals. At the same time, Beck asserts that individualisation is a 'macro-sociological phenomenon, which possibly – but then again perhaps not – results in changes in attitude in individuals. That is the *crux of contingency* – how individuals deal with it remains an open question' (2007, p 681, original emphasis). If so, it is not clear why they might not respond, among other ways, collectively and in class terms. Beck continues, however, that the 'instance of falsification' is not to be found in the 'contingency and modes of behaviour of individuals', but in the state reforms leading to 'institutionalized individualization'. In other words, the 'objective' class structure remains intact and individuals may conceivably act as if they are part of a class. Yet, this does not matter because the primary factor is not the decline of the class structure or even class consciousness, but the neoliberal reform of the state. Here, Beck ties the rise and fall of social classes to the rise and fall of the Keynesian welfare state. This claim is confusing because it moves the analytical goalposts from the realm of underlying social change to policy change. But, even if we ignore that, Beck never explains why policy change should matter more in determining the fate of classes than the relationship between profit seeker and wage labourer.

Problems such as these suggest that like network governance theorists Beck conflates attitudinal and institutional change with change in the social structure, fudging the 'relationship between the macro, objective elements of the social cosmos (social structures) and micro or subjective elements (attitudes, behaviours, perceptions)' (Atkinson, 2007, p 709). Again, this critique does not itself invalidate the claim that class is a 'zombie category'. However, it does leave open the possibility that the so-called 'me generation' might, faced with the end of debt-fuelled consumption, the return of scarcity, the attack on jobs, wages and welfare and the massive upward redistribution of wealth in response to the sovereign debt crisis, reconstitute itself as the 'us generation'. Such would seem to be the objective of demonstrators attending possibly the largest trade union march ever held in the UK on 26 March 2011 and those engaged in waves of general strikes across parts of Africa, Europe and the Middle East.

The cybertariat

Chapter One highlighted claims that the demise (more accurately the spatial redistribution) of manufacturing and the rise of the flexible knowledge economy were powerful contributory factors in the decline of the western working class. In the UK, it is true that the Thatcherite assault shrunk the manufacturing base of the economy and with it the industrial working class. Processes such as financialisation, the rise of the 'service economy' and Third Way-style claims about 'post-capitalism' found their echoes on the left in the work of Hardt and Negri (2000, 2004), who see the traditional structures of capitalism being supplanted by the smooth, networked configurations of Empire and its nemesis,

Multitude. The essence of these claims is that the rise of immaterial or knowledge labour transforms the economy, as discussed earlier in this chapter, and dissolves or circumvents class in favour of network power. As Beck conflates capitalism with industrial society, so Hardt and Negri conflate the working class with industrial labour. They argue that because immaterial labour is inherently cooperative and affective and cannot be subordinated to the value chain it escapes capture by Empire and has immanent emancipatory power.

Like the impact of the information revolution on capitalism discussed earlier, its alleged implications for class are increasingly subject to critical scrutiny. Critics note firstly that the concept of immaterial labour ignores that all human labour is simultaneously material and immaterial and thus tends to exaggerate distinctions between different kinds of work. Even the most sophisticated forms of knowledge production depend on material infrastructure and physical inputs. Conversely, the most repetitive, standardised and monotonous tasks involve some cognitive input (Camfield, 2007, p 24). Second, by ignoring the different kinds and degrees of knowledge work, informationalists conflate radically dissimilar kinds of labour such as that of call centre workers, government administrators and elite software designers. As Camfield argues in his critique of Hardt and Negri, citing Dyer-Witherford, 'analysis that puts under one roof multimedia designers, primary-school teachers ... and strippers ... may reveal valuable commonalities, but can also cover up chasmic differences, fault lines of segmentation, veritable continental rifts that present the most formidable barrier for the organization of counterpower' (2007, p 34). Third, the notion that the knowledge economy represents an epochal break with 'industrialism' and cannot be subordinated to the value chain understates the capacity of capitalists to recuperate, standardise and render calculable the fruits of many kinds of labour. Huws (2003) sees this process occurring in the knowledge economy, where she detects an emerging 'cybertariat'. De-skilling, Taylorisation and nascent unionisation are rife in knowledge work, patterns that recur in the roll-out of new-wave technologies from early capitalism onwards. Rather than leading to the rise of affective, communicative and networked labour, the informational realm may be subject to the same top-down management–worker relations and the same instrumental rationalities as other industries. As Mosco (2008, p 124) suggested, we should take seriously the possibility that the information age is 'plain old capitalism with a new set of technologies'.

Class (re)formation

Chapter One discussed Beck's view that there have been several waves of individualisation in modernity. During the rise of industrial capitalism, for example, Engels discerned the 'dissolution of mankind into monads, of which each one has a separate essence and a separate purpose', becoming 'more repellent and offensive, the more these individuals are crowded together' (cited in Merrifield, 2002, p 35). Yet, previous waves of individualisation were accompanied by the emergence of new traditions and class subjectivities. The question posed by the theory of reflexive modernisation is whether the wave of individualisation unleashed by post-scarcity and the neoliberal offensive is unique and final, or conjunctural and potentially reversible (Callinicos, 2007b, p 308).

Recent research suggests that class formation proceeds apace, not least in the so-called 'Brazilianised' spaces that Beck and Giddens see arising in the developing world (Davies, 2010). Cammack (2006, p 6) highlighted a World Bank report predicting an increase in the global labour force from 3 billion to 4 billion by 2030, almost all in developing countries. Cammack further reveals that what Beck sees as underlying sociological change is, in fact, a neoliberal class strategy for creating a proletariat without class consciousness:

> The principal objective of this sustained effort was the systematic transformation of social relations and institutions in the developing world, in order to generalise and facilitate proletarianisation and capitalist accumulation on a global scale, and build specifically capitalist hegemony through the promotion of legitimating schemes of community participation and country ownership.

Zeilig and Ceruti (2008) support the view that neoliberalism fosters class formation, casting light on the complex class composition of African townships. In Soweto, for example, they found the distinction between the formal working class and the 'Brazilianised' slum-dweller of reflexive modernisation to be excessively simplistic. They discovered that 78.3% of Sowetan households contained a mix of formally employed, unemployed and self-employed family members. Rather than forming a labour aristocracy, those in formal employment have duties of kinship to those who are not. The class composition of Soweto is thus fluid.

Moreover, there is evidence that class formation and emerging class consciousness go hand-in-hand. Zeilig and Ceruti's picture of class formation 'in itself' is complemented by the recent return of class struggle and militancy to South Africa. If they are right, such developments signify the emergence of a new working class capable of acting 'for itself'. They conclude that similar patterns of class composition, formation and resistance occur in cities across Africa. The 2010 strike wave in China is the latest vivid example of class formation in a fast-developing nation subjecting ever-greater swathes of population and territory to capital accumulation. According to Dunn (2008, p 24), official Chinese statistics reported a ten-fold increase in strikes in a decade, even before the recent unrest. More broadly, the explosion of militant struggles across Europe and the Arab world draws attention to the potential for concerted class resistance, perhaps on an unprecedented global scale. Even in the UK, where the unions suffered some of the worst defeats of the 1980s and the ideological offensive against class has been unremitting, most people believed at the turn of the millennium that society was still divided along class lines and were emphatic that it is not a classless society (Savage, 2002, p 63). Savage did not find strong individual identification with particular classes, unsurprising in light of the crushing union defeats of the 1980s. However, a MORI survey in 2002 discovered that 68% agreed with the statement 'at the end of the day, I'm working class and proud of it', up from 51% in 1994 (Mortimore, 2002). According to Marks and Baldry (2009, p 54), 90% of people in Britain recognised the existence of social classes and saw themselves occupying a class position. Importantly, they found knowledge workers beginning to use class-related concepts to describe their position and status (2009, p 61).

Class remains important at the subconscious level too. Bourdieusian research demonstrates that the cultural signatures of class remain indelible as the habitus structures the way individuals engage with their social fields. According to Reay (2005, p 911), 'feelings of ambivalence, inferiority and superiority, visceral aversions, recognition, abjection and the markings of taste constitute a psychic economy of social class'. Davies' (2007) study of collaboration in Dundee and Hull, discussed in Chapter Three, found the clashing class-cultural habitus of state managers and citizen-activists to be crucial in explaining how interlocutors can share a common language yet fail to communicate meaningfully.

Thus, when post-traditionalists talk about the demise of class and claim that one can 'no longer' read social and political ideas or identities from class position, they overlook four powerful objections: that this reductionist, a-historical claim is a straw man, that wherever capital goes there is evidence of new class formation, that there has been a significant revival in class militancy globally and that even if individuals do not associate themselves with a social class, the subtle imprints of class in the habitus provide compelling cues for social conduct. In Bourdieu's (2003, p 30) words, by extolling the 'myth of the transformation of all wage earners into dynamic small entrepreneurs', Beck and Giddens merely peddle 'as societal norms those rules imposed on the dominated by the needs of the economy'. Individualisation and networks do not define the condition of late modernity; they are elements of a political strategy to undermine class consciousness in a period of vigorous class formation. This claim is developed in Chapter Five.

Dunn (2004) concluded his study of the modern workplace by arguing that nothing in the conjuncture makes working-class struggle inherently less likely today than it was in 1900 or 1950. As Harvey (2006, p 65) put it, referring to the massive transfer of wealth to the rich under neoliberalism: 'if it looks like class struggle and acts like class struggle then we have to name it for what it is' and organise accordingly. Restating class in this way changes the question posed by network governance theory. Instead of looking at how de-traditionalised actors cooperate to solve problems and mobilise resources in pursuit of notionally shared objectives, the challenge is to explore how the ideologies and practices of governance seek to reorganise class relations.

Summary

Jessop (2007a, p 244) noted the 'dialectic between the complexity of the real world and the manner in which the real world comes to be interpreted as complex'. He cautions: 'Do not multiply complications beyond what is necessary but do introduce as many as are necessary' (Jessop, 2007a, p 225). The challenge posed by the ideology of network governance is to think clearly about what is disorganised, distributed and complex, what is not, and who has an interest in asserting that complexity renders obsolete any attempt to organise and plan society collectively and democratically. If structures still have causal powers, if capitalism is still prone to devastating crises, if nation states are pivotal actors in the global political economy and if class is still a centrally important social cleavage, then the post-traditional conception of network governance based on trust among autotelic personalities in an increasingly differentiated polity is vulnerable to fundamental challenge. The concept of network governance as hegemony developed in Chapter Five builds on these alternative background assumptions, arguing that the ideology of networks is a significant facet of the flawed neoliberal hegemonic project.

Notes

[1] Rhizomorphous capacity is the ability to form and navigate a burgeoning complex of fluid network relations

[2] www.compassonline.org.uk/uploads/documents/WhatIsTheDemocraticLeft.doc.

FIVE

From network governance to hegemony

Introduction

To recap, Chapter Three argued that actual-existing governance networks appear dysfunctional from the standpoint of post-traditional governance theory, tending to replicate practices they were meant to surpass. Chapter Four argued that the basis for explaining this puzzle is that the social, political and economic conditions for widespread and sustainable network governance do not exist. If so, the phenomenon of governance networks must be explained in terms other than those of network governance theory. Chapter Five develops a Gramscian account, grounded in Marxist political economy. It argues that the promotion of governance networks can fruitfully be understood as a dimension of neoliberal hegemonic strategy, part of the 'regulative, cultural work of producing ideal neo-liberal subjects' (Johnson, 2007, p 107). However, as the critique of Foucauldian governance theory in Chapter Three and the discussion of the relationship between states and capitals in Chapter Four suggested, hegemony exists in a dialectical relationship with domination, formulated in Gramsci's theory of the integral state. The chapter argues that the everyday politics of governance networks represent the dialectics of the integral state in microcosm. These dialectics explain why roll-forward governmentalisation seems to trump the connectionist project and, hence, why the neoliberal hegemonic strategy confronts structural limits in everyday political encounters.

This chapter begins with a brief discussion of the post-Marxist Gramscian tradition before exploring the orthodox Gramscian conception of hegemony, focusing on the historic bloc, the integral state and passive revolution. Adapting Boltanski and Chiapello (2005a, 2005b), it then develops a historical account of how the synthesis of 'free market' economics and network ideology occurred in the fashioning of neoliberalism. The chapter proceeds to develop a preliminary assessment of the efficacy of the ideology of networks. It argues that viewed through the prism of the integral state, the everyday politics of governance networks point to the incompatibility of connectionism and neoliberal political economy. It finally contextualises the connectionist hegemonic project with the broader repertoire of governing technologies that constitute any concrete social formation.

Post-traditional Gramscian analysis

Chapter One argued that Gramscian influence in governance and public policy declined as post-traditional theory gained ground. Post-Gramscians (Lash, 2007; Thoburn, 2007) go so far as to announce the era of 'post-hegemonic' power, defined as the dispersion of collective traditions and the general meltdown of institutions, making the organisation of hegemony impossible. In governance theory, the Differentiated Polity Model is an example of post-hegemonic theory, emphasising the dispersion of structural power. The Danish School, by contrast, is influenced by Laclau and Mouffe's post-Marxist Gramscianism (for example Torfing, 1999), where recognition and voice in networks and other institutions is a struggle over meaning. Laclau and Mouffe's approach is distinguished from post-hegemony by the claim that it is possible, despite the proliferation of identities, to mobilise counter-hegemonic power around relatively stable counter-hegemonic discourses.

Chapter Four argued that interpretive governance theory is prone to epistemological slippage. Laclau and Mouffe's *Hegemony and Socialist Strategy* further exemplifies. They assert (2001, p vii) that there have been 'drastic transformations of the social structure' such as globalisation, multiculturalism and de-territorialisation, only then to conflate 'the social' with discourse. Attempts to confine hegemony to discourse power are seriously compromised when prefaced with positivistic generalisations about 'change'. From the perspective of Chapter Four, moreover, Laclau and Mouffe exaggerate and misinterpret structural changes, leading to the abandonment of classical theories that retain considerable analytical and explanatory power. As Joseph (2002, p 104) argued, 'hegemony loses its true meaning once it is separated from its material location in social practices and structures and is confined to the role of a discursive articulator'. Accordingly, Chapter Five develops an 'orthodox' Gramscian account of governance networks focusing on the material and ideological dimensions of the neoliberal project, and its limits.

The Gramscian conception of hegemony

Gramsci's great achievement was to grasp how bourgeois power is organised and maintained in different kinds of capitalist society. He found that the advent of formal equality in the West with universal suffrage and the ideological production and reproduction of public consent through education, the mass media and other institutions of civil society, were powerful instruments of hegemony (Gramsci, 1971). For Gramsci, the ideal-typical moment of hegemony occurs when all social resources are marshalled by the historic bloc whose objective is, as he put it (1971, pp 181-2), the unity of economic and political goals and, furthermore, 'intellectual and moral unity ... on a "universal" plane'. Comprehensive hegemony is the '*additional* power that accrues to a dominant group in virtue of its capacity to lead society in a direction that not only serves the dominant group's interests but is also perceived by subordinate groups as serving a more general interest' (Arrighi, 2005, p 32, original emphasis). However, hegemony is a continuous struggle in the Gramscian interpretation and 'pure' hegemony is unattainable. The empirical challenge is therefore to understand the dynamics of coercion, consent and resistance that constitute any hegemonic configuration.

The historic bloc

Jessop (1997, pp 56-7) defines the historic bloc as the 'historically constituted and socially reproduced correspondence between the economic base and the politico-ideological superstructures of a social formation', exercising (in addition) political, intellectual and moral leadership over dominant and dominated classes alike. Moral and political hegemony is rooted in the dominant mode of production and 'must necessarily be based on the decisive function' of the capitalist class (Gramsci, 1971, p 161). If the perspective developed in Chapter Four is accurate, then the form of the historic bloc will be mediated by the structural interdependencies and conflicts between states and capitals. The question addressed in this chapter is how the governing bloc seeks to coordinate dominant class fractions, political elites and more-or-less successfully mobilises civil society activists (Jessop, 2007a, p 25).

The neo-Gramscian approach to this question is 'weakly dialectical', positing the development of a transnational ruling class and transnational hegemony to which the nation state is increasingly subordinate. Cox developed the concept of 'nébuleuse' to describe how the 'transnational and international network of state elites, corporate representatives and intellectuals' coalesced into a historic bloc responsible for cultivating a 'policy consensus for global capitalism' (Cox with Schechter, 2002, p 33). The nébuleuse has no fixed institutional structure, but is constituted informally by the triumvirate of the World Bank, the World Trade Organization and the IMF, plus private authorities such as credit ratings agencies (Sinclair, 2005). To the extent that it is able to set strategic priorities and exercise global leadership the nébuleuse has hegemonic power. Grounded in class analysis, the neo-Gramscian approach nevertheless occupies some common ground with post-traditional theory, highlighting the decline of the effective power of both nation states and the working class as a potential counter-hegemonic force (Cox and Schechter, 2002, p 107). Schwartzmantel (2009, p 12), for example, argued that we approach Gramsci today in a context where 'the idea of a cohesive movement based on the working class belongs to "old style politics" which have no purchase in a more diverse society, in which different identities and movements compete for people's attention'.

According to Gramscians of a more orthodox Marxist persuasion, however, neo-Gramscians overstate hegemonic integration and downplay the persistence of crisis-tendencies, geopolitical rivalries and class struggle (Budd, 2007). As Chapter Four argued, global political economy remains grounded in the international system of competing nation states, and the ruling class is inherently (and viciously) heterodox. Chapter Four further argued that the state–capital relationship is best understood in terms of the structural interdependence of economic and political-territorial imperatives and the homology between the goals and functions of capitalists and state managers. If this perspective is right it would suggest that the national governing bloc, with spatiotemporal variations according to historical development and local political economy, must be taken seriously as an agent of hegemony. Importantly, nation states are still primary agents of coercive power, at least in the West. Taking coercion seriously inevitably brings the state back in (yet again) as a pivotal player. As Chapter Four argued, the relationship between the national and the supranational is dialectical and both terms are integral to it.

The integral state

For Anderson (1976, p 30), democracy has been crucial in the manufacture of hegemony in capitalist societies. He sees the widespread belief that people '*exercise an ultimate self determination* within the existing order' as the primary source of consent for it (original emphasis). The democratic foundations of consent are supplemented with ideological nostrums including the bourgeois appeal to technological rationality and the idea of civil society as the realm of free association and/or counter-power. Thus, observes Jessop (2007a, p 4), modern democratic states tend not to resort to violence and where they do, it is 'a sure sign of crisis or state failure'. Jessop points to a pivotal analytic distinction in Gramscian theory between hegemony and coercion, but the struggle for hegemony means that in practice coercion is the ever-present condition of consent. The study of hegemony is therefore about the changing form and relationship between coercion, resistance, active assent and passive consent for the goals of a prevailing hegemonic bloc.

Thomas (2009, p 137) argues that Gramsci's unique contribution to Marxist theory was not hegemony, but the concept of the integral state. His reading is significant because it resituates Gramsci within the classical Marxist tradition and rejects the concept of civil society autonomy for that of dialectical unity. Gramsci (1971, pp 262-3) defined the integral state as 'political society + civil society, in other words hegemony protected by the armour of coercion', where 'political society' denotes the coercive power of the state. Civil society is not conceived in liberal terms as the domain of free association, in democratic terms as the source of the public sphere or in Third Way terms as a partner of the state. It is rather the 'terrain upon which social classes compete for social and political leadership or hegemony over other social classes'. Hegemony is guaranteed 'in the last instance, by capture of the legal monopoly of violence embodied in the institutions of political society' (Thomas, 2009, p 137). However, hegemony and domination are not qualitatively distinct, but 'strategically differentiated forms of a unitary political power' (Thomas, 2009, p 163). Miéville (2005, p 126) argued that because contracts have to be enforceable, violence is integral to the commodity form and the realisation of exchange value. Coercion is not merely deployed in the 'last instance'; it is immanent to the relationship between governments, corporations and citizens (Frazer and Hutchings, 2011). It is situated in dialectical relationship with consent on a continuum from the everyday compulsion of juridical enforcement, the carceral state and routine, petty-fogging bureaucratic control-freakery to physical violence and warfare. The difference between consent and coercion is not, therefore, adequately captured by a simple distinction between governmentality and armed violence. The distinction is rather that between internal or biopolitical regulation (governmentality) and external regulation (disciplinary power), which includes but is not limited to violence. Just as consent operates on a continuum from passive and grudging to active and enthusiastic, so compulsion is a continuum from bureaucratic obstruction to armoured force. As in the market transaction, consent in the integral state is partly '*constituted by* a silent, absent force', the threat of violence without which 'the system of cultural control would be instantly fragile, since the limits of possible actions against it would disappear' (Anderson, 1976, p 43, original emphasis). Hegemony or consent in civil society is always mediated by coercion or tacit threat – the 'shadow of hierarchy'. In this reading, the integral state is the dialectical unity of hegemony-domination or coercion-consent.

Why is the continuum of coercion inescapable? As suggested earlier, hegemony is a struggle, not an accomplished fact. The flaw in any hegemonic strategy, argues Anderson (1976, p 29), is that as a system prone to accumulation crises capitalism tends to generate expectations among subordinate classes as the condition of consent to it that it cannot fully meet. Hence, contradictions accumulate, consent tends to be fragile and universal assent is never achieved. Or, as Poulantzas put it, the limits of capitalist power are inherent in the ways that 'its mechanisms incorporate and condense the struggles of the dominated classes without being fully able to fully integrate and absorb them' (cited in Jessop, 2007a, p 146). In other words, crises mark the point at which open material, physical and discursive struggles are most likely to be the determinants of future development. In Anderson's terms, capitalist power is a 'topological system' with a 'mobile centre', so that in a political crisis 'capital re-concentrates from its representative into its repressive apparatus' (1976, p 44). Yet there is much ground between armoured coercion and comprehensive hegemony in which coercion and consent coexist in dialectical unity. As will be argued later, this expanded conception of coercion means that governance networks can fruitfully be understood as a form of the integral state in microcosm.

Passive revolution and the hegemonic apparatus

The term 'passive revolution' was originally coined to describe the post-Jacobin era of bourgeois revolutions when the capitalist class ascended to power without revolutionary violence, such as in the Italian Risorgimento (Thomas, 2009, p 147). The term has also been used to describe significant moments of struggle and transformation within capitalist states, when hegemony is threatened or an established configuration of the integral state no longer facilitates the expansion of capital and/or the maintenance of social order (Townshend, 2009, p 156). Gramsci used it to describe developments as diverse as the fascist counter-revolutions of the 1920s and 30s and sociotechnical modifications in the labour process leading to Fordism. The shift to neoliberalism discussed in the following section is another good example. Passive revolution therefore refers to a movement seeking to carry out transformation by non-revolutionary means within the confines of capitalism.

Given its crisis-prone nature, the capacity of the hegemonic bloc to organise passive revolution is essential for capitalist development. Gramsci saw the construction of hegemony as a dynamic concept 'a continuous process of formation and superseding of unstable equilibria' (Gramsci, 1971, p 182). In a successful passive revolution, established ways of thinking and acting are unlearned and replaced with new habits and norms such that a renewed 'second nature' is constructed (Fontana, 2002, p 163). Leys (1990, p 127) commented that 'for an ideology to be hegemonic, it is not necessary that it be loved. It is merely necessary that it have no serious rival'. However, as Fontana intimates, competition places constant pressure on hegemonic actors to *further* enrol consenters and *re-enrol* dissenters. Importantly, where the old ways become an impediment the bloc must, as well as disciplining dissenters, *disenrol* consenters as the condition of *re-enrolling* them in new ways forged in the passive-revolutionary process. The global and hyper-competitive phase of capitalism, particularly in a prolonged crisis, places acute pressure on the dominant bloc to mobilise and remobilise, mining every available human resource. Thus, while citizen passivity or grumbling of the kind discussed in Chapter Three is a form of subjection from the standpoint of counter-hegemonic politics, it is subversive from the standpoint of hegemonic leadership. Despite the improbability of comprehensive hegemony, 'love' is precisely what the neoliberal project strives for through connectionist ideology. Conversely, in Marxist crisis-theoretical terms any hegemonic moment, however encompassing, will be limited in space-time. If it is not then remade from the top down, or overthrown from the bottom up, decline is the likely outcome. As was the case with neoliberalism (discussed later), passive revolution also entails a struggle among fractions within the hegemonic bloc itself, such as between old- and new-wave enterprises or between Weberian and post-Weberian bureaucrats. The struggle for hegemony is therefore as much about episodic 'disenrolment' as it is 'enrolment', both inside and outside the hegemonic bloc.

One of the non-coercive strategies used in passive revolutions is 'trasformismo' (Paterson, 2009, pp 45-7), a term describing the capacity of the hegemonic bloc to 'cream off' opposition leaders. Clientalism is one example, what Jessop (2007a, p 113) calls 'force-fraud-corruption' another. Post-war corporatism was also a powerful medium of trasformismo investing workplace trade union officials with privileges unavailable to grass-roots members. For Paterson, it plays a pivotal role in passive revolutions as an 'ideological strategy that attempts to win over protesting popular movements as a whole so that they consent to the dictates of existing political institutions' (2009, p 47). Trasformismo therefore operates through a 'hegemonic apparatus', the means by which the integral state 'ascends to power through the intricate network of social relationships of civil society'. The ascent cannot be taken for granted, but 'must be repeated each day', if a prevailing bloc is to maintain its power (Thomas, 2009, pp 224-5).

Hegemony, thus described, requires no rational elite to manipulate the consciousness of the masses. It is inherently precarious, and where hegemonic forces achieve leadership, they do so 'honestly' precisely because they see their own interests as the general interest (Marx and Engels, 1998, pp 52-3). In Gramscian terms, the hegemonic bloc 'exercises power by presenting itself as "ethico-political", as the representative of universal values, independent of narrow economic, social or class interests' (Fontana, 2002, p 161). The discussion now turns to the emergence of the connectionist hegemonic strategy of neoliberalism.

Neoliberalism, networks and hegemony

Neoliberalism is here understood as a globalising hegemonic project, emerging contingently from the economic and social crises of the 1960s and 70s. At its core is the passive-revolutionary attempt to revitalise capital accumulation, whose Keynesian form began faltering in the late 1960s amid a global wave of social and political instability. It is contested and spatiotemporally variable in form and outcome, but distinguished by the overriding commitment to expanding markets, refashioning states and enrolling civil societies. Neoliberalising regimes achieved decisive victories during and after the crises that engulfed the world from the late 1960s. Naomi Klein's conception of neoliberalism as the 'shock doctrine' depicts it as a 'fundamentalist form of capitalism', consistently 'midwifed by the most brutal forms of coercion, inflicted on the collective body politic as well as on countless individual bodies' (2007, p 18; see also Žižek, 2009, pp 18-19). While it arguably endowed the neoliberal avant-garde with excessive a priori ideological and organisational coherence, the shock doctrine is a salutary corrective to accounts that downplay the role of states as coercive agents of neoliberalisation.

By way of example, the infamous fiscal crisis in New York represented the neoliberal passive-revolutionary moment in microcosm, highlighting the mix of crisis, coercion, class-conscious mobilisation and ideological struggle that enabled new governing principles to be established as the norm. By the mid-1970s, New York had accumulated significant debts in the context of a weakening economy. In 1975, 'a powerful cabal of investment bankers ... refused to roll over the debt and pushed the city into technical bankruptcy' (Harvey, 2005, p 45), the urban equivalent of a sovereign debt crisis. After this Kulturkampf, city revenues were reallocated to debt payment funded by wage freezes, cuts in employment and welfare and the imposition of service user fees. Humiliatingly, municipal unions were compelled to invest pension funds in the purchase of city bonds, creating a structural incentive to moderation. Journalist Ken Auletta, writing in *The New York Magazine*, described the process in quasi-Gramscian terms as a 'bloodless revolution' of the kind that 'just slip in like fog' (1976, p 32), changing the 'language and even the nature of power' (1976, p 33).

The federal state was pivotal to the Kulturkampf. Supporting Klein's idea of neoliberalisation as shock therapy, Harvey (2005, p 46) reported William Simon, Secretary of the US Treasury, saying that the terms of any bailout should be 'so punitive, the overall experience so painful, that no city, no political subdivision would ever be tempted to go down the same road' of debt-financed spending. Harvey remarked that this strategy was 'every bit as effective as the military coup ... in Chile', redistributing wealth 'to the upper classes in the midst of a fiscal crisis' (2005, p 45). Powerful economic actors mobilised in the face of a crisis of profitability, increasing competition and declining confidence in the city's ability to pay its debts. They were encouraged by a cash-strapped federal government faced with unrest at home and military defeat overseas. When Mayor Abraham Beame proved unable to implement stringent enough measures, he was side-lined. The Governor of New York, Hugh Carey, effectively became 'both Governor and Mayor' (Auletta, 1976, p 35). Carey established the Municipal Assistance Corporation to manage the crisis, appointing Democrat financier Felix Rohatyn to lead the rescue. According to Berman (2007, p 24), Rohatyn conceded 'we have balanced the budget on the backs of the poor'. This process fundamentally changed the political landscape. Liberal New Yorkers reluctantly conceded 'new realities', creating conditions in which the neoliberal common sense of the feasible and desirable – competitiveness and fiscal responsibility - could crystallise and acquire hegemonic form. More cautious local state actors were overridden (for example Beame), removed by fiat or nurtured into 'pragmatic' dispositions as their choice horizons narrowed.

Neoliberalisation in its many guises involved more or less decisive passive-revolutionary interventions of this kind based on variable configurations of coercion–consent. Chile was among the most brutal passive-revolutionary moments. The UK's IMF bailout in 1976, and subsequent retrenchment, was analogous to New York at the national scale, a decisive moment in the neoliberal turn and a prequel to the Thatcherite assault on an increasingly bitter and demoralised working class. Both processes involved state coercion short of military violence. Peck and Tickell (2002, pp 397-8) argue that neoliberalisation has led to 'fast policy transfer'. Ideas propagated in the US, the UK or through the international organisations are copied by other countries and domestic policy scrutiny is curtailed in favour of 'off the shelf' solutions, 'leading to a deepening and intensification' of neoliberalisation. The contingent neoliberalisation of leading capitalist states created the conditions for an internally differentiated supra-national bloc, articulated by the international organisations, providing incentives to adaptors and creating increasing difficulties for non-adaptors. Successful cases of neoliberalisation represented sunk-investment, narrowing choice horizons and opportunity structures for further neoliberalisation. Using 'off the shelf' neoliberal policies became common sense, part of a positive feedback loop in which 'the shock doctrine' could begin retreating to the shadows – at least in the West.

Cox (1994, p 99) argued that global political economy 'is characterized by a "new capitalism" which opposes any form of state or interstate control or intervention'. However, state power was pivotal to processes described in the preceding paragraphs. As was noted in Chapter Four, Cammack described neoliberalism as an attempt to foster class relations without class consciousness. He further argued (2004, p 190) that neoliberalism seeks to 'equip the poor for their incorporation into and subjection to competitive labour markets and the creation of an institutional framework within which global capital accumulation can be sustained, while simultaneously seeking to legitimate the project through participation and a pro-poor agenda'. Neoliberalism is not anti-state, but an active state project. It was always perceived as such by agents of neoliberalisation. Cammack (2010, p 270) records that the World Bank 'necessarily took the view that the state had to be an active agent of change rather than a passive conduit for uncontained market forces'. It stated that competitive markets 'cannot operate in a vacuum — they require a legal and regulatory framework that only governments can provide'. Hence, 'it is not a question of state or market: each has a large and irreplaceable role' (World Bank, 1991, p 1), including Thomas L. Friedman's 'hidden fist'.

As Chapter Two suggested, the idea that states must re-acculturate citizens was also integral to neoliberal thinking from the outset (Retort, 2004). Coercive neoliberalism paved the way not for the postmodern or post-national state and the unfettering of civil society, but for regulatory neoliberalism where states use a variety of technologies, including governmentalities and harder or softer forms of coercion, to foster hegemonic conditions in which they can retreat to the shadows. From an integral state perspective, then, 'coercive' and 'regulatory' neoliberalism are not pure 'types' or 'periods'. They coexist in a dialectical relationship. Which term of the relationship is most prominent depends on circumstance; it is the 'dialectical mix that matters'.

Connectionist ideology can be understood as a key facet of regulatory or roll-out neoliberalism. Although they do not formulate it in these terms, Boltanski and Chiapello's (2005a) *New Spirit of Capitalism* draws attention to the synthesis of neoliberalism and the ideology of informational capitalism as its justificatory medium. Boltanski and Chiapello record how corporations reflexively appropriated the 'artistic critique' motivating the 1968 generation of activists. Whereas 'social critique' condemned the inequalities of capitalism, the artistic critique lamented the routine and standardisation imposed by Fordism, castigating it for obliterating individuality, demanding increased personal autonomy and reasserting the creative spirit. In place of the sclerotic Fordist system and its industrial hulks, authors of the artistic critique advanced a new 'connectionist' paradigm inspired by the emerging knowledge economy, what Boltanski and Chiapello call the 'project-oriented justificatory regime'. This justificatory order heralds the virtues of creativity, individual adaptability, communication and the art of connecting laterally in project-based teams built around shared goals and affective trust. Hence, power is constructive: 'the balance of power is no longer a salient issue when the main objective is the creation of a sense of belonging, a feeling of satisfaction with and trust in one another' (Boltanski and Chiapello, 2005b, p 183).

As Chapters Two and Four highlighted, the global capitalist renaissance of the 1980s and 1990s was inflected by this connectionist legitimating discourse, a new justificatory regime seeking to cultivate belief in the avant-garde practices of informational capitalism throughout economy and society. According to Žižek (2009, p 52):

> In such ways, capitalism is transformed and legitimized as an egalitarian project: accentuating auto-poetic interaction and spontaneous self-organization, it has even usurped the

> far left's rhetoric of workers' self-management, turning it from an anti-capitalist slogan into a capitalist one.

The origins of the artistic critique lay in the political and aesthetic avant-garde of the 1950s (Boltanski and Chiapello, 2005, p 170), when informational capitalism was beginning to incubate through ideas such as Bernal's (1957) scientific-technical revolution. These ideas were recuperated to political ideology, for example by Harold Wilson's 'white heat' and John F. Kennedy's 'New Frontiers'. According to Wilson (1963):

> In all our plans for the future we're redefining and we're restating our socialism in terms of the scientific revolution. But that revolution cannot become a reality unless we are prepared to make far-reaching changes in economic and social attitudes which permeate our whole system of society. The Britain that is going to be forged in the white heat of this revolution will be no place for restrictive practices or for outdated methods on either side of industry.

Wilson conceived the 'white heat' as a scientific paradigm shift, making socioeconomic 'modernisation' imperative and rendering old class conflicts obsolete. Modernisation, in the Wilsonian vision, held out the promise of prosperity for all, heralding the end of class domination. The parallels with the later informational fetish of the Third Way are obvious. Randall (2009) argued that announcing a new epoch is a common strategy, particularly for 'revisionist' or right-moving social democrats. In Gramscian terms it is the trademark of passive-revolutionary strategies that imbue technical innovations with emancipatory potential. In the hands of Kennedy and Wilson, scientific-technical and informational boosterism was inflected with the same irrational exuberance that Alan Greenspan later attributed to financial markets. Randall (2009, p 203) further commented that, like speculative bubbles, ideological bubbles tend to pop. Harold Wilson's new paradigm failed to halt relative economic decline, save Old Labour from electoral defeat in 1970 or prevent a wave of class struggles under Edward Heath's Tories. The 'New Frontiers' project lost its progressive aura when Richard Nixon won the Presidency in 1968. Informational capitalism could not save the Third Way when the 'weightless economy' collapsed under the burden of its own contradictions in 2008.

Neoliberalism did not, therefore, appropriate the artistic critique in a vacuum. It recuperated and transformed modernisation agendas and ideologies that were already prevalent. Corporate and state managers were able to appropriate it in the context of a burgeoning scientific-technical paradigm where nascent informational capitalism was already discernible. It was the already-existing 'good news' from which social democrats and avant-garde neoliberals alike drew inspiration for their modernisation strategies.

The potential Gramscian affinities of Boltanski and Chiapello's account are obvious. The flaw in their analysis is arguably its excessive credulity towards connectionist ideology. They claim (2005a, p 173) that the transformation of capitalism since the 1960s has brought the connectionist world into existence. The project-oriented justificatory regime seeks to legitimise an established reality 'and restrict its practices in such a way as to substantiate the affirmation of a justificatory constraint that acts on behalf of the common good'. However, Boltanski and Chiapello wrongly conflate the justificatory regime with the condition it seeks to legitimise, exaggerating the rise of the network and ignoring the profound disjuncture between hegemonic ideology and contemporary political economy.

Chapter One quoted Lowndes' (2001, p 1962) claim that network governance was promoted by governments in a 'strategically selective' context that favoured networks but where hierarchies and markets remained part of the 'mix'. It is argued here, instead, that networks became the favoured ideology of markets and states in a crisis-ridden context that, given the retreat of the left, became strategically selective towards ideas like the New Spirit of Capitalism. Gramsci (1971, p 133) argued that if a particular configuration of the historic bloc is to become hegemonic, it must successfully link political struggle with a programme of economic reform. Connectionist ideology fulfilled a vital part of this condition for western neoliberalism and its Third Way variants in the aftermath of social conflict and structural adjustment.

If the promise of a flexible, creative and networked economy served as a powerful justification for neoliberal capitalism, it has been used with equal enthusiasm to legitimise neoliberal state modernisation. Boltanski and Chiapello explain how the 'new spirit' inspired middle-class champions of the artistic critique in France, many of whom later became part of the state elite. Influenced by connectionist intellectuals like Giddens, Third Way governments also sought to reinvent themselves in the language of networks deemed 'peculiarly appropriate to the operation of the enabling state' (Bevir, 2005, p 46). Talk of 'complexity', 'whole systems thinking', 'adaptivity', 'diversity' and 'inclusivity' is pervasive in Anglophone public sector discourse (Blake et al, 2008; Benington and Hartley, 2009). Aided and abetted by consultants, senior managers exhort local authorities to 'think like Google' and become 'the networked council'.[1] This ideology has been cultivated, not least, by business schools where post-traditional leadership and management ideologies are taught to rising public service leaders, reinforcing the orthodoxy. The British National School of Government described one programme for fast-trackers in the language of the New Spirit of Capitalism as being designed for those 'leading people in non-hierarchical ways, for example, members of project or special teams'. It elaborated:

> It is crucial for those on the Fast Stream to develop their ability to lead not only those they manage but also others with whom they work collaboratively. The increased demands on organisations to deal effectively with ambiguity, unpredictability, complexity and turbulence means that leaders must be proactive and take their people with them.[2]

A society of networks based on trust is thus the visionary regulative ideal of neoliberalism, a hegemonic ambition inspiring states, markets and civil societies alike. To the extent that it could actually be achieved beyond the ideational and discursive fields, connectionism would vindicate the informationalist modernisation strategy, solve the problem of 'community cohesion' by forging reflexive 'social capital', give a further lease of life to capital accumulation and enable hierarchy to retreat into the shadows. It would represent the strategic triumph of 'soft power' and a new hegemony, at least until the next round of crises. However, as Chapter Three demonstrated, the hegemonic ideology of network governance encounters intractable barriers in the attempt to transform the governing landscape. The neoliberal hegemonic project remains flawed, or incomplete. The following sections use the Gramscian framework to explain why.

Governance networks and the integral state

To recap again, the grounds for a Gramscian account are two-fold: first, network governance is an important dimension of hegemonic ideology operating across economy, state and society. However, there is a pronounced tendency for the hegemonic ideology and the institutional practices associated with it to fail, insofar as the outcome is the roll-forward of practices such as hierarchy, creeping managerialism and network closure. Thus, Chapter Three argued that the universe of governance networks points not to the dawn of a new connectionist epoch, the condition of 'network governance', but to substantive continuity and governance as usual. It therefore highlighted the need to rethink the foundations of network governance theory in contemporary political economy, the task undertaken in Chapter Four. The second premise for the Gramscian account is that the concept of the integral state, understood as the dialectics of coercion-consent, can add value in explaining the conundrum: why is it that the universe of governance networks designed to advance the connectionist vision seems often to subvert it? Why, in other words, does the combinard not turn up in practice (McKee, 2009, p 474)? The following paragraphs begin to develop an answer to this question at the systemic level and in the micropolitics of governance networks. Chapter Six then explores possible parameters for a Gramscian governance research agenda.

Part of the reason why collaborative governance structures fail to institutionalise the dispositions and practices of the combinard must be, as argued earlier, that the 'network state' is a *project* not an accomplished outcome, a project undermined by its material foundations in competition, conflict and crisis. That this is so is evidenced not only by the critical literatures on governance networks discussed in Chapter Three, but also the burgeoning critique of the transformation thesis across the social sciences. In management, for example, Grint (2010, p 103) notes the 'desperate search for the post-heroic' form of leadership, which he claims is untenable because sacralisation of the leader is inherent in the role. Bolden et al's (2009) study of the 'distributed leadership' discourse in British university management supports Grint, finding that it was 'most powerful as a rhetorical device' disguising the demise of collegiality and consensual decision making. Or, as Clarke and Butcher (2009, p 590) put it in a study of business school management, managerial discourse perpetrates 'an illusion of participation that obscures institutionalized power relationships'. The *Times Higher Education Supplement* went so far as to argue that the British university system is engulfed by 'hyper-bureaucracy', increasingly consumed by a 'bureaucratic nightmare' of rankings, rapacious performance management and audit overload (Mroz, 2010). Critical management studies further argue that the dominant trends are increased audit, surveillance and the attempt by managers to enrol subjectivities in pursuit of improved performance (for example Costea et al, 2008), alongside old-fashioned bullying and coercion (McCarthy et al, 2001), reportedly at its highest level in a decade across the corporate, public and voluntary sectors. From the perspective of labour studies, Alonso (2001, p 284) argued powerfully that the ideology of networks propagated by corporations has created a 'fog of ignorance' obscuring the vigorous formation of hierarchies by the very managers who proselytise networking. Perhaps most powerfully of all, given his earlier position, Stoker (2011, p 29) now argues:

> Local government systems need a substantial amount of hard power in order to exercise soft power. You can't win with the losing hand. That is the fatal flaw in the community governance vision.

It is hard to imagine a pithier expression of the dialectical relationship between coercion and consent.

As Chapter Four intimated, one barrier to authentic network governance is the condition of neoliberal political economy itself. Johnson (2007, p 105) argued that because of the 'congealment' of events, such as climate change, the global war on terror, neo-imperialism, growing concentrations of wealth, power and inequality and now the economic and sovereign debt crises, 'models of a fragmented world do not have the ontological purchase to grasp realities of power or guide transformative practices'. Hobsbawm (1989, p 46) formulated the problem in terms similar to Polanyi's, arguing:

> The state must henceforth, in the interests of withering away, give ever more precise directions about how its funds should and should not be spent … central power and command are not diminishing but growing, since 'freedom' cannot be achieved but by bureaucratic decision.

Hobsbawm's dialectic highlights a structural barrier to the neoliberal hegemonic project and, by extension, a major impediment to network governance. If there is a fundamental contradiction between neoliberal ideology and neoliberal political economy, then hierarchy cannot but emerge from the shadows, whether in the guise of administrative coercion to deal with mildly recalcitrant citizens or the violence of state-led imperialist adventuring and economic shock therapy.

This may be the most compelling explanation why, to invoke Arrighi (2005), hegemony may now be tending to give way to dominance and resistance from the scale of international political economy to the daily politics of the state–civil society interface. The attempt to synthesise neoliberal political economy with network governance fails because the relationship is dialectical, not constructive. The conditions of late capitalism preclude the realisation of the neoliberal hegemonic project, if this is understood as a utopian attempt to escape the confines of modernity and dissolve the integral state. This contradiction manifests, in different ways, throughout the universe of governance networks.

The micropolitics of the integral state

Authentic Marxian inquiry entails a continual movement between theory, evidence and transformative practice. Hence, claiming that the universe of governance networks can be understood as a form of the integral state under neoliberalism raises the question of how it helps make sense of specific cases, such as those discussed in Chapter Three. It was argued earlier that political leaders, corporate elites, intellectuals and state managers all play a prominent role in propagating connectionist ideology. The concept of the integral state draws particular attention to the role of state managers and citizen-activists in governance networks. Connectionist ideology is pervasive in contemporary public administration. Yet, as Du Gay (2003) highlights, aspirations for a post-Weberian public service coexist with the neoliberal culture of 'responsiveness' or 'partisanship' towards policy delivery, the shift from ostensible neutrality to policy 'enthusiasm' and control freakery. The tendency towards 'creeping managerialism' discussed in Chapter Three points to the enactment of this dialectic in the work of the state manager: someone committed to disavowing their own coercive power, fostering adaptive behaviour and networking in a complex environment, but also 'responsive' to ever-increasing pressures to 'deliver' in the face of public dissatisfaction and scarce resources. Du Gay's analysis draws attention to the possibility that in day-to-day sense making, the connectionist impulse is commonly trumped by the managerialist impulse. Whereas the post-traditional administrator is a 'bricoleur' (Innes and Booher, 1999), encouraging citizen-activists to express themselves as the medium of innovative governance solutions, the New Public Management (NPM) technocrat censors it in the name of efficiency. Whether and how this contradiction is enacted by individual managers working at the civil society interface through governance networks is a potential topic for further research, but the tenor of the critique in Chapter Three is that the dilemma is commonly resolved in favour of administrative domination, albeit of a different kind than the studied neutrality of the ideal-typical Weberian bureaucrat. Where the dilemma plays out in this way, state managers cannot be effective agents of the hegemonic practices they espouse.

Considering the day-to-day production and contestation of hegemony also invites reflection on the manner in which dispositions and dilemmas are reinforced, contested and remade. As Chapter Four highlighted, Bourdieusian research shows how the cultural signatures of class and profession become inscribed as the habitus acquired through lived experience regulates the way individuals engage with social fields like governing institutions. These constitute Reay's 'psychic economy of social class' (2005, p 911). The present author's study of governance networks (Davies, 2007, 2009), discussed in Chapter Three, found the clashing habitus of network managers and citizen-activists to be crucial in explaining how interlocutors ostensibly sharing a common agenda could fail to communicate meaningfully about it. Whereas administrator discourse emphasised stakeholder responsibility for contributing to the governing effort, the citizen-activist tended to draw on a rights-based discourse, the right to a political voice and investment in the community. The depoliticisation of the collaborative space meant that value conflicts never surfaced there, making the 'consensus' brittle and shallow and fostering mutual suspicion. Despite depoliticisation (Geddes, 2006), tacit conflict undermined the ethical virtues required for networking and effectively prevented the desired anthropological transformation. This example points to the possibility that one reason for the roll-forward of hierarchy is the clash between the 'good sense' of distrusting citizen-activists and the dilemmas and sense-making activities of network managers, which reflect pressures in contemporary political economy that brook neither slack nor pause for reflection.

Bourdieu (1984, p 462) further observed that collaborating with dominant groups 'discredits and destroys the spontaneous political discourse of the dominated'. The language of the dominant group imposes 'a total but totally invisible censorship on the expression of the specific interests of the dominated, who can only choose between the sanitised word of official discourse and inarticulate grumblings'. The enactment of symbolic power in discourse is itself a powerful medium of governmentality. Diamond's (2004) study of community regeneration partnerships found that the network managers' relationship with citizen-activists was marked indelibly by cultural capital: education, language, income and physical distance from the communities they were meant to serve. The official was further separated from community 'partners' by security barriers, code-locked doors, CCTV and other symbols of managerial and professional power. Diamond's example thus illustrates how the cultural trappings of management operate as forms of symbolic power reinforcing the 'otherness' of the professional habitus, again undermining the potential for cultivating ethical virtues required for network governance.

In Davies' study (2007, 2009), the tacit struggle over meaning led network managers to erect administrative barricades against dissenters, using the 'inarticulate grumblings' of citizen-activists as grounds for excluding them through 'restructuring'. In this case, roll-forward hierarchy arose from the combination of value conflict, mutual incomprehension and the reflexively technocratic practices of state managers trying to deal with citizen-activists incapable of fulfilling the role of the ideal-typical 'good partner', the sociable, problem-solving entrepreneur. The Bourdieusian insight is that if cultivating the connectionist disposition is understood as the attempt to nurture a particular habitus among social groups who are incapable of assimilating it in virtue of their own class cultures and aspirations, then it is self-limiting and prone to foundering on the rocks of misrecognition evident in governance networks. Misrecognition, deriving from the clashing habitus, may therefore be another trigger for the dilemma facing network managers, resulting in roll-forward hierarchy and network closure. In Gramscian terms, the attempt to make a specific set of interests 'ethico-political', to translate them into the general interest, overreaches itself where the sociocultural conditions of translation do not exist and cannot be cultivated. As Chapter Six argues, processes of this kind could also be an interesting area for research on the micropolitics of the integral state.

Governance networks and the institutionalisation of neoliberal hegemony

Notwithstanding these limits it is important to recognise the hegemonic power of neoliberalism and the more consensual moment of the integral state. Crouch (2011) rightly argues that it has so far proven extraordinarily resilient. Despite its manifest failures and disastrous consequences there is as yet no organised counter-hegemonic movement (although this might emerge from burgeoning mass strikes, anti-cuts movements or indeed the wave of revolutions in Africa and the Middle East) or alternative passive-revolutionary accumulation strategy. Hay (2011) calls this condition 'pathology without crisis': the seemingly precarious situation of an ideology whose accumulation strategy is bankrupt remaining, for the time being, dominant. The political segue from financial crisis to crisis of public spending and sovereign debt crisis is emblematic of Crouch's puzzle.

Within the world of governance networks, there are many studies suggesting that the connectionist ethos has indeed contributed to recuperating civil society activists. As suggested earlier, one of the most significant ways that governance networks fulfil a connectionist mission is by fostering depoliticised discourses. Geddes (2006, p 93) argues:

'[w]hile local partnerships are weak in their ability to change the way in which powerful interests and organizations act, they seem much stronger in their ability to restrict local policy and politics within narrow parameters'. Davies (2009) concurs that partnerships have cultivated a consensual ethos, rendering adversarialism taboo and establishing a depoliticised problem-solving discourse as the norm (see also Skelcher et al, 2005), although this ethos obscures underlying value conflicts.

Parts of the community-organising literature in the US reach similar conclusions. Stoecker (2003), for example, considered the respective merits of community organising (dissidence) and community development (participation). He argued that communities must organise to 'get the power' but that collaboration to procure further investment and expertise is necessary to keep it. However, he also found that where community organisations simultaneously engage in organising and partnerships, organising capacity suffers (2003, pp 496-7). To this extent, Stoecker lends support to the idea that governance networks recuperate organising potential and undermine the potential for dissident community leadership.

Research on the World Bank-funded Kecamatan Development Programme provides further insights into the cultivation of neoliberal governmentalities in the developing world. Kecamatan is a village-based programme in Indonesia to alleviate poverty, strengthen local government and community institutions and improve local governance. It has disbursed US$1.3 billion since 1998. Key principles include broad-based community participation, transparency and information sharing, an open agenda where villagers may propose any activity 'except for ones on a negative list', competition between villages for KDP funds and simplicity – 'no complex rules, just simple strategies and methods'. According to the World Bank, all KDP activities 'aim at allowing villagers to make their own choices about the kinds of projects that they need and want'. It says that the KDP has been implemented in some 49% of all Indonesian villages.[3]

This project is a good example of regulatory neoliberalism in action, seeking to imbue communities simultaneously with connectionist (build community and partnership) and competitive norms (connected communities must compete). According to Carroll (2009, p 449), 'the KDP, drawing upon the political technology of "participatory development", constitutes a distinctly different and temporarily effective delivery device for extending capitalist social relations and the institutions that the development orthodoxy posits should accompany such relations'. Cammack (2010, p 276) extends the point, noting that in countries like Brazil leaders with once 'impeccable radical credentials' embrace World Bank projects of this kind. He cautions that the recuperative powers of regulatory neoliberalism should not be underestimated, as they present 'a considerable analytical and existential challenge to advocates of other more radical forms of politics'.

Such studies suggest that while there might indeed be a prominent trend towards the governmentalisation of governance networks and a disjuncture between neoliberal ideology and neoliberal political economy, it does not preclude the emergence of something like connectionism locally, for example in areas where stronger economic growth makes more generous redistribution affordable and/or the habitus of administrators and civil society activists is more closely aligned, such as where activists are from the professional classes. Yet inclusivity is the raison d'être of hegemonic strategy and, as Chapters One and Three argued, networks of like-minded interlocutors are more likely to be exclusionary than inclusionary. However, exploring and explaining variable configurations of the integral state in different governing institutions could be a fruitful objective for future comparative research, discussed further in Chapter Six.

Connectionism in context

The purpose of this volume is to establish that the ideologies and practices of network governance can fruitfully be understood as a facet of the neoliberal hegemonic project and its limits. It is beyond the scope of the present work to offer comprehensive place-based accounts of hegemony, domination and resistance. However, it is important to recognise network governance as just one, albeit important, element of any concrete hegemonic strategy. Connectionist policies, such as cultivating social capital, are concerned with the re-acculturation of society as a whole. However, participation in governance networks is generally limited to a cadre of leading civil society activists. This fact does not reduce their importance as potential agents of trasformismo, but it does mean that any hegemonic strategy must rely on a mix of other tactics, including coercion and concessions. One task for place-based Gramscian research is therefore to assess the juxtapositions of connectionism and other strategies and tactics within specific state, suprastate and subnational governing blocs.

In the 1980s, for example, Jessop et al (1988) found that Thatcherism adopted a 'two-nations' hegemonic strategy, enrolling two-thirds of the nation behind the promise of shared prosperity and confining the other third to the margins and coercive supervision. Chapter Two argued that the subsequent Tory turn to active citizenship represented the beginnings of a strategy to enrol the other third. Third Way policy was 'inclusive', at least to the extent that it promised a place in the 'big tent' for all responsible citizens. An important tool for maintaining working-class acquiescence to neoliberalism, particularly in the UK, Europe and the US, was 'privatised Keynesianism' (Crouch, 2008). This term refers to the financing of consumption through personal debt, a strategy made necessary by low personal incomes and viable by the combination of rising asset prices, trading risk in the financial sector and transferring responsibility for defaults from lender to borrower. Crouch depicts privatised Keynesianism as a strategy to convince working-class people that their mortgaged houses and credit card debts constituted a share in national 'prosperity' and square the tension between the need to maintain consumer demand on the one hand and low wages, upward redistribution and the pathologies of the neoliberal accumulation model on the other. The management and celebration of debt-financed consumption created the purchasing power necessary for keeping the economy afloat and worked as a hegemonic mechanism. 'Consumerism' is therefore better understood as a duty of neoliberal citizenship and a form of 'individual economic chivalry' (Hilton, 2004, p 106) than as the rational choice of prosperous autotelic personalities.

The collapse of privatised Keynesianism poses the double-dilemma of how to sustain any sense of belonging forged through these hegemonic mechanisms and how to restore economic growth. Whether consumption can somehow be sustained in the face of defaults, austerity, wage cuts, stagnant house prices, the credit squeeze, high unemployment and potential 'double-dip' recessions remains to be seen. However, until the crash it fulfilled an important economic condition of connectionist neoliberalism. The promise of a connected society inspired by informational capitalism needed a credible prosperity narrative, made possible by the combination of sustained growth before 2008, and privatised Keynesianism.

For Crouch, privatised Keynesianism was partly a means of sustaining the economic bubble and partly a substitute for the redistributive policies of the Keynesian era. Neoliberalism has been the era of upward redistribution. Harvey (2005, p 17) shows a rough correlation between the severity of defeats inflicted on the organised working class and inequality in the form of rising Gini coefficients, the increasing share of national income allocated to the top 1% of wage earners and the declining proportion of national income allocated to labour. However, Gramsci (1971, p 161) argued that 'the fact of hegemony presupposes that account be taken of the interests and the tendencies of the groups over which hegemony is to be exercised'. The nature of concessions depends on economic conditions and the balance of hegemonic and counter-hegemonic forces locally, but even trenchantly neoliberal regimes make them, as the Thatcher government did to pay off certain groups during the confrontations of the mid-1980s and Gordon Brown did for New Labour (on a more principled basis) by introducing the minimum wage and 'redistribution by stealth'.[4]

If comprehensive hegemony is an ideal where coercion and concessions would both be unnecessary, real-world governing regimes rely on a variety of techniques in the material and ideological spheres and along the consensus–coercion continuum, depending in part on the extent of counter-hegemonic resistance and the relative health of the economy. Spatiotemporal variation in the degree and form of neoliberalisation (Ferguson, 2010) testifies not only to differences in the local balance of forces and the capacity for resistance, but also to the historical and geographical specificities of capitalist development – the unevenness characteristic of global political economy and the rate at which accumulation strategies become exhausted. Empirical research on specific hegemonic formations must be sensitive to the reflexive, hybrid and mutative character of neoliberalism and undertake 'historical geographies' of concrete cases (Peck and Tickell, 2002, p 48). Neoliberal regimes may make substantive material concessions, whether under duress and without ideological compromise or by recuperating concessions to the ideology of the governing bloc. However, if capitalism is ageing, substantive concessions will tend over time to undermine the system and become more precarious, challenged through passive-revolutionary processes by forward-looking elements of the hegemonic bloc and liable to reversal unless counter-hegemonic forces prove equal to the struggle. One question posed by the ongoing crisis is whether 'zombie capitalism' (Harman, 2009) will ever again in the West be able to afford the concessions required for authentically progressive social democratic governance. In this context, governance networks are one terrain in the struggle for hegemony situated in a broader mix of hegemonic technologies, each prone to contradictions and contestation.

Summary

The cultivation of governance networks can be understood simultaneously as a hegemonic regulative ideal, as part of a hegemonic apparatus and as institutionalising the integral state. Roll-out 'governmentalisation' highlights how administrative compulsion pervades everyday state–civil society interactions. If so, post-traditional governance theory is based on a category error, the analytical separation of spheres that are dialectically related. It assumes the dissolution of structures and contradictions that are integral to capitalist modernity. Under capitalism, the integral state is always with us and 'political society' will always be 'coming back in' (Thomas, 2009, p 452). One vector of the dialectic is the apparent incompatibility of neoliberal ideology and neoliberal political economy, manifesting in the roll-forward of hierarchy in governance networks, where the experience of routine dilemmas and culture clashes undercuts connectionist aspirations. Chapter Six further explores the research implications of reframing network governance as the struggle for hegemony.

Notes

[1] http://johnshewell.com/?p=141. John Shewell is Head of Communications at Brighton & Hove City Council in the UK.

[2] www.nationalschool.gov.uk/programmes/programme.asp?id=25430

[3] web.worldbank.org/WBSITE/EXTERNAL/COUNTRIES/EASTASIAPACIFICEXT/EXTEAPREGTOPSOCDEV/0,,print:Y~isCURL:Y~contentMDK:20477526~pagePK:34004173~piPK:34003707~theSitePK:502940,00.html

[4] Brown's redistributive measures did not prevent income inequality from rising between 1997 and 2009 to the highest levels since records began in 1961.

SIX

Gramscian governance research

Introduction

As was suggested in Chapter Five, a key challenge for research influenced by Marxism is to move between the domains of theory, empirical inquiry and struggle. The first part of this chapter develops a research framework drawing on the tradition of 'dialectical network analysis' (Benson, 1977; Marsh and Smith, 2000). The chapter then explores the challenges of critical inquiry in the governance field, focusing on three issues: the case for seeing research as a critical intervention in public discourse, the choices at stake in adopting 'insider' or 'outsider' perspectives on governance network participation and potential avenues for comparative inquiry. The final part of the chapter considers the strengths and limitations of the network as a medium of counter-hegemonic power beyond the state–civil society interface.

Dialectical network analysis

Chapters Four and Five argued for a 'strongly dialectical' account of the development of governance networks as part of the flawed neoliberal hegemonic strategy. Paterson (2009, p 46) observes that neo-Gramscian research in international political economy calls for a 'new multilateralism', the democratisation and transformation of international organizations from the bottom up through the struggles of social movements. He notes that this agenda derives from a non-deterministic (arguably weak) dialectic, which specifies no necessary end point to conflict between social forces and depicts nothing as inevitable. In contrast, the strongly dialectical perspective maintains that the contradictory and conflictual nature of an emergent, emerging totality makes crises inevitable and transformation and democratisation highly improbable without first transforming the relations in question. It introduces no other determinism, but points to the manner in which ageing capitalism increasingly impedes the construction of stable institutions capable of realising goods such as trust, sustainability, equality and democracy.

How, then, does the strongly dialectical approach differ from the post-dialectical and weakly dialectical accounts? The following sketch draws from dialectical network analysis in political science (Marsh and Smith, 2000; Evans, 2001), organisational studies (Benson, 1977) and neo-institutionalism (Davies and Trounstine, 2012). Benson's (1977) dialectical framework sought to build on Marxism, considering how contradictions in organisational life might be exploited for emancipatory ends. He identified four elements of dialectical network analysis: social construction, totality, contradiction and praxis. Benson's concept of social construction refers to the 'production of social structure ... within a social structure' (1977, p 3). These are the dialectics of structure and agency, where social structures endow the actors attempting to maintain and transform them with causal powers. The second element, totality, explores the relationship between 'complex, interrelated wholes with partially autonomous parts' – the idea of dialectical unity or structural interdependence. The third element, contradiction, is the essence of a dialectical account, including contradictions constitutive of a social order and contingent or secondary contradictions capable of resolution without threatening the order itself. Praxis, finally, refers to the 'free and creative reconstruction of social arrangements on the basis of a reasoned analysis of both the limits and the potentials of present social forms' (Benson, 1977, p 5), the prospects for conscious resistance and transformation.

Building on Benson, Evans (2001, p 545) argued that the task of dialectical network analysis is to consider how a network is produced, mechanisms through which it is maintained and its ongoing reproduction and reconstruction. As dialectical analysis is concerned with contradictory social relations, it is inherently longitudinal. Even policy communities, relatively stable alliances of powerful actors dominating a policy field, are not static. Exogenous accounts of network change see the policy community breaking up or resolving into an issue network, either with the eruption of a crisis, such as the salmonella in eggs affair in agriculture, or the intervention of actors hitherto outside the network, such as the intrusion of health interests into the agricultural policy community following the salmonella scandal (Smith, 1991).

However, dialectical analysis must also incorporate networked relations themselves and the manner in which contradictions manifest and are transformed through critique and praxis. Recent developments in neo-institutionalism recognise that potential instability is often embedded in the very rules and norms that enable institutions to function. Exogenous factors explain some change, but endogenous contradictions are also crucial to understanding why institutions implode (Lindner and Rittberger, 2003, p 468). Dialectical institutionalism remains underdeveloped, but Hay (1999b) explored the relationship between path dependency and path shaping, the moment of institutional instability, as 'punctuated evolution'. He built on the evolutionary concept of punctuated equilibrium appropriated to international relations by Krasner (1984), denoting a social world characterised by stasis and sudden change. In Hay's model there is no stasis. During times of 'normal' policy the gradual accumulation of contradictions (evolution) is the precondition for crises (punctuation). Accumulated pathologies must achieve 'narration', the political and ideological articulation at which point they become full-blown crises. While dialectical institutionalism entails no necessary rapprochement with Marxism, it lends itself to the idea that multiple dialectical determinations are at work in the governance field. Thus, for example, Marsh and Smith (2000) argue that dialectical explanations attributing causal power to policy networks must consider contradictions between the network and the social whole, the network and the outcome of network-mediated action, the network and network actors and (we might add) between asymmetrically powerful network actors themselves.

Chapter Five drew attention to salient contradictions at each level. One contradiction between governance networks and the social whole is that between the neoliberal hegemonic project and the neoliberal political economy that subverts it. A contradiction between the network as a causal structure and network actors is that while the collaborative architecture cultivates the depoliticisation of public policy, this is at the expense of an authentic consensus because it occludes underlying value conflicts between participants. A prominent contradiction between network and outcome is the tendency for networks to morph into closed hierarchies – roll-forward governmentalisation.

Benson noted that his dialectical principles do not constitute a 'developed substantive theory' of organisations or a 'conceptual framework to guide research'. He rather saw dialectical network analysis as a 'critical-emancipatory stance towards organizational studies' and the 'active reconstruction of organizations' (1977, p 19). This volume embraces Benson's critical-emancipatory stance, but goes further than he in making substantive claims about the dialectical relationship between connectionist ideology and the material conditions undermining it. **Table 6.1** illustrates elements of the strongly dialectical account of network governance, applying Benson's four criteria at the macro-, meso- and micro-levels of analysis. **Table 6.2** is a schematic representation of orthodox Gramscian, neo-Gramscian and post-Gramscian perspectives.

Table 6.1: Governance networks: a strongly dialectical analysis

	Social construction	Totality	Contradiction	Praxis
Macro	Connectionist hegemonic project emerges from the crisis of the 1960s and 1970s	Contradictory totality centred on the expansion of the capital relation and geopolitical competition	Acute accumulation crisis amid cut-throat economic and geopolitical competition	From the defeat of organised labour and the rise of civil society to the no-global movement and the return of class militancy
Meso	State and market strategies for constructing governance networks	The networked polity as a facet of the integral state	Roll-forward governmentalisation trumps connectionism	Technocratic managerialism dominates in conflict with connectionist dispositions
Micro	Resourcing, embedding norms, practices and tensions. Contesting and remaking civil society	Governance networks	Clashing rationales and dispositions, endemic distrust, networks resolve into hierarchies	Depoliticisation, tacit resistance – relative ungovernability

In reality, there is some blurring across **Table 6.2**, particularly the second and third columns.

Provan and Kenis (2008, p 233) criticise what they see as the tendency for scholars to treat governance networks 'as undifferentiated forms, as if they all could be characterized in the same general way'. Certainly, the suggestion that there is or has been a move from hierarchies (via markets) to networks, however qualified, is a case of generalisation. The alternative generalisation that 'the celebration and cultivation of governance networks is an important moment in the struggle for hegemony under neoliberalism' does not specify spatiotemporal variety or trajectory, the precise configuration of actors, the manner in which contradictions manifest, or their outcome in specific cases. Nor is it to suggest that the governance network is the only kind of network, or the only kind of governance that matters. The central claim is that considering governance networks from the standpoint of hegemony and the integral state tells us something useful that alternative generalisations do not. It is possible that the task of generalisation is

Table 6.2: Competing Gramscian interpretations of contemporary governance

	Orthodox Gramscian	Neo-Gramscian	Post-Gramscian
Perspective on the transformation thesis	Rejection	Critical adaptor	Agent and enthusiast
Totality	Contradictory emergent-emerging totality	Sceptical towards theories of totality – social structures are loosely coupled ecologies	Dispersion, post- or anti-totality
Social structure	Exercises emergent causal power in stratified reality	Reciprocal structuration	Post-structural analysis or traditions as weak structures
Dialectics	Strong, particularly in late capitalism	Weakening. Structural contradictions softened by globalisation and the decline of class cleavages	None, or that between beliefs and traditions
State-capital conjuncture	Structural interdependence	Relative autonomy or autopoesis	'State' and 'capital' are reifications
Civil society	Part of the integral state and the dialectics of coercion-consent	Relative autonomy or autopoesis	'Civil society' is reification. Myriad forms of sociability
Hegemony	Incomplete and always contested	Provisional but strong and weakly contested	Post-hegemony
Coercion-consent	Coercion the condition of consent	Emphasises consent and underplays coercion	Coercion redundant amid rampant subjectivities
Privileged actors	Capitals, states and classes	Global 'nébuleuse' and social movements	Individual connectionists and fluid networks
Agency	Agents endowed with powers through position in the social structure	Agents act reflexively on relatively malleable social structures	The subject unfettered from the yoke of tradition

Table 6.2: continued

	Orthodox Gramscian	**Neo-Gramscian**	**Post-Gramscian**
Agent of transformation	Class	Social movement	Multitude, swarm, network
Organised governance networks	Hegemonic strategy of states and markets in neoliberal passive revolution	Rise of networks in a 'mix' with states and markets	Networks emblematic of the connectionist epoch
Informal governance networks	Closed power networks, for example policy communities, are the medium of exclusion and domination	Rise of heterodox networks in a 'mix' with hierarchies and markets	Networks exemplify the postmodern condition
Prominent network type	Power networks: policy communities, closed networks	Governance networks	Empire, multitude – network governance
Governance trends	Governance networks recuperated by hierarchies, from hegemony to dominance	More networks in a mix with market and hierarchy: towards metagovernance	De-traditionalisation, dispersion and the proliferation of networks
Concepts	Marxism, Orthodox Gramscianism	Neo and Post-Marxist Gramscianism, Regulation theory, Metagovernance, Neo-institutionalism	Actor Network Theory, Differentiated Polity Model, Post-hegemony, Reflexive modernisation
Key thinkers	Benson	Cox, Jessop	Beck, Bevir, Lash, Rhodes

indeed futile, but determining this requires us to investigate claims for similarity, such as the tendency alleged in Chapter Three for networks to resolve into hierarchies, and consider other generalisations and particularisations. In Barry's formal terms (1975, p 86):

> Our understanding of a subject may be advanced if concepts and processes can be translated into other terms more readily grasped and fruitful analogy will suggest new lines of enquiry by provoking the speculation that relationships found in the one field may hold, mutatis mutandis, in the other as well.

Tables 6.1 and **6.2** highlight the implications of changing 'orthodox' background assumptions underpinning the transformation thesis and express them in terms amenable to empirical inquiry.

A Gramscian perspective on network variety

A key argument of Chapters Three to Five is that governance networks are promoted in a context where 'traditional' structures and conflicts are not being superseded by any incipient postmodern or reflexively modern condition. If we consider the universe of governance networks as existing within a contradictory totality characterised by chronic instability, vast concentrations of power and wealth and ever-intensifying competition at every interstice, then it behoves us also to consider the possibility that institutions and practices mediate these conditions. From this vantage point, the problems with governance networks highlighted in Chapter Three make more sense if we start with Marx and Gramsci than if we begin with network governance theory. It would explain why, for example, networks comprised of powerful actors with similar material and cultural endowments and congruent interests (like policy communities) seem more likely to flourish than open and inclusive ones. As Kenis and Oerlemans (2008, p 292) put it, the centrally positioned actors in any network are more likely than not to form ties with organisations of similar status or interest. Those most likely to be central are those with the most resources. A key question here is whether factors such as de-traditionalisation, the rise of the autotelic personality and the universalising nature of risk tends to reduce social distance, as the theory of reflexive modernisation suggests. If not, it remains unlikely that we will find governance networks capable of forging sustainable affective relationships between otherwise unequal actors in pursuit of common goals. Accordingly, we need to ask what evidence there is that governance networks moderate, dissolve or otherwise overcome the social context of structural inequality in which they are situated.

Conversely, following the principles of critical realism, no substratum of reality should be conflated with the stratum from which it emerged. In nature, the laws of chemistry are not reducible to, but are only intelligible through, the temporally and analytically prior laws of physics. In the social world, institutions may work with the grain of the social structure or come into conflict with it. There is no a priori theoretical reason why institutions cannot subvert or transform the larger structures within which they operate. Perhaps governing networks can cultivate affective trust, thus demonstrating the 'theory effect' but the onus is on celebrants to demonstrate this far more convincingly than they have done hitherto in the face of considerable evidence to the contrary. If the relationship between institution and structure is dialectical, it seems reasonable to posit, in light of the evidence, that institutions that are egalitarian, democratic, collectively oriented and seeking to develop the connectionist ethos are likely to be unsustainable as long as the social conditions of ageing capitalism subsist. The Bolivarian revolutions discussed later in the chapter, contesting neoliberalism and trying to build egalitarian and inclusive governance, pose an ongoing empirical test of this conception of the relationship between institutional reform and social structure.

Flawed hegemony

Table 6.3 develops a broad heuristic to help guide comparative governance research based on Gramscian principles. It foregrounds the flawed hegemonic 'type' as this is a highly prevalent form of governance network. Here, the network seeks to mobilise governing resources and enrol citizen-activists, but with limited success, leading to 'governmentalisation'. The tendency for network coordination to degenerate into hierarchical coordination (if it occurs at all) derives, in part, from the failure of networks to cultivate the dispositions envisioned by the neoliberal hegemonic project: connectionist citizen-activists capable of energetically solving policy and management problems through a de-politicised, trust-based discourse. To the extent that the connectionist disposition fails to develop, we see the incremental roll-forward of managerialism, or administrative coercion; an incremental reconfiguration of the integral state on the coercion-consensus continuum, from hegemonic leadership towards domination.

Governance by exclusion

The comparative literature draws attention to the fact that not all forms of governance network are concerned directly with hegemony. The theory of the Growth Machine (Molotch, 1976) and Urban Regime Theory, for example, both suggest another archetype, 'governance by exclusion'. In Stone's (1989) account, American city officials and down-town market elites use their superior resources to pre-empt the governing agenda to the exclusion of citizens and lower-class interests, creating stable governing regimes with relatively impermeable boundaries. Like policy communities, the regime and growth machine archetypes are instances of exclusionary governance networks comprised of powerful social groups.

Moreover, as Davies and Pill (2012) found in Baltimore, there has barely been any attempt to construct inclusive governance networks, other than those led by private foundations. Whereas in UK cities the tapestry of organised governance networks is very dense, in Baltimore it is not. However, this does not mean the terrain of hegemonic struggle has been vacated for laissez faire; rather that it is organised differently. The carceral state, ghettoisation and the strong culture of church-inspired voluntarism combine with market discipline and operate as alternative hegemonic mechanisms (Harvey, 2005, p 50). This form relies on grass-roots interconnectivity and evidently entails networking of a kind, but this has no particular ideological currency. It is not celebrated as the work of the 'great man', or necessarily organised consciously as 'networking'. If the more 'inclusive' form of neoliberalism associated with the flawed hegemonic archetype fails, or states no longer have the resources to deploy expensive soft control technologies, then the drift to self-help and coercion may continue, perhaps tempered or undermined by the scale and ferocity of resistance. Governance by exclusion is best understood as a form of economic, spatial and symbolic violence, where hegemonic actors do not see the potential or need for an inclusionary strategy.

The interregnum

Stone (1989, p 236) further points out that regime building and maintenance is difficult and suggests that governing regimes are rare. Governing inertia or non-governance is possible at any scale, if no social force proves capable of organising the requisite leadership associated with a hegemonic project or outright domination. Loopmans' (2008) study of gentrification in Antwerp highlights the alternation of hegemonic and non-hegemonic phases in the governance of the city. He demonstrates how, in the latter phase, alternative would-be hegemonic strategies competed for leadership in an interregnum where no clear policy trajectory could be established. The interregnum is thus a further archetype, which may occur at any geopolitical scale. It may reflect vacillation or uncertainty within a constellation of hegemonic forces, or a finely balanced struggle between forces contending for hegemony.

Counter-hegemony

The counter-hegemonic archetype might take a number of forms including movements that seek to engage and transform the state and those that oppose it directly, either through distributed forms of struggle or traditional class-based coercive resistance. The English Community Development Projects (CDPs) of the late 1960s and 1970s are an instance of the first kind. Geddes (2009) described how the CDPs were set up in deprived urban areas in the late 1960s. In a famous report, *Gilding the Ghetto* (CDP, 1977), they developed a critique of the social pathology model underpinning the programme and instead elaborated a critique of capitalist political economy. The CDPs were interesting because a number of junior state managers 'went native' in developing a radical public critique of the programme they were meant to be delivering. Their actions highlighted both the heterogeneity of the state, as critical officials decided to respond to local demands over those of their superiors, and its limits as programme funding was withdrawn by the Callaghan government in 1978.

The second counter-hegemonic type is 'networked outsider resistance', the preferred mode of organising among leading elements in the 'no global' movement. Just as the network is the organising principle of the neoliberal knowledge economy it is also, for theorists like Hardt and Negri (2000), the organising principle of post-traditional resistance. Here, struggle can swarm, flow around or swamp power, creating new emancipatory practices without confronting underlying structures, themselves perceived as undergoing profound transformation. The third counter-hegemonic type, class-based coercive resistance, recognises the possibility, discussed in Chapter Four, that the decline in the political power of the working class during the neoliberal offensive is reversible. The growing propensity for militant working class action globally is evidence of this.

Comprehensive hegemony and post-hegemony

The heuristic allows, finally, that both post-hegemonic and comprehensively hegemonic forms of network governance could emerge, thereby refuting the central arguments developed in this volume. In the post-hegemonic worldview, flexible structures of trust-based collaboration form and dissolve, bringing together a fluid plurality of interests to debate and pursue an assortment of goals that are likely to be in constant flux. In the comprehensively hegemonic form, governmental and non-governmental actors are self-regulating under a unified logic of rule. They achieve practical mastery of the demands, tasks, conventions, dispositions and symbols of connectionism. They are at ease in the company of others, trusting and capable of advocating and contributing vigorously to networks. They happily channel the expressive drive into a post-political discourse and practice of resource mobilisation, common interest and problem solving.

Real cases are likely to be hybrid, with 'types' competing in a dialectical relationship. One interesting research task is to explore this relationship. For example, which archetypes are most prominent, which secondary archetypes serve as ideological justifications for the dominant ones and which ones clash? When and how do institutions switch between formality and informality (Crouch, 2005, p 52) and how is this movement related to the evolving dialectics of coercion and consent? However, the point is not merely to assign cases to categories in or across heuristics but also, as **Tables 6.1** and **6.2** emphasise, to posit the conditions in which different institutions develop, or not, and with what implications for the variety of theoretical perspectives on offer.

With this cautionary note, the asymmetric continuum in **Table 6.3** highlights six possible archetypes considered from the standpoint of hegemony, domination and resistance. To operationalise the framework it is necessary, finally, to consider what it means for the study of power. Arguably, it supersedes the debate over whether to study 'power over' (domination), or 'power to' (production) (Stone, 1989), since it has been argued in the vernacular of the integral state that 'power to' operates in the shadow and exercise of 'power over'. Rather, studying governance through a Gramscian lens poses the question of what resources are, or are not, mobilised by whom and how effectively they are deployed in support of any hegemonic, post-hegemonic or would-be counter-hegemonic formation. If governance networks generate new governing capacity, how is it mobilised? To what ends is it deployed and at the expense of what alternative interests, agendas and capacities? What contradictions manifest in the enactment of network relations, or in

Table 6.3: Six governance archetypes from a Gramscian perspective

	Flawed hegemony	Exclusion/ domination	Interregnum	Counter-hegemony	Comprehensive hegemony	Post-hegemony
Actors	Managerialist administrators, 'ungoverned' civil society activists	Informal alliance of local business elites, politicians and administrators	A variety of actors struggle for leadership.	Social movements, Re-emergent class conflicts	Connectionist administrators, business leaders and civil society activists	Network enthusiasts of all kinds
Characteristics	Networks tend to resolve into closed hierarchies	Control through exclusion. Elite closure.	Inertia, fragmentation, struggle, non-governance	Project-oriented resistance. Possible concessions to resistance	Adaptive, homogenous, inclusive network: post-pluralist, post-political	Adaptive, heterodox, inclusive network: pluralist and/or democratic
Integral State Form	De-politicization, but roll-forward governmentalization (administrative coercion)	The carceral state, high surveillance, laissez faire	Variable/contested	High coercion, high resistance	Hierarchy in the shadow, high levels of social assent	The integral state is dissolved
Dispositions	Mutual suspicion	Instrumental trust among elites	Variable	Distrusting and antagonistic	Affective trust through acculturation	Affective trust through empowered reflexivity
Struggle	Contested governance institutions 'from within'	Balkanised/ ghettoised, eg favellas, townships and US style spatial segregation	Variable	High and project-oriented	Very low	Everywhere and nowhere
Examples	Organised governance networks	Urban Regimes, Policy Communities, Growth Machines	Policy and leadership interregnum in Antwerp	Emerging global movement against austerity	Counterfactual – possibly the 'remaking' of civil society in Kecatamen.	Counterfactual – possibly network-conscious elite information workers

the relationship between network, context and outcome? And, how are contradictions deferred, resolved, or aggravated? The central claim of this volume is that, in considering these questions, the Gramscian approach casts light on important questions that post-traditional theory takes for granted or dismisses as 'zombie categories'.

Critical scholarship and governance networks

Marxist and Gramscian scholarship is concerned not only with theory and evidence, but also with transformation. It is therefore important to consider the role of the critical scholar in the study and practice of governance institutions, while conceding that, sadly, the academy as a whole feeds dominant paradigms and generally contributes little to emancipatory politics. Even professed radicals often write in an idiom that makes their work difficult for non-specialists (the current work is no exception). Like other fields, knowledge production is governed by historically rooted power relations and discourses (Kincheloe and McLaren, 2000, p 280). For Bourdieu (1990b), this idiom is part of the symbolic capital that constitutes recognition and membership of the academic field. From some points of view, the current salience of 'relevance' and 'impact' in assessing academic work might be positive because it challenges scholasticism, which is a real problem. However, from the standpoint of emancipatory politics it is profoundly reactionary. Making 'impact' a criterion of research excellence, or following governmental cues as to what should be researched will, by definition, squeeze non-mainstream research funding and cause critical work to slide even further down the journal rankings proselytised and enforced by university technocrats, and which increasingly determine academic cultural capital. The current political economy of university life undoubtedly makes research conducted with a view to challenging power structures difficult, but it is not impossible. The next part of the chapter further explores the research challenge facing critical governance scholars: the problem of 'relevance', the dilemmas associated with taking a critical intellectual stance on governance networks and potentially fruitful avenues for future inquiry. It is written from the standpoint of a researcher who has hitherto failed to follow the suggested principles very well, but would like to do better in future.

Impact, relevance and intervention in public discourse

In his successful campaign for the Presidency of the American Sociological Association, Michael Burawoy (2002) developed a powerful distinction between 'policy sociology' in the service of a client and 'public sociology' as a critical intervention in the public domain. He stated:

> As mirror and conscience of society, sociology must define, promote and inform public debate about deepening class and racial inequalities, new gender regimes, environmental degradation, market fundamentalism, state and non-state violence. I believe that the world needs public sociology – a sociology that transcends the academy – more than ever. Our potential publics are multiple, ranging from media audiences to policy makers, from silenced minorities to social movements. They are local, global, and national. As public sociology stimulates debate in all these contexts, it inspires and revitalizes our discipline. In return, theory and research give legitimacy, direction, and substance to public sociology. Teaching is equally central to public sociology: students are our first public for they carry sociology into all walks of life. Finally, the critical imagination, exposing the gap between what is and what could be, infuses values into public sociology to remind us that the world could be different.

Critical research embraces the label 'political' and is 'unafraid to consummate a relationship with emancipatory consciousness. Whereas traditional social scientists cling to the guard rail of neutrality, critical researchers frequently announce their partisanship in the struggle for a better world' (Kincheloe and McClaren, 2000, p 291). This is the outlook of Gramsci's organic intellectual. In the academic field, the would-be organic intellectual acknowledges the class character of the university system, is reflexive on the illusion of professional autonomy while resisting further encroachments, and seeks to become immersed in day-to-day struggles alongside working-class organic intellectuals, following the example of scholars like Bourdieu and Burawoy. This is a way of viewing the relationship between the academic world and the world of 'practice' that challenges the orthodoxy around research 'impact' without retreat to the ivory tower. It focuses on the duty of the critical scholar to intervene in public discourse, such as by making difficult and specialised research accessible to a public readership or by putting it at the service of struggle. Such research is 'relevant' in searching for ways to transform social life but shuns client relationships that make knowledge creation liable to capture by elites.

The critical insider

The principles of public sociology are a benchmark for critical scholarship on governance networks. From the perspective of Benson, Bourdieu or Burawoy, such research begins by celebrating resistance. Chapter Three concluded with the distinction between critique from within the orthodoxy ('propositional critique') and critique of the orthodoxy with a view to overturning it ('oppositional critique') (Cooke and Kothari, 2001, pp 5-6). Either way, the challenge is to step outside what appears common sense in the interests of critical, or good, sense. As Johnson (2007, p 108, original emphasis) put it, if we are not to 'operate *within* these hegemonic categories, we need to go beyond them'. Arguing that network governance theory is part of a hegemonic ideology is one starting point for doing this. Callinicos (2007b, p 306) suggests, for example, that the theory of reflexive modernisation represents the hypostatisation 'into social trends' of 'the life-experiences of a generation of Western intellectuals who came to adulthood in the 1960s'. Such intellectuals became demoralised in the ebb-tide of class struggle and the crisis of Marxism. Embracing ideas like the New Spirit of Capitalism, they became agents of connectionist hegemony, part of the ethico-political apparatus (Fontana, 2002).

Like Cooke and Kothari, McDonald (2005, pp 581-2) identified two critical traditions in response to governance networks: 'critical pragmatists' or reformists, who argue for conditional and critical engagement with collaborative structures; and 'structuralists', who examine the 'deep structures' of power and their fissures with a view to overturning them. The choice of whether to take an 'insider' or 'outsider' perspective recalls the 'in and against the state' debate (Holloway, 2005), the question of how those engaged in a struggle for socialism but occupying positions inside or close to the state machine should operate. For neo-Gramscian thinkers and theorists of relative autonomy, the 'war of position' requires activists to fight for the transformation of the state from within; it is a vital terrain of struggle. Whether struggle can be concluded 'in and against the state' or eventually has to move 'outside and against' remains the subject of considerable controversy and depends on how the relationship between states, capitals and civil societies is understood. Where all Gramscians would agree is that to the extent 'participation' is appropriate its purpose is not consensus but to foster struggle, challenge and transformation.

One research objective available to both 'insider' and 'outsider' positions is that of 'catalytic validity'. Catalytic validity occurs when researchers and respondents challenge each other to reflect on and transform their practices (Kincheloe and McClaren, 2000, p 297) and in doing so determine how power structures might also be transformed. In other words, one goal of critical research is to consider how different forms of public action, from critical engagement in governance networks through to militant confrontations with the state, 'contributes to a sense of self-transformation and learning' among researchers and respondents alike (Dwyer, 2004).

The 'in and against' perspective also addresses the question of how critical scholars should manage relationships with political leaders and state managers. Lotia and Hardy (2008, p 381) argue that since management is not monolithic, it can (at least in theory) be recuperated for progressive or emancipatory goals. The case of state managers 'going native' in the CDPs supports their position. In critical management studies, Alvesson and Willmott (1996, p 18) suggest that one condition for doing research in partnership with managers should be that they commit themselves to fostering organisations in which 'communications are less distorted by socially oppressive and asymmetrical relations of power'. Or, for McDonald (2005, p 597), 'receptive professionals' should be alerted to the legitimising strategies that they unwittingly use to 'reproduce their dominance', exploring with them the 'contradictions, fissures and cracks presented by the rhetoric of "empowerment" and "partnerships"' and trying to 'generate a more realistic understanding of the limits and possibilities of partnership working'.

The critical outsider

Insider and outsider positions are not necessarily mutually exclusive, and which to take will depend on context and disposition. However, if the analysis of governance networks developed in preceding chapters holds water, it suggests that there is a good case for organising 'outside and against' state- and market-led institutions. This stance draws attention to the case for insurgent modes of organising to exploit fissures in the integral state. In a critique of deliberative theory, Kohn (2000, p 425) argued that separation or critical distance enables the creation of protected space where social movements can 'explore and test genuinely alternative ways of framing collective problems'. Dorling (2010, p 316) concurs: 'Almost every time that there is a victory for humanity against greed it has been the result of millions of small actions mostly undertaken by people not in government'. If governing institutions entrench the interests of dominant groups, the disempowered must develop alternatives (see also Fraser, 1990).

Yet it is not separation itself that empowers, but re-engagement on the terrain of insurgency. Kohn (2000, p 426) argued that '[r]ealizing abstractions such as reciprocity, equality and opportunity is usually a process of historical struggle rather than theoretical consensus'. This struggle takes place not primarily through discourse, but at 'concrete sites of resistance, the literal, symbolic, and imaginary barricades, forums, and fortresses where the people mount challenges to currently hegemonic visions of collective life'. Or, as Touraine put it (1995, p 274, original emphasis), asserting the autonomous subject is 'always the antithesis of socialization, of adaptation to a role or status ... It is the gesture of refusal, of *resistance*, that creates the subject ... It is the more restricted ability to stand aside from our own social role, our non-belonging and our need to protest that allows each of us to live as a subject'. In Marxist terms, revolutionary class consciousness can be forged only in the struggle against capitalism.

Separation is a form of resistance, but if the perspective in Chapters Four and Five is correct, effective resistance, such as to austerity, will require the mobilisation of coercive counter-power. The case for coercive action against state and capital is made powerfully by Medearis (2005), who rejects the prohibition on force in deliberative democratic theory. He argues that since hierarchical power is pervasive in public discourse, subaltern groups have no choice but to act coercively to achieve democratic goals. If it is true that governance structures reproduce the inequalities they nominally seek to overcome, then those who value inclusive politics can be sympathetic towards non-participation and coercion. Legitimate coercive action is 'necessarily strategic and non-deliberative but still thoroughly entwined in public discourse' (Medearis, 2005, p 55). Medearis contends, against Habermas, that coercion is justified when it is 'reasonably oriented' towards democratising institutions and social relations which 'oppress and disadvantage some groups, hindering their inclusion in political contention on equal terms' (2005, p 74).

Neither Kohn nor Medearis considers the question posed in Chapters Four and Five of whether coercion exercised within the confines of capitalist democracy can be sufficient to achieve comprehensive and sustainable democratic inclusion, or whether these structures must themselves be transformed. Either way, if it is true that the transformative potential of discourse is subverted by capitalist political economy, then collaboration with its agents should be treated with suspicion, encouraging what Crossley (2003, p 52) approvingly called 'perceptual-cognitive schemas which dispose agents to question, criticize and distrust political elites and processes'. The latter perspective poses the question of whether it is time for a comprehensive break with the ideology of network governance and to argue, as critical scholars do, for separation and insurgency – what the present author (Davies, 2007) calls 'exit-action' strategies. Davies (2007, p 795) further argues that scholars and activists have invested a great deal of time and effort in exploring how inclusive and democratic governance networks might be fostered. Similar energy might fruitfully be invested in advocating and analysing practices such as renewed class and community struggles and insurgent planning, which is 'utopian in spirit and transformative in practice', 'counter-hegemonic, transgressive and imaginative' as it challenges established structures of power through re-claiming historical consciousness and imagines 'the concept of a different world as being ... both possible and necessary' (Miraftab, 2009, p 33).

Future directions in comparative critical governance research

Critical governance research can make use of a wide repertoire of research methods. It is true that mainstream political science in the US has long favoured rational choice theory and quantitative techniques, whereas urban studies tend to favour qualitative research and case studies (Davies and Imbroscio, 2010). However, Wyly (2010) critiques the backlash against positivism, making a powerful case for critical scholars to use the full spectrum of research techniques, including quantitative methods. Rigorous observation and measurement plays a very important role in radical social inquiry. Journals such as *Radical Statistics* and fine-grain studies of poverty and inequality (for example Dorling, 2010) are undoubtedly powerful weapons in the armoury of critics. Moreover, Hayward (2004, p 18) suggests that the methods of cognitive science can generate important insights into the production and reproduction of power in discursive encounters.

The advantage of dialectical analysis is that it can encompass spatiotemporally diverse modes of networking from the formal to the informal – organised inclusionary networks as well as informal exclusionary networks. The claim that many different kinds of network are comparable and can be understood through a common analytical prism is supported, in part, by the global diffusion of western governance ideologies. As Chapters Two and Three sought to demonstrate, the celebration and critique of governance networks are both global phenomena widely incorporated into the economic, political and managerial fields. They are also incorporated into the research programmes of governance scholars. Thus, academic discourse for and against governance networks is itself common analytical terrain.

However, policy and discourse convergence also begs the question of how far imported western values, goals and meanings become embedded in day-to-day collaborative and cultural practices. The south–north transfer of programmes, like participatory budgeting, poses the same question in reverse. For example, comparative research on governance networks in the UK and South Africa and undertaken by a British scholar needs to be cognisant of important similarities and differences. Similarities include the use of English as the official language and the self-confessed adaptation of Anglo-American policy frameworks and public management techniques to the South African context. Differences include South Africa's character as a democratising and developing nation, such as the fact that former anti-apartheid activists hold office and many civil society organisations retain close links with the governing party, and the impact of mass poverty and the HIV-AIDS epidemic on the potential for 'inclusive' governing institutions. In addition, the researcher would need to be sensitive to subcultural pluralism, for example questioning the potential effects of competing notions of 'Africanness' on governing ethos, practice and power (Filatova, 1997). If, for example, the concept of 'social inclusion' is mediated through local values such as Ubuntu, how does this affect the configuration of collaborative institutions, practices and outcomes? Similar questions might be asked of any incipient movement towards the cultivation of governing networks, such as in China.

One task of comparison is therefore to ascertain whether the global convergence of policy discourses and practices (arguably a 'totalising' trend) is tending to obliterate subcultural differences, or not. Part of the challenge is to develop macro-scale accounts of how far the global ideology of networks penetrates national and subnational governance cultures in the form of hegemonic strategies and alliances, intermingling with and challenging local custom and practice. Such studies could consider how the ideology of networks rises and falls in particular contexts including local, country-specific and cross-national accounts of the emergence and forms of network governance – such as that written about the UK in Chapter Two. An important element of this task is to specify the configuration of hegemonic forces, the relationship between the supranational and the national and the manner in which constellations of social forces are organised into national and subnational blocs including (for example) business leaders, political leaders, intellectuals, administrators and layers of civil society activists. Historical geographies of specific cases (Peck and Tickell, 2002, p 48) could, furthermore, consider how far resistance is reflexive on the local governing bloc and vice-versa, potentially creating hybrid justificatory regimes and governance institutions. Each account could then be compared and considered from the standpoint of the frameworks in **Tables 6.1–6.3**.

At the other end of the analytical spectrum, a pressing gap in network governance scholarship is the lack of ethnographic research of the kind conducted by scholars concerned with emancipation and the microdynamics of power. As Huxham and Beech (2008, pp 566-8) argue, studies of power at the micro level are a 'missing link' in research on interorganisational relations, despite these being vital to our understanding of how networks function. Thus, ethnographers could address the continuing need for research on the internal dynamics, or software, of governance networks (Skelcher, 2007) and their efficacy as vehicles for hegemonic leadership. In public administration, Rethemeyer and Hatmaker (2008, p 642) argue for 'micro level event histories of actual network systems in action'. Such research is very expensive and time consuming, but the most insightful way of getting to grips with the performativities of governance networks, the manner in which strategy is enacted, contested and transformed. Bourdieu (1984, p 453) cites a further compelling reason for conducting empirical research in this manner: that differences in the way they are conceived, uttered and justified can make 'nominally identical opinions really incommensurable'. Consensual discourses in governance networks can disguise deep differences in meaning that unintentionally destabilise or subvert the network (Davies, 2009). Ethnographies might therefore be a particularly fruitful way of casting comparative light on the encounter between would-be hegemonic ideologies and local culture and practice. On this terrain, there is common ground with interpretivism, which highlights the value of decentred research through telling rich and textured 'governance stories' (Bevir and Rhodes, 2006). However, the critical realist refuses to confine the analysis to discourse and stories, always drawing attention back to the conditions of their enactment and their material affects.

A key challenge for future studies of governance networks will therefore be to develop historically grounded but fine-grain understandings of how they serve, or fail to serve, the ends of the connectionist project (or its successor) and to chart how the ideology of networks rises and falls in concrete settings. This means that the study of networks should be placed squarely in the political economy tradition, examining how they reproduce and embed power asymmetries or generate conflict and resistance. Ethnographic research might focus particularly on the nature and quality of communication, the power of symbols, the reflexivity and non-reflexivity of network actors. It might further explore the relationship between discourse, practice and structure. It could also re-engage with the literatures on the causal power of networks discussed earlier in this chapter and explore how they mediate, reproduce and perhaps transform structural antagonisms.

One other possible area for new research on governance networks is the applications and limits of 'nudge', the ostensibly soft technologies being deployed to transform public behaviour and encourage citizen resilience in the face of deep cuts and fears of another round of social retrenchment (John et al, 2009; Kerswell and Goss, 2009). In some ways the 'behavioural turn' is also 'governance as usual'. It arguably extends and rebrands Third Way acculturation strategies and has long been integral to corporate and political marketing. 'Nudge' reopens the questions posed in this volume. Does it represent a significant change in the dominant hegemonic strategy? What dispositions does it seek to foster and how successfully? How are 'cues' absorbed and resisted by target groups? How might 'nudge' be used in the political arena such as to cultivate the connectionist disposition? The behavioural turn is one further challenge posed by a resilient neoliberal conjuncture, calling for the rereading of classics in Marxist psychology (for example Pavlov, 1927) and linguistic theory (Voloshinov, 1986). Collins (1999) provides a good example of their application in governance research.

Emancipation through networks

What of the wider potential of networks as insurgent mechanisms beyond the governance arena? The present volume cannot do justice to such an important question, but it seems appropriate briefly to discuss the impact of social networks as an organising medium and their limits. Influential voices on the left, such as Hardt and Negri (2004), Holloway (2005) and Klein (2007) have argued that it is possible to swarm around structures of domination, dissolving them in an emancipatory tide of networked counter-power rather than confronting them with concentrated and coercive counter-power. Callinicos (2006) notes, for example, that as part and parcel of the revitalisation of social critique in the 1990s, the 'no-global' movement adopted the metaphor of networks to describe itself, indicative of an interesting homology between the goals of new protest movements and the hegemonic strategy of neoliberalism. The meaning of networks is itself the terrain of ideological struggle (Callinicos, 2006, p 63).

There is no doubt that the digital age opens up new avenues for networking, including the organisation of online and street protests. One oft-cited example is the public response to the 2004 Madrid railway bombing, for which the Aznar government tried to blame Basque separatists. A series of spontaneous demonstrations erupted, involving millions of people angry at both the attack and the mendacity of the Spanish government in the face of compelling evidence that the atrocity was perpetrated by Al Qaida in revenge for Spain's part in the war on Iraq.[1] Inspired by mobilisations of this kind, the social forums movement was suspicious of any attempt to develop collective strategy or form a coherent counter-hegemonic project, fearing that to do so would undermine democracy, spontaneity and creativity. Social movements have long occupied a privileged empirical and intellectual position within the resistance to neoliberalism, constituting a 'critical orthodoxy' celebrated by organisations such as Attac and the autonomists influenced by Hardt and Negri.

These ideas have also influenced Bolivarian revolutionaries such as the Marxist Vice President of Bolivia, Garcia Linares, who reportedly sees the 'multitude' as the source of revolutionary creativity. According to Postero (2010, p 23), Linares and his allies see Bolivia as a 'multicolored formation (*formación abigarrada*) in which several very different forms of social and economic relations coexist in an unequal and disarticulated way'. Their analysis is influenced by the post-traditional view that a new form of 'plebeian organization is evolving'. Pre-existing 'forms of organization such as guilds and peasant organizations, "rooted in local spaces and concerns," play a greater role, bringing collective demands and forms of knowledge to the fore'. Postero continues (2010, p 23):

> Bolivia's new 'multitude' formations are not as rigid as previous union-style formations but rather bring together people and groups in 'affiliational relationships' and 'assembly-style democracy'. In contrast to traditional forms of association, which control and mobilize their members, they suggest, these forms maintain their power through moral authority, relying on participants' commitment to the cause. This is the new plebeian Bolivia.

This is a paradigm statement of post-traditional theory in its emancipatory guise. 'Old' forms of association are clunky and controlling, new ones are fluid, reflexive and heterogeneous. In a neoliberal world, the Bolivarian revolution is, like Mexico's Zapatista movement, a source of true inspiration for the left. Both eschew direct confrontation with state and capital and instead try to maintain popular coalitions in a situation of effective dual power. In Bolivia, this compromise entails a non-aggression pact with the 'autonomy' movement in the rich eastern provinces, which predictably enough enjoys the support of the US government. The Bolivarians have made significant inroads against neoliberalism. Perhaps the most famous victory was in the Cochabamba water wars, where in 2000 the World Bank and the Bolivian government were defeated in their attempt to privatise the municipal water supply by the coalition of forces that later became part of the 'Movement Towards Socialism' (MAS). The MAS was elected to power under the leadership of Evo Morales in 2005 (Guarneros-Meza and Geddes, 2010). It is clear, therefore, that the looser, network style of social movement does have teeth. It was influential in the recent uprisings in Egypt and Tunisia. According to Hardt and Negri:

> The organisation of the revolts resembles what we have seen for more than a decade in other parts of the world, from Seattle to Buenos Aires and Genoa and Cochabamba, Bolivia: a horizontal network that has no single, central leader … the multitude is able to organise itself without a centre … being co-opted by a traditional organisation would undermine its power.[2]

However, this intervention provoked great controversy in the left blogosphere, some commentators arguing that it was a very one-sided analysis and that the revolutions were not all about networks and swarm resistance. If the street movements were vital catalysts, strikes and occupations were decisive or just as important (as was the army in Egypt) as they were in the revolutions in the 20th century.[3] Moreover, the sustainability of the Bolivarian model is a source of constant scrutiny. Lopez Maya (2010) is pessimistic, arguing that its inability to radicalise and undertake more substantive redistributive measures is eroding the social base of the revolution in Venezuela. Here, the by now familiar argument is that participatory reforms are being recuperated and that the Chavez regime is losing interest in bottom-up innovation, instead favouring the institutionalisation and homogenisation of participatory structures. Lopez Maya sees these developments as the 'recentralising tendencies of the state and the concentration of powers in the president' (2010, p 125).

There is, therefore, a significant unanswered question about whether networked counter-power can continue to extend social, political and economic rights, so moving further towards substantive equality and ultimately socialism-of-a-kind, or is vulnerable to counter-revolutionary offensives of the kind conducted by General Pinochet and his armies in Chile in 1973.

Moreover, while they enjoyed considerable success following the birth of the 'no-global' movement at the WTO protests in Seattle in 1999, the social forums have now virtually disappeared, perhaps because of their failure to achieve any decisive breakthrough and perhaps because participants had incompatible goals that the network form of resistance prohibited them from debating properly, let alone resolving into common priorities. The underlying problem may be that theories of network resistance underestimate both the continuing concentration of political and economic power and the concentrated force required to displace it. Consequently, the critique of network governance theory may be as important for understanding the tasks of the opposition as for understanding the hegemonic ambitions of neoliberal capitalism.

This is the tenor of the rather precarious attempts to rehabilitate Leninism (for example Budgen et al, 2007) and the 'idea of communism' spearheaded by the likes of Callinicos (2006) and Žižek (2009). The Leninist Gramsci certainly argued, in the elliptical manner he cultivated to escape fascist censorship, that any revolutionary conjuncture requires 'the degree of homogeneity that is necessary and sufficient to generate an action that is coordinated and simultaneous in the time and geographical space in which the historical event takes place' (1971, p 194). If so, it will not be sufficient simply to forge autonomous spaces or fluid movements swarming around the power structures of capitalist political economy. These must be confronted at the point of production, distribution and exchange. The question then is whether it is possible to create a movement capable of doing so spearheaded by the organised working class or some other constellation of forces, one also capable of rescuing communism from the totalitarian stigma of Stalin and Mao. With the no-global movements waning and more traditional forms of workers' struggle re-emerging, critical scholars might find themselves drawn back to such unfashionable ideas as the need for a democratically determined 'hierarchy' of priorities and actions (Eagleton, 1996). These debates continue on the left, gaining a new lease of life in the UK with the birth of the student movement against the cuts in late 2010 and its trade union counterpart in 2011. They form a vital part of the terrain upon which the emancipatory potential and limits of networked resistance will be determined.

Summary

Governing networks are highly unlikely to engage the vast majority of citizens, or to be the locus of insurgency. From the perspective of resistance, it might be better for critical scholars to concern ourselves with other spheres of social life, such as networked and other forms of resistance. However, governing networks remain very important for understanding power, the pursuit of hegemony and, if critical insiders are right, the subtle means by which power can be contested and transformed at the state–civil society interface. For as long as the ideology of networks prevails, critical research on governance networks will help us understand the relationship between state, corporation and civil society, whether or not the Gramscian perspective advanced here finds favour. The concluding chapter reflects again on the central themes developed throughout the volume.

Notes

[1] www.brookings.edu/testimony/2004/0331europe_gordon.aspx

[2] www.guardian.co.uk/commentisfree/2011/feb/24/arabs-democracy-latin-america?INTCMP=SRCH

[3] http://the19thbrumaire.blogspot.com/2011/02/arab-revolution-and-coming.html

SEVEN

Conclusion

The wider context for the Marxist-Gramscian perspective developed in this book is what Callinicos (2007b, p 345) sees as the changing of the subject away from postmodernism back towards capitalism, class and resistance – themes that the transformation thesis dismissed amid the crisis of Marxism, the global capitalist renaissance and its fetish for networks. The purpose, therefore, has been to show how the Marxist and Gramscian traditions are relevant in rethinking governance today. Harvey comments that although postmodernism promised aesthetic emancipation, working with the grain of capital accumulation meant that its initially spectacular designs soon took on a predictably monotonous quality (cited in Merrifield, 2002, p 150). Similarly, post-traditional faith in the transformative quality of networks founders in the face of 'governance as usual'. Connectionist ideology lent vision and promise to the global capitalist renaissance, transposed by governments into the language of opportunity and inclusion and strategies for cultivating governance networks. This is the vision that founders as creeping governmentalisation trumps connectionism, amid more or less overt recalcitrance among distrusting civil society insiders and burgeoning crisis and resistance elsewhere in the social system.

Consequently, what is different about the past 40 years or so is not so much de-traditionalisation, dispersion and the rise of the network society, as the celebration of networks spearheading neoliberalism. Gramscian concepts, particularly the hegemonic project, the historic bloc, passive revolution and the integral state can contribute much to our understanding of the connectionist conjuncture as a moment in the struggle for hegemony. This struggle takes place on the terrain of the integral state, the dialectics of coercion–consent enacted in the day-to-day politics of institutions like governance networks. The idea of a contradictory totality central to Marxism is not a theory of 'final suture' as Laclau and Mouffe (2001, p 125) argued but of its impossibility, which is why hegemony is a relentless struggle and coercion remains the inescapable condition of consent. The neoliberal struggle has been partly about the shock doctrine and expanding markets, but also about transforming and enrolling civil society, attempting to cultivate the connectionist ethos.

In some cases this strategy may have succeeded in enrolling civil society activists, but in many others the dialectics of the integral state clearly undermine it. Participation in governance networks may foster relative political quiescence and depoliticised discourses, but subaltern good sense means that the activist also remains distrustful, truculent, wedded to obsolete values and practices and mired in a non-connectionist habitus. At a time when hegemony means ownership of mind and body, neuron and synapse, such dispositions are far from revolutionary, but they are subversive. They are one reason why, instead of inclusion and enrolment, we see exclusion and network closure – the incremental resolution of collaborative structures into relatively impermeable hierarchies.

If this argument holds water, networks cannot fulfil the hegemonic function envisioned by the 'irrationally exuberant' champions of neoliberal capitalism and neoliberal governance. Achieving genuinely diverse, pluralistic and reflexive governance would require nothing less than the comprehensive transformation of capitalist political economy. However, the contradictions inherent in the neoliberal formation are profound, alerting us once more to the explanatory power of the Marxist Gramsci. The major flaw in the transformation thesis is therefore that what Beck erroneously calls 'zombie categories' are fundamental to contemporary social life. The constant backsliding from the rhetoric of networks into 'authoritarian high modernism' (Moran, 2010, p 37) cannot be dismissed simply as the futile attempt to manage the problems of reflexive modernisation using the methods of first modernity, or as the intractability of the old Weberian elite. It is rather symptomatic of the contradiction between the ideology of reflexive modernisation and capitalist modernity itself. Reflexive modernisation is the vague premonition of one possible post-capitalist condition mistaken for emergent reality (Wetherly, 2000).

It is worth repeating the point made in the introduction, that the critique of network governance theory does not mean denying the existence of networks or abandoning network analysis per se. On the contrary, network analysis draws attention to the production, reproduction and contestation of power and the manner in which alliances forged around congruent interests and resource interdependencies reinforce asymmetric power relations. The target of critique is the proposition that network-like institutions and practices are proliferating, that they are based on novel forms of sociability and that they transcend structures of power and domination. Networks can be a powerful organising tool, but whether cooptive or insurgent, they have no special potential.

This conclusion highlights the point made in Chapter Three that characterising institutions as 'hierarchies' or 'networks' is misleading. As Hood (2000, p 6) observed, one of the paradoxes of New Public Management (NPM) was that 'new' systems tended to develop the practices they were meant to transcend to an even higher degree. Governance networks are rightly charged with behaving like hierarchies, but hierarchies depend on networking. As was suggested in Chapter One, network analysis could reveal as much about the 'relational' dimensions of a dictatorship as any fluid, self-coordinating social movement, showing how the dictator's position in a network enables him to exercise command power. The challenge is therefore less to allocate institutions to types or periods, valuable as these heuristics can sometimes be, than to discern how and why an institution or system of institutions embodies a particular 'mix' of coordination mechanisms. The concept of the integral state is also, therefore, a means of moving beyond the government–governance impasse by positing that all governance institutions are likely to embody the dialectics of coercion, consent and resistance in some form. Beyond the celebration of networks and the denunciation of hierarchies, exploring how the dialectic plays out would be a worthwhile research challenge, and perhaps the basis for new and better classifications.

Whether the fashion for networks is now passing is unclear. There are, however, reasons for thinking that it may be starting to wane. The reflexive self-criticisms of Bevir and Rhodes (2010) and Stoker (2011) are striking examples in the academic world. In more practical terms, sustaining governing networks is costly. Since the connectionist project rests on the post-materialist and post-crisis narrative of the (relative) abolition of scarcity, the return of crisis and austerity pose obvious questions about its sustainability. One possible trend identified by Davies and Pill (2012) is the withdrawal of investment in governance networks and a retreat to privatism. If disinvestment continues, the elaborate system of state-organised governance networks created in the era of the Third Way might be dismantled or wither on the vine.

Such developments could herald a move towards laissez faire or roll-back neoliberalism in debt-strapped economies. To be viable, laissez faire would require a combination of unfettered market discipline and socially resilient, self-reliant citizens either acculturated during previous rounds of social investment or through the amorphous diffusion of governmentalities capable of sustaining entrepreneurialism without further state intervention. However, Gramsci (1971, pp 159-60) argued that laissez faire is an illusion:

> Thus it is asserted that economic activity belongs to civil society, and that the State must not intervene to regulate it. But since in actual reality civil society and State are one and the same, it must be made clear that laissez-faire too is a form of State 'regulation', introduced and maintained by legislative and coercive means. It is a deliberate policy, conscious of its own ends, and not the spontaneous, automatic expression of economic facts. Consequently, laissez-faire liberalism is a political programme ... to change the economic programme of the State itself ... the distribution of the national income.

Like Hobsbawm and Polanyi, Gramsci here draws attention to the intractability of the integral state, as much for laissez faire as any inclusionary hegemonic project. It may signal the retreat of hegemonic politics, the escalation of state violence and, potentially, ghettoisation in the face of widespread public anger and social strife. However, whether a strategy for disinvestement and coercive management can be sustained in the face of rising struggle, or is capable of restoring the neoliberal accumulation model to profitability, remains to be seen.

It does not follow from the discussion in Chapter Six that critical scholars should be advising anyone to refuse participation in organised governance networks. Nevertheless, the case for insurgency and organised resistance is very strong in a period of severe crisis and where governments are implementing cuts in wages, jobs and services, in effect another enormous upward transfer of wealth from labour to capital. As Harvey put it, 'the mass of the population has either to resign itself to the historical and geographical trajectory defined by overwhelming and ever-increasing upper-class power or respond to it in class terms' (2005, p 202). Thomas (2009, p 452) warned in similar terms that if the labouring classes do not develop their own hegemonic apparatus capable of challenging political society and the integral state, they will remain 'subaltern to its overdeterminations'. A class response is now beginning to gather momentum across much of the world, and the struggle against neoliberal austerity will depend on it deepening and radicalising.

Early on, critical scholars cautioned against interpreting the proliferation of governance networks through the lens of idealised network theories (Lowndes and Skelcher, 1998, p 324). According to Davies (2000, p 422), writing in the context of a relatively new Blair government in the UK, 'it is not surprising that there is no firm trend in the direction of governance by network and there is no reason at present to believe that networking will become "pervasive"'. As Harding (1997, p 292) commented, scholars might 'wittingly or unwittingly' be colluding in particular representation of changes 'as if they were in some way natural or unavoidable' when they are not what they seem to be and 'a range of other representations and options is possible'. Despite many cautionary voices, network governance theory did become the orthodoxy. It is fatally flawed. As Joseph (2010b, pp 141-2) argued: 'No, networks have not replaced these more fundamental social relations. But they, and their ideologues, give these relations a renewed life, and consequently have to be challenged, both in theory and in practice'. The Gramscian conception of 'governance as hegemony' is one response to the call for challenges to an orthodoxy now deservedly falling into disrepute. Its purpose is to encourage research and activism that contemplates governance from the standpoint of resistance and transformation.

References

Abrahamson, P. (2003) 'Different social Europes, different partnership contexts', in L. Kjaer (ed) *Local partnerships in Europe: an action research project*, Copenhagen: Copenhagen Centre, pp 17-28.

Agger A. Sorensen, E. and Torfing, J. (2008) 'It takes two to tango: when public and private actors interact', in K. Yang and E. Bergrud (eds) *Civic engagement in a network society*, Charlotte, NC: IAP – Information Age Publishing, pp 15-40.

Alonso, L.E. (2001) 'New myths and old practices: postmodern management discourse and the decline of Fordist industrial relations', *Transfer: European Review of Labour and Research*, vol 7, no 2, pp 268-88.

Alvesson, M. and Willmott, H. (1996) *Making sense of management: a critical introduction*. London: Sage.

Amin, A. (ed) (1994) *Post-Fordism: a reader*, Oxford: Blackwell.

Anderson, P. (1976) 'The antinomies of Antonio Gramsci', *New Left Review*, no 1/100, pp 5-78.

Ansell, C. and Gash, A. (2008) 'Collaborative governance in theory and practice', *Journal of Public Administration Research and Theory*, vol 18, no 4, pp 543-571.

Archer, M. (2000) 'For structure: its realities, properties and powers: a reply to Anthony King', *The Sociological Review*, vol 48, no 3, pp 464-72.

Arnstein, S. (1969) 'A ladder of citizen participation', *Journal of American Institute of Planners*, vol 35, no 4, pp 216-24.

Arrighi, G. (2005) 'Hegemony unravelling – 1', *New Left Review*, no 2/33, pp 23-80.

Atkinson, R. (1999) 'Discourses of partnership and empowerment in contemporary British urban regeneration', *Urban Studies*, vol 36, no 1, pp 59-72.

Atkinson, W. (2007) 'Beck, individualization and the death of class: a critique', *The British Journal of Sociology*, vol 58, no 3, pp 349-66.

Auletta, K. (1976) 'The new power game', *The New York Magazine*, vol 9, no 2, pp 32-42.

Baccaro, L. and Papadakis, K. (2009) 'The downside of participatory-deliberative public administration', *Socio-Economic Review*, vol 7, no 2, pp 245-76.

Bachmann, R. and Zaheer, A. (2008) 'Trust in inter-organizational relations', in S. Cropper, M, Ebers, C. Huxham and P. Smith Ring (eds) *The Oxford handbook of inter-organizational relations*, Oxford: Oxford University Press, pp 533-54.

Balakrishnan, G. (2010) 'The coming contradiction', *New Left Review*, no 2/66, pp 31-53.

Bang, H. (2008) *Political science in a swing: between democracy and good governance*, Paper presented at the 58th Political Studies Association Annual Conference, Swansea University, 1–3 April 2008.

Bang, H. and Esmark, A. (2009) 'Good governance in the network society: reconfiguring the political from politics to policy', *Administrative Theory & Praxis*, vol 31, no 1, pp 7-37.

Barker, C. (1991) [1978] 'A note on the theory of capitalist states', in S. Clarke (ed) *The state debate*, Basingstoke: Palgrave-Macmillan, pp 182-91.

Barry, B. (1975) 'On analogy', *Political Studies*, vol xxiii, nos 2 and 3, pp 208-24.

Bauman, Z. (2002) 'Foreword: individually, together' in U. Beck, *Individualization: institutionalized individualism and its social and political consequences*, London: Sage, pp xiv-xix.

Beck, U. (1992) *Risk society: towards a new modernity*, London: Sage.

Beck, U. (2007) 'Beyond class and nation: reframing social inequalities in a globalizing world', *British Journal of Sociology*, vol 58, no 4, pp 679-705.

Beck, U. and Beck-Gernsheim, E. (2002) *Individualization: institutionalized individualism and its social and political consequences*, London: Sage.

Beck, U. and Grande, E. (2007) *Cosmopolitan Europe*, Cambridge: Polity Press.

Beck, U., Giddens, A. and Lash, S. (1994) *Reflexive modernization: politics, tradition and aesthetics in the modern social order*, Stanford: Stanford University Press.

Beebeejaun, Y. (2010) 'Do multicultural cities help equality?', in J.S. Davies and D.L. Imbroscio (eds) *Critical urban studies: new directions*, New York: SUNY Press, pp 121-34.

Bell, S. and Hindmoor, A. (2009) *Rethinking governance: the centrality of the state in modern society*, Cambridge: Cambridge University Press.

Bellamy-Foster, J. (2000) *Marx's ecology: materialism and nature*, New York: Monthly Review Press.

Benington, J. and Hartley, J. (2009) *"Whole systems go"! Improving leadership across the whole public service system*, Sunningdale: National School of Government.

Benson, J.K. (1977) 'Organisations: a dialectical view', *Administrative Science Quarterly*, vol 22, no 1, pp 1–21.

Bentley, T. and Halpern, D. (2003) '21st century citizenship', in A. Giddens (ed) *The progressive manifesto: new ideas for the centre-left*, London: Policy Network (Polity), pp 73-96.

Bentley, T. and Wilsdon, J. (2003) 'Introduction: the adaptive state', in T. Bentley and J. Wilsdon (eds) *The adaptive state*, London: Demos, pp 13-36.

Berman, M. (2007) ' Introduction', in M. Berman and B. Berger(eds) *New York calling: from blackout to Bloomberg,* London: Reaktion.

Bernal, J. D. (1957), *Science in history*, 2nd edn, London: Watts.

Bevir, M. (2005) *New Labour: a critique*, London: Routledge.

Bevir, M. (2010) *Democratic governance*, Princeton: Princeton University Press.

Bevir, M. and O'Brien, D. (2001) 'New Labour and the public sector in Britain', *Public Administration Review*, vol 61, no 5, pp 535-47.

Bevir, M. and Rhodes, R.A.W. (2006) *Governance stories*, London: Routledge.

Bevir, M. and Rhodes, R.A.W. (2008) 'The differentiated polity as narrative', *British Journal of Politics and International Relations*, vol 10, no 4, pp 729-34.

Bevir, M. and Rhodes, R.A.W. (2010) *The state as cultural practice*, Oxford: Oxford University Press.

Bieler, A. and Morton, A.D. (2003) 'Globalisation, the state and class struggle: a "Critical Economy" engagement with Open Marxism', *British Journal of Politics and International Relations*, vol 5, no 4, pp 467–99.

Bieler, A., Bruff, I. and Morton, A. D. (2010) 'Acorns and fruit: from totalization to periodization in the critique of capitalism', *Capitalism and Class*, vol 34, no 1, pp 25-37.

Birchall, J. (ed) (2001) *The new mutualism in public policy*, London: Routledge.

Blair, T. (1996) *New Britain: my vision of a young country*, London: Fourth Estate.

Blair, T. (1998) *Leading the way: a new vision for local government*, London: Institute for Public Policy Research.

Blair, T. (2005) 'We are the change-makers', Speech to the Labour Party conference, 27 September (available at http://news.bbc.co.uk/1/hi/uk_politics/4287370.stm).

Blake, G., Diamond, J., Foot, J., Gidley, B., Mayo, M., Shukra, K. and Yarnit, M. (2008) *Community engagement and community cohesion*, York: Joseph Rowntree Foundation.

Bockmeyer, J. L. (2000) 'A culture of distrust: the impact of local political culture on participation in the Detroit EZ', *Urban Studies*, vol 37, no 13, pp 2417-40.

Boddy, M. and Fudge, C. (eds) (1984) *Local socialism*, Basingstoke: Macmillan.

Bogason, P. (2000) *Public policy and local governance: institutions in postmodern society,* Cheltenham: Edward Elgar.

Bolden, R., Petrov, G. and Gosling, J. (2009) 'Distributed leadership in higher education', *Educational Management, Administration & Leadership*, vol 37, no 2, pp 257-77.

Boltanski, L. and Chiapello, E. (2005a) *The new spirit of capitalism*, London: Verso.

Boltanski, L. and Chiapello, E. (2005b) 'The new spirit of capitalism', *International Journal of Politics, Culture and Society*, vol 18, nos 3 and 4, pp 161-88.

Bonefeld, W. and Holloway, J. (eds) (2005) *Global capital, national state and the politics of money*, Basingstoke: Macmillan Press.

Borgatti S. P., Mehra, A., Brass, D.J. and Labianca G. (2009) 'Network analysis in the social sciences', *Science,* vol 323, pp 892-5.

Bourdieu, P. (1984) *Distinction: a social critique of the judgement of taste*, London, Routledge.

Bourdieu, P. (1990a) *In other words: essays towards a reflexive sociology*, Cambridge, Polity Press.

Bourdieu, P. (1990b) *Homo academicus*, Stanford, CA: Stanford University Press.

Bourdieu, P. (1998) *Practical reason*, Stanford, CA: Stanford University Press.

Bourdieu, P. (2003) *Firing back: against the tyranny of the market 2*, London: Verso.

Boyer, R. (1990) *The Regulation School: a critical introduction*, New York: Columbia University Press.

BPD (Business Partnerships for Development) (2002) *Putting partnering to work*, Business Partners for Development (available at www.bpdweb.com/products.htm).

Bray, D. (2006) 'Building "community": new strategies of governance in urban China', *Economy and Society*, vol 35, no 4, pp 530-49.

Budd, A. (2007) 'Transnationalist Marxism: a critique', *Contemporary Politics*, vol 13, no 4, pp 331-47.

Budgen, S. Kouvelakis S. and Žižek, S. (eds) (2007) *Lenin reloaded: towards a politics of truth*, Durham, NC: Duke University Press.

Burawoy, M. (2002 'Candidates announced for ASA officers', *Footnotes*, vol 30, no 3 (available at www.asanet.org/footnotes/mar02/fn11.html).

Cabinet Office (2010) *The coalition: our programme for government*, London: Cabinet Office.

Callinicos, A.T. (1999) ' Social theory put to the test of politics: Anthony Giddens and Pierre Bourdieu', *New Left Review*, no 1/ 236, pp 77-102.

Callinicos, A. T. (2000) 'Impossible anti-capitalism'? *New Left Review*, no 2/2, pp 117-4.

Callinicos, A.T. (2001) *Against the Third Way*, Cambridge: Polity Press.

Callinicos, A.T. (2006) *The resources of critique*, Cambridge: Polity Press.

Callinicos, A.T. (2007a) 'Does capitalism need the state system?', *Cambridge Review of International Affairs*, vol 20, no 4, pp 533-49.

Callinicos, A.T. (2007b) *Social theory: a historical introduction*, Cambridge: Polity Press.

Callinicos, A.T. (2009) *Imperialism and global political economy*, Cambridge: Polity Press.

Camfield, D. (2007) 'The multitude and the kangaroo. A critique of Hardt and Negri's theory of immaterial labour', *Historical Materialism*, vol 15, no 2, pp 21-52.

Cammack, P. (2004) 'What the World Bank means by poverty reduction, and why it matters', *New Political Economy*, vol 9, no 2, pp 189-211.

Cammack, P. (2006) *The politics of global competitiveness*, Papers in the Politics of Global Competitiveness, no 1, Manchester: Institute for Global Studies, Manchester Metropolitan University.

Cammack, P. (2010), 'The shape of capitalism to come', *Antipode*, vol 41, no s1, pp 262-80.

Carlin, N. and Birchall, I. (1983) 'Kinnock's favourite Marxist', *International Socialism*, vol 2, no 21, pp 88-116.

Carroll, T. (2009) '"Social Development" as a neoliberal Trojan Horse: the World Bank and the Kecamatan development program in Indonesia', *Development & Change*, vol 40, no 3, pp 447–66.

Castells, M. (1977) *The urban question: a Marxist approach*, London: Edward Arnold.

Castells, M. (1996) *The rise of the network society: the information age, economy, society and culture*, Oxford: Blackwell.

Catlaw, T. J. (2007) 'From representations to compositions: governance beyond the three-sector society', *Administrative Theory & Praxis*, vol 29, no 2, pp 225-59.

CDP (Community Development Programme) (1977) *Gilding the ghetto: the state and the poverty experiments*, London: CDP Inter-project Editorial Team.

Chandler, D. (2001) 'Active citizens and the therapeutic state: the role of democratic participation in local government reform', *Policy & Politics*, vol 29, no 1, pp 3-14.

Clarke, M. and Butcher, D. (2009) 'Political leadership, bureaucracies and business schools: a comfortable union?', *Management Learning*, vol 40, no 5, pp 587-607.

Coates, D. (2001) 'Capitalist models and social democracy: the case of New Labour', *British Journal of Politics and International Relations*, vol 3, no 3, pp 284-307.

Collins, C. (1999) 'Applying Bakhtin in urban studies: the failure of community participation in the Ferguslie Park Partnership', *Urban Studies*, vol 36, no 1, pp 73-90.

Cook, K.S., Hardin, R. and Levy, M. (2007) *Cooperation without trust?* New York: Russell Sage Foundation.

Cooke, B. and Kothari, U. (2001) *Participation: the new tyranny?*, London: Zed Books.

Costea, B., Crump, N. and Amiridis, K. (2008) 'Managerialism, the therapeutic habitus and the self in contemporary organizing', *Human Relations*, vol 61, no 5, pp 661-85.

Cox, K.R. (1993) 'The local and the global in the new urban politics: a critical view', *Environment and Planning D: Society and Space*, vol 11, no 4, pp 433–48.

Cox, R.W. (1994) 'The crisis in world order and the challenge to international organisation', *Cooperation and Conflict*, vol 29, no 2, pp 99-113.

Cox, R. W. with Schechter, M.G. (2002) *The political economy of a plural world: critical reflections on power, morals and civilization*, London: Routledge.

Creaven, S. (2000) *Marxism and realism: a materialist application of realism in the social sciences*, London: Routledge.

Cropper, S., Ebers, M., Huxham, C. and Smith Ring, P. (eds) (2008) *The Oxford handbook of inter-organizational relations*, Oxford: Oxford University Press.

Crossley, N. (2003) 'From reproduction to transformation: social movement fields and the radical habitus', *Theory, Culture and Society*, vol 20, no 6, pp 43-68.

Crossley, N. (2004) 'On systematically distorted communication: Bourdieu and the socio-analysis of publics', in N. Crossley and J.M. Roberts (eds) *After Habermas: new perspectives on the public sphere*, Oxford: Blackwell, pp 88-112

Crouch, C. (2005) *Capitalist diversity and change: recombinant governance and institutional entrepreneurs*, Oxford: Oxford University Press.

Crouch, C. (2008) 'What will follow the demise of privatised Keynesianism?', *Political Quarterly*, vol 79, no 4, pp 476-87.

Crouch, C. (2011) *The strange non-death of neoliberalism*, Cambridge: Polity Press.

Davies, J.S. (2000) 'The hollowing-out of local democracy and the fatal conceit of governing without government', *British Journal of Politics and International Relations*, vol 2, no 3, pp 414-28.

Davies, J.S. (2002) 'The governance of urban regeneration: a critique of the "governing without government" thesis', *Public Administration*, vol 80, no 2, pp 301-22.

Davies, J.S. (2004) 'Conjuncture or disjuncture? An institutionalist analysis of local regeneration partnerships in the UK', *International Journal of Urban and Regional Research*, vol 28, no 3, pp 570-85.

Davies, J.S. (2007) 'The limits of partnership: an exit-action strategy for local democratic inclusion', *Political Studies*, vol 55, no 4, pp 779-800.

Davies, J.S. (2009) 'The limits of joined up government: towards a political analysis', *Public Administration*, vol 87, no 1, pp 80-96.

Davies, J.S. (2010) 'Back to the future? Marxism and urban politics', in J.S. Davies and D.L. Imbroscio (eds) *Critical urban studies: new directions*, New York: SUNY Press, pp 73-88.

Davies, J.S. (2011, forthcoming) 'Active citizenship: navigating the Conservative heartlands of the New Labour project', *Policy & Politics*.

Davies, J.S. and Imbroscio, D.L. (2010) 'Introduction', in J.S. Davies., and D.L. Imbroscio (eds) *Critical urban studies: new directions*, New York: SUNY Press, pp 1-8.

Davies, J.S. and Pill, M. (2012, forthcoming) 'Hollowing-out neighbourhood governance? Re-scaling revitalization in Baltimore and Bristol', *Urban Studies*.

Davies, J.S. and Trounstine, J. (2012, forthcoming) 'Urban politics and the new institutionalism', in S. Clarke., P. John and K. Mossberger (eds) *The Oxford handbook of urban politics*, Oxford: Oxford University Press.

DCLG (Department of Communities and Local Government) (2006) *Strong and prosperous communities: the local government White Paper*, Cm 6939, London: HMSO.

Deakin, N. and Taylor, M. (2002) *Citizenship, civil society and governance*, Paper presented to the Third Sector from a European Perspective Conference, ISTR European Network Meeting, Trento Italy, December 2002.

De Jager, N. (2006) 'The South African government and the application of cooptive power', *Politikon*, vol 33, no 1, pp 101-12.

Denters, S.A.H. and Rose, L.E. (2005) *Comparing local governance: trends and developments*, Basingstoke: Palgrave Macmillan.

Devine, P., Pearmain, A. and Purdy, D. (2007) *Feel-bad Britain: how to make it better*, London: Lawrence & Wishart.

Diamond, J. (2004) 'Local regeneration initiatives and capacity building: whose "capacity" and "building" for what'?', *Community Development Journal*, vol 39, no 2, pp 177-89.
Dinham, A. (2005) 'Empowered or over-powered? The real experiences of local participation in the UK's New Deal for Communities', *Community Development Journal*, vol 40, no 3, pp 301-12.
Doogan, K. (2009) *New capitalism? The transformation of work*, Cambridge: Polity Press.
Dorling, D. (2010) *Injustice: why social inequality persists*, Bristol: The Policy Press.
Dryzek, J. (2010) *Foundations and frontiers of deliberative governance*, Oxford: Oxford University Press.
Du Gay, P. (2003) 'The tyranny of the epochal: change, epochalism and organizational reform', *Organization*, vol 10, no 4, pp 663-84.
Dunn, B. (2004) *Global restructuring and the power of labour*, Basingstoke: Palgrave.
Dunn, B. (2008) 'Accumulation by dispossession or accumulation of capital? The case of China', *Journal of Australian Political Economy*, no 60, pp 5-27.
Dwyer, P. (2004) *The contentious politics of the concerned citizens forum (CCF)*, Durban: University of KwaZulu-Natal.
Eagleton, T. (1996) *The illusions of postmodernism*, Oxford: Blackwell.
Edwards, M. (2009) *Civil society*, 2nd edn, Cambridge: Polity Press.
Edwards, R., Armstrong, P. and Miller, N. (2001) 'Include me out: critical readings of social exclusion, social inclusion and lifelong learning', *International Journal of Lifelong Education*, vol 20, no 5, pp 417-28.
Elkin, S.L. (1985) 'Pluralism in its place: state and regime in liberal democracy', in R. Benjamin and S.L. Elkin (eds) *The democratic state*, Lawrence, KA: University of Kansas Press, pp 179-212.
Elliott, G. (1993) *Labourism and the English genius*, London: Verso.
Evans, M. (2001) 'Understanding dialectics in policy network analysis', *Political Studies*, vol 49, no 3, pp 542-50.
Evans, M. and Davies, J. (1999) 'Understanding policy transfer: a multi-level, multi-disciplinary perspective, *Public Administration*, vol 77, no 2, pp 361-85.
Fairclough, N. (2000) *New Labour, new language*, London: Routledge.
Fairlie, J.A. (1926) 'Advisory committees in British public administration', *American Political Science Review*, vol 20, no 4, pp 812-22.
Ferguson, J. (2010) 'The uses of neoliberalism', *Antipode*, vol 41, no s1, pp 166-84.

Filatova, A. (1997) 'The rainbow against the African sky or African hegemony in a multi-cultural context', *Transformation*, vol 34, no 2, pp 47-56.

Finlayson, J. G. (2005) *Habermas: a very short introduction*, Oxford, Oxford University Press.

Fisher, R. (1977) 'Community organizing and citizen participation: the efforts of the people's institute in New York City, 1910–1920', *The Social Service Review,* vol 51, no 3, pp 474-90.

Flichy, P. (2005) 'Internet: the social construction of a "network ideology"', in O. Coutard., R.E. Hanley and R. Zimmerman (eds) *Sustaining urban networks*, Oxford: Routledge, pp 103-16.

Flinders, M. (2005) 'Majoritarian democracy in Britain: New Labour and the constitution', *Western European Politics*, vol 28, no1, pp 62–94.

Flores, A. (2005) *Local democracy in modern Mexico: a study in participatory methods*, Bury St Edmonds: Arena Books.

Fontana, B. (2002) 'Gramsci on politics and state', *Journal of Classical Sociology*, vol 2, no 2, pp 157-78.

Foucault, M. (1982) 'Subject and power', *Critical Inquiry*, vol 8, no 4, pp 777-95.

Frances, J. Levačić, R. Mitchell, J. and Thompson, G.F. (1991) 'Introduction', in G.F. Thompson, J. Frances, R. Levačić and J. Mitchell (eds) *Markets, hierarchies and networks: the coordination of social life,* Buckingham: Open University Press, pp 1-20.

Fraser, N. (1990) 'Rethinking the public sphere. A contribution to the critique of actually existing democracy', *Social Text*, vol 25/26, pp 56-80.

Frazer, E. and Hutchings, K. (2011) 'Virtuous violence and the politics of statecraft in Machiavelli, Clausewitz and Weber', *Political Studies*, vol 59, no 1, pp 56-73.

Frederickson, G.H. (2005) 'Whatever happened to public administration? Governance, governance everywhere', in E. Ferlie, L.E. Lynn and C. Pollitt (eds), *The Oxford handbook of public management*, Oxford: Oxford University Press, pp 282-304.

Friedman, T.L. (2000) *The lexus and the olive tree*, New York: Random House.

Fung, A. and Wright, E. O. (2001) 'Deepening democracy: innovations in empowered participatory governance', *Politics and Society*, vol 29, no 1, pp 5-41.

Gamble, A. (1994) *The free economy and the strong state*, 2nd edn, Basingstoke: Macmillan.

Gaventa, J. (2004) 'Towards participatory governance: assessing the transformative possibilities', in S. Hickey and G. Mohan (eds) *Participation: from tyranny to transformation*, London: Zed Books, pp 25-41.

Geddes, M. (2006) 'Partnership and the limits to local governance in England: institutionalist analysis and neo-liberalism', *International Journal of Urban and Regional Research,* vol 30, no 1, pp 76–97.

Geddes, M. (2008) 'Inter-organizational relationships in local and regional development partnerships', in S. Cropper, M. Ebers, C. Huxham and P. Smith Ring (eds) *The Oxford handbook of inter-organizational relations*, Oxford: Oxford University Press, pp 203-30.

Geddes, M. (2009) 'Marxism and urban politics', in J. S. Davies and D.L. Imbroscio (eds) *Theories of urban politics*, 2nd edn, London: Sage, pp 55-72.

Gerstenberger, H. (2010) 'The historical constitution of the political forms of captialism', *Antipode*, vol 43, no 1, pp 60-86.

Giddens, A. (1984) *The constitution of society*, Berkeley: University of California Press.

Giddens, A. (1994) *Beyond left and right: the future of radical politics*, Cambridge: Polity Press.

Giddens, A. (1995) *Politics, sociology and social theory: encounters with classical and contemporary social thought*, Stanford, CA: Stanford University Press.

Giddens, A. (1998) *The third way*, Cambridge: Polity Press.

Giddens, A. (2000) *The third way and its critics*, Cambridge: Polity Press.

Giddens, A. (2007) *Europe in the global age*, Cambridge: Polity Press.

Giddens, A. (2010) 'The rise and fall of New Labour', *New Perspectives Quarterly*, vol 27, no 3, pp 32-7.

Gilbert, J. (2004) 'The second wave: the specificity of New Labour neoliberalism', *Soundings*, no 26, pp 25-45.

Gilchrist, A. (2009) *A networking approach to community development*, 2nd edn, Bristol: The Policy Press.

Goldsborough, J. O. (1977) 'Eurocommunism after Madrid', *Foreign Affairs*, vol 55, no 4, pp 800-14.

Gramsci, A. (1971) *Selections from prison notebooks*, translated by Q. Hoare and G. Nowell-Smith, London: Lawrence & Wishart,.

Granovetter, M. (1973) 'the strength of weak ties', *American Journal of Sociology*, vol 78, pp 1360-80.

Grant, J. (2010) 'Foucault and the logic of dialectics', *Contemporary Political Theory*, vol 9, no 2, pp 220-38.

Gray, J. (2000) 'Inclusion: a radical critique', in P. Askonas and A. Stewart (eds) *Social inclusion: possibilities and tensions*, New York: St Martin's Press, pp 19-36.

Grint, K. (2010) 'The sacred in leadership: separation, sacrifice and silence', *Organization Studies*, vol 31, no 1, pp 89-107.

Guarneros-Meza, V. (2008) 'Local governance in Mexico: the case of two historic-centre partnerships', *Urban Studies*, vol 45, nos 5 and 6, pp 1011-35.

Guarneros-Meza, V. and Geddes, M. (2010) 'Local governance and participation under neoliberalism: comparative perspectives', *International Journal of Urban and Regional Research*, vol 34, no 1, pp 115-29.

Habermas, J. (1971) *Knowledge and human interests*, Boston, Beacon Press.

Habermas, J. (1984) *The theory of communicative action*, vol 1, Cambridge: Polity Press.

Habermas, J. (1987) *The philosophical discourse of modernity*, Cambridge, MA: MIT Press

Habib, A. (2005) 'State-civil society relations in post-apartheid South Africa', *Social Research*, vol 72, no 3, pp 671-92.

Hall, S. (1988) *The hard road to renewal*, London: Verso.

Hall, S. and Jacques, M. (eds) (1983) *New times: the changing face of politics in the 1990s*, London: Lawrence & Wishart.

Hall, P., Kettunen, P., Lofgren, K. and Ringholm, T. (2009) 'Is there a Nordic approach to questions of democracy in studies of network governance?', *Local Government Studies*, vol 35, no 5, pp 515-38.

Harding, A. (1994). 'Urban regimes and growth machines: toward a cross national research agenda', *Urban Affairs Quarterly*, vol 29, no 3 pp 356–83.

Harding, A. (1997) 'Urban regimes in a Europe of the cities', *European Urban and Regional Studies*, vol 4, no 4, pp 291-314.

Hardt, M. and Negri, A. (2000) *Empire*, Harvard: Harvard University Press.

Hardt, M. and Negri, A. (2004) *Multitude: war and democracy in the age of empire*, New York: Penguin Books.

Harman, C. (2007) 'The rate of profit and the world today', *International Socialism*, no 115 (available at www.isj.org.uk/?id=340).

Harman, C. (2009) *Zombie capitalism*, London: Bookmarks.

Harrison, P. (2006) 'Integrated development plans and third way politics', in U. Pillay, R. Tomlinson and J. du Toit (eds) *Democracy and delivery: urban politics in South Africa*, Cape Town: HSRC Press, pp 186-207.

Hart, K. (2003) 'Epilogue: studying world society', in T. H. Eriksen (ed) *Globalisation: studies in anthropology*, London: Pluto Press, pp 217-27.

Hartley, J. and Allison, M. (2000) 'The role of leadership in the modernization and improvement of public services', *Public Money & Management*,vol 20, no 2, pp 35-40.

Harvey, D. (2003a) 'City and justice: social movements in the city', in L.F. Girard., B. Forte, M. Cerreta., P. De Toro and F. Forte (eds) *The human sustainable city*, Aldershot: Ashgate, pp 235-54.

Harvey, D. (2003b) *The new imperialism*, Oxford: Oxford University Press.

Harvey, D. (2005) *A brief history of neoliberalism,* Oxford: Oxford University Press.

Harvey, D. (2006) *Spaces of global capitalism*, London: Verso.

Harvey, D. (2010) *The enigma of capital and the crises of capitalism*, Exmouth: Profile Books.

Hay, C. (1999a) *The political economy of New Labour*, Manchester: Manchester University Press.

Hay, C. (1999b) 'Crisis and the structural transformation of the state: interrogating the process of change', *British Journal of Politics and International Relations*, vol 1, no 3, pp 317-44.

Hay, C. (2010) 'Introduction: political science in an age of acknowledged interdependence', in C. Hay (ed) *New directions in political science*, Basingstoke: Palgrave Macmillan, pp 1-24.

Hay, C. (2011) 'Pathology without crisis? The strange demise of the Anglo-liberal growth model', *Government and Opposition,* vol 46, no 1, pp 1-31.

Hay, C. and Rosamond, B. (2002) 'Globalization, European integration and the discursive construction of economic imperatives', *Journal of European Public Policy*, vol 9, no 2, pp 147-67.

Hayward, C. R. (2004) 'Doxa and deliberation', *Critical Review of International Social and Political Philosophy*, vol 7, no 1, pp 1-24.

Heifetz, R.A., Grashow, A., and Linsky M. (2009) *The practice of adaptive leadership*, Cambridge, MA: Harvard Business Press.

Heller, P. (2001) 'Moving the state: the politics of democratic decentralization in Kerala, South Africa and Porto Alegre', *Politics and Society*, vol 29, no 1, pp 131-63.

Hickey, S. and Mohan, G. (eds) (2004) *Participation: from tyranny to transformation*, London: Zed Books.

Hilton, M. (2004) 'The legacy of luxury: moralities of consumption since the 18th century', *Journal of Consumer Culture*, vol 4, no 1, pp 101-23.

Hobsbawm, E. (1978) 'The forward march of labour halted?', *Marxism Today*, September, pp 279-85.

Hobsbawm E.J. (1989) *Politics for a rational left: political writings 1877–1988*, London: Verso.

Holloway, J. (2005) *Change the world without taking power*, 2nd edn, London: Pluto Press.

Hood, C. (2000) 'Paradoxes of public-sector managerialism, old public management and public service bargains', *International Public Management Journal*, vol 3, no 1, pp 1-22.

Hunt, S. (2005) *Whole of government: does working together work?*, Policy and Governance Discussion Paper no 05-01, Asia Pacific School of Economics and Government, The Australian National University.

Huws, U. (2003) *The making of a cybertariat: virtual work in a real world*, New York: Monthly Review Press.

Huxham, C. and Beech, N. (2008) 'Inter-organizational power', in S. Cropper, M. Ebers, C. Huxham and P. Smith Ring (eds) *The Oxford handbook of inter-organizational relations*, Oxford: Oxford University Press, pp 555-79.

Innes, J.E. and Booher, D.E. (1999) 'Consensus building and complex adaptive systems: a framework for evaluating collaborative planning, *Journal of the American Planning Association*, vol 65, no 4, pp 412-23.

James, T. (2009) 'Whatever happened to regulation theory? The regulation approach and local government revisited', *Policy Studies*, vol 30, no 2, pp 181-201.

Jansen, E. (2002) *NetLingo: the internet dictionary*, California: NetLingo.

Jessop, B. (1997) 'A neo-Gramscian approach to the regulation of urban regimes: accumulation strategies, hegemonic projects and governance', in M. Lauria (ed) *Reconstructing urban regime theory: regulating urban politics in a global economy*, London: Sage, pp 51-73.

Jessop, B. (2000) 'Governance failure', in G. Stoker (ed) *The new politics of British local governance*, Basingstoke: Macmillan, pp 11-32.

Jessop, B. (2003a) 'Governance and meta-governance: on reflexivity, requisite variety and requisite irony', in H.P. Bang (ed) *Governance as social and political communication*, Manchester: Manchester University Press, pp 101-16.

Jessop, B. (2003b), 'Putting hegemony in its place', *Journal of Critical Realism*, vol 2, no 1, pp 138-48.

Jessop, B. (2007a) *State power*, Cambridge: Polity Press.

Jessop, B. (2007b) 'What follows neoliberalism? The deepening contradictions of US domination and the struggle for a new global order', in R. Albritton, R. Jessop and R. Westra (eds) *Political economy and global capitalism*, London: Anthem Press, pp 67-88.

Jessop, B., Bonnett, K., Bromley, S. and Ling, T. (1988) *Thatcherism: a tale of two nations,* London: Verso.

John, P., Smith, G. and Stoker, G. (2009) 'Nudge nudge, think think: two strategies for changing civic behaviour', *The Political Quarterly*, vol 80, no 3, pp 361-70.

Johnson, R. (2007) 'Post-hegemony? I don't think so', *Theory, Culture and Society*, vol 24, no 3, pp 95-110.

Jordan, B. (2001) 'Tough love: social work, social exclusion and the third way', *British Journal of Social Work*, vol 31, no 4, pp 527-46.

Jordan, G. (1990) 'Sub-governments, policy communities and networks', *Journal of Theoretical Politics*, vol 2, no 3, pp 319-38.

Joseph, J. (2002) *Hegemony: a realist analysis*, London: Routledge.

Joseph, J. (2003) 'Restating hegemonic theory', *Journal of Critical Realism*, vol 2, no 1, pp 127-37.

Joseph, J. (2010a) 'The limits of governmentality: social theory and the international', *European Journal of International Relations*, vol 16, no 2, pp 223-46.

Joseph, J. (2010b) 'The problem with networks theory', *Labour History*, vol 51, no 1, pp 127-44.

Kearns, A. (1995) 'Active citizenship and local governance: political and geographical dimensions', *Political Geography*, vol 14, no 2, pp 155-75.

Kenis, P. and Oerlemans L. (2008) 'The social network perspective: understanding the structure of cooperation', in S. Cropper, M. Ebers, C. Huxham and P. Smith Ring (eds) *The Oxford handbook of inter-organizational relations*, Oxford: Oxford University Press, pp 289-312.

Kerswell, C. and Goss, S. (2009) *Challenging behaviour*, London: Solace Foundation Imprint.

Kickert, W.J.M, Klijn, E.H. and Koppenjan, J. (eds) (1997) *Managing complex networks: strategies for the public sector*, London: Sage.

Kincheloe, J.S. and McLaren, P. (2000) 'Rethinking critical theory and qualitative research', in N.K. Denzin and Y.S. Lincoln (eds) *Handbook of qualitative research*, London: Sage, pp 279-313.

Kjaer, A.J. (2004) *Governance*, Cambridge: Polity Press.

Klein, N. (2007) *The shock doctrine: the rise of disaster capitalism*, New York: Picador.

Klijn, E.H. (2008) 'Policy and implementation networks: managing complex interactions', in S. Cropper, M. Ebers, C. Huxham and P. Smith Ring (eds) *The Oxford handbook of inter-organizational relations*, Oxford: Oxford University Press, pp 118 -46.

Kohn, M. (2000) 'Language, power and persuasion: toward a critique of deliberative democracy', *Constellations*, vol 7, no 3, pp 408-29.

Kooiman, J. (2000) 'Societal governance: levels, models and orders of social-political interaction', in J. Pierre (ed) *Debating governance: authority, steering and democracy*, Oxford: Oxford University Press, pp 138-64.

Kokx, A. and van Kempen, R. (2009) 'Joining forces in urban restructuring: dealing with collaborative ideals and role conflicts in Breda, The Netherlands', *Environment and Plannning A*, vol 41, no 5, pp 1234-50.

Krasner, S. D. (1984) 'Approaches to the state: alternative conceptions and historical dynamics', *Comparative Politics*, vol 16, no 2, pp 223-46.

Kunkel, B. (2011) 'How much is too much', *London Review of Books*, vol 33, no 3, pp 9-14.

Laclau, E. and Mouffe, C. (2001) *Hegemony and socialist strategy*, 2nd edn, London: Verso.

Lambright, K.T., Mischen, P.A., and Laramee, C.B. (2010) 'Building trust in public and nonprofit networks: personal, dyadic, and third-party influences', *The American Review of Public Administration*, vol 40, no 1, pp 64-82.

Lash, S. (2002) 'Foreword: individualization in a non-linear mode', in U. Beck and E. Beck-Gernsheim, *Individualization: institutionalized individualism and its social and political consequences*, London: Sage, pp vii–xiii.

Lash, S. (2007) 'Power after hegemony: cultural studies in mutation'? *Theory, Culture and Society*, vol 24, no 3, pp 55-78.

Lash, S. and Wynne, B. (1992) 'Introduction', in U. Beck *Risk society: towards a new modernity*, London: Sage, pp 1-8.

Latour, B. (2005) *Reassembling the social: an introduction to actor-network theory*, Oxford: Oxford University Press.

Lauria, M. (ed) (1997) *Reconstructing urban regime theory: regulating urban politics in a global economy,* Thousand Oaks, CA: Sage.

Lawless, P. (1994) 'Partnership in urban regeneration in the UK: the Sheffield central area study', *Urban Studies*, vol 31, no 8, pp 1303-24.

Lawless, P. (2004) 'Locating and explaining area-based urban initiatives: New Deal for Communities in England', *Environment and Planning C: Policy and Politics*, vol 22, no 3, pp 383-99.

Leadbeater, C. (2000) *Living on thin air: the new economy*, London: Penguin Books.

Leggett, W. (2009) 'Prince of modernisers: Gramsci, New Labour and the meaning of modernity', in R. McNally and J. Schwarzmantel (eds) *Gramsci and global politics: hegemony and resistance,* London: Routledge, pp 137-55.

Leys, C. (1990) 'Still a question of hegemony', *New Left Review*, no 1/181, pp 119-28.
Limerick, D., Cunnington, B. and Crowther, F. (1993) *Managing the new organisation: collaboration and sustainability in the post corporate world*, San Francisco, CA: Jossey Bass Publishers.
Lindblom, C.E. (1977) *Politics and markets*, New York: Basic Books.
Lindner, J. and Rittberger, B. (2003) 'The creation, interpretation and contestation of institutions – revisiting historical institutionalism', *Journal of Common Market Studies*, vol 41, no 3, pp 445-73.
Loopmans, M. (2008) 'Relevance, gentrification and the development of a new hegemony on urban policies in Antwerp, Belgium', *Urban Studies*, vol 45, no 2, pp 2499-519.
Lopez Maya, M. (2010) 'Caracas: the state and peoples' power in the barrio', in J. Pearce (ed) *Participation and democracy in the twenty-first century city*, Basingstoke: Palgrave Macmillan, pp 100-26.
Lotia, N. and Hardy, C. (2008) 'Critical perspectives on collaboration', in S. Cropper, M, Ebers, C. Huxham and P. Smith Ring (eds) *The Oxford handbook of inter-organizational relations*, Oxford: Oxford University Press, pp 366-89.
Lowndes, V. (2001) 'Rescuing Aunt Sally: taking institutional theory seriously in urban politics', *Urban Studies*, vol 38, no 11, pp 1953-71.
Lowndes, V. and Skelcher, C. (1998) 'The dynamics of multi-organizational partnerships: an analysis of changing modes of governance', *Public Administration*, vol 76, no 2, pp 313-33.
Lowndes, V. and Wilson, D. (2003), 'Balancing revisability and robustness? A new institutionalist perspective on local government modernisation', *Public Administration*, vol 81, no 2, pp 275-98.
Lynn, L.E. (2001) 'The myth of the bureaucratic paradigm: what traditional public administration really stood for', *Public Administration Review*, vol 61, no 2, pp 144-60.
Magnette, P. (2003), 'European governance and civic participation: beyond elitist citizenship?, *Political Studies*, vol 51, no 1, pp 144-60.
March J.G. and Olsen J.P. (1989) *Rediscovering institutions: the organizational basis of politics*, New York: Free Press.
Marinetto, M. (2003a) 'Governing beyond the centre: a critique of the Anglo-Governance School', *Political Studies*, vol 51, no 3, pp 592-608.
Marinetto, M. (2003b) 'The governmentality of public administration: Foucault and the public sphere', *Public Administration*, vol 81, no 3, pp 621-49.
Marks, A. and Baldry, C. (2009) 'Stuck in the middle with who? The class identity of knowledge workers', *Work, Employment & Society*, vol 23, no 1, pp 49-65.

Marquand, D. (2004) *The decline of the public*, Cambridge: Polity Press.

Marsh, D. (2008) 'Understanding British government: analysing competing models', *British Journal of Politics and International Relations*, vol 10, no 2, pp 251-68.

Marsh, D. and Rhodes, R.A.W. (1992) *Policy networks in British government*, Oxford: Oxford University Press.

Marsh, D. and Smith, M. (2000) 'Understanding policy networks: towards a dialectical approach', *Political Studies*, vol 48, no 1, pp 4-21.

Marsh, D., Richards, D. and Smith, M. (2003) 'Unequal plurality: towards an asymmetric power model of British politics', *Government and Opposition*, vol 38, no 3, pp 306-32.

Marx, K. and Engels, F. (1998) [1846] *The German ideology*, New York: Prometheus Books.

Mathur, N., Skelcher, C. and Smith, M. (2003) *Towards a discursive evaluation of partnership governance*, Paper presented to European Consortium for Political Research Joint Sessions, Edinburgh, March 2003.

Mayer, M. (1994) 'Post-Fordist city politics', in A. Amin (ed) *Post-Fordism: a reader*, Oxford: Blackwell, pp 316-37.

McAnulla, S. (2006) 'Challenging the new interpretivist approach: towards a critical realist alternative', *British Politics*, vol 1, no 1, pp 113-38.

McCarthy, P., Rylance, J., Bennett, R. and Zimmermann, H. (eds) (2001) *Bullying: from backyard to boardroom*, 2nd edn, Leichardt, NSW: The Federation Press.

McClary, M. (1991) *Feminine endings: music, gender and sexuality*, Minneapolis, MN: University of Minnesota Press.

McDonald, I. (2005) 'Theorising partnerships: governance, communicative action and sports policy', *Journal of Social Policy*, vol 34, no 4, pp 579-600.

McGuigan, J. (2009) *Cool capitalism*, London: Pluto Press.

McKee, K. (2009) 'Post-Foucauldian governmentality: what does it offer critical social policy analysis?', *Critical Social Policy*, vol 29, no 3, pp 465-86.

Medearis, J. (2005) 'Social movements and deliberative democratic theory', *British Journal of Political Science*, vol 35, no 1, pp 53-75.

Meredith, S. and Catney, P. (2007) 'New Labour and associative democracy: old debates in new times'? *British Politics*, vol 2, no 3, pp 347-71.

Merrifield, A. (2002) *Metromarxism: a tale of the city*, London: Routledge.

Miéville, C. (2005) *Between equal rights: a Marxist theory of international law*, Leiden: Brill Academic Publishers.

Milburn, A. (2006) 'We can't let the right be the voice of the "me generation"', *The Guardian*, 21 February.
Miliband, D. (2006) 'Empowerment not abandonment', Speech to the National Council of Voluntary Organisations annual conference, 21 February.
Miliband, R. (2009) [1968] *The state in capitalist society*, London: Merlin Press.
Miraftab, F. (2009) 'Insurgent planning: situating radical planning in the global south', *Planning Theory*, vol 8, no 1, pp **32-50.**
Molotch, H. (1976) 'The city as a growth machine', *American Journal of Sociology*, vol 82, no 2, pp 309-32.
Moran, M. (2010) 'Policy-making in an interdependent world, in C. Hay (ed) *New directions in political science*, Basingstoke: Palgrave Macmillan, pp 25-42.
Morgan, K., Rees, G. and Garmise, S. (1999) 'Networking for local economic development', in G. Stoker (ed) *The new management of British local governance*, Basingstoke: Macmillan, pp 181-96.
Mortimore, R. (2002) *Working class and proud of it!*, MORI Social Values, 16.8.2002 (available at www.ipsos-mori.com/newsevents/ca/296/Working-Class-And-Proud-Of-It.aspx).
Mosco, V. (2008) 'Knowledge workers of the world unite?', *Canadian Journal of Communication*, vol 33, no 1, pp 121-25.
Mroz, A. (2010) 'Leader: Red tape – a form of distrust', *Times Higher Education Supplement*, 4 March (available at www.timeshighereducation.co.uk/story.asp?storycode=410626).
Mulgan, G. (1998) *Connexity: how to live in a connected world*, Cambridge, MA: Harvard Business School Press.
Nelson, J. and Zadek, P. (2000) *Partnership alchemy: new society partnerships in Europe*, Copenhagen, Copenhagen Centre.
Newman, J. (2004) 'Modernizing the state: a new form of governance?', in J. Lewis and R. Surender (eds) *Welfare state change: towards a third way?*, Oxford: Oxford University Press, pp 69-88.
Newman, J. (2005) 'Participative governance and the remaking of the public sphere', in J. Newman (ed) *Remaking governance: peoples, politics and the public sphere*, Bristol: The Policy Press, pp 119-38.
Nickel, P.M. (2007) 'Network governance and the new constitutionalism', *Administrative Theory & Praxis*, vol 29, no 2, pp 198-224.
Nickel, P.M. (2009) 'Text, portrayal and power: a critique of the transformation of the state thesis', *Journal of Power*, vol 2, no 3, pp 383-401.
Offe, C. and Keane, J. (1985) *Disorganized capitalism: contemporary transformations of work and politics*, Boston, MA: MIT Press.

Oliver, D. (1991) 'Active citizenship in the 1990s', *Parliamentary Affairs*, vol 44, no 2, pp 157-71.

Osmani, S.R. (2008), 'Participatory governance: an overview of issues and evidence', in United Nations (ed) *Building trust through civic engagement*, New York: United Nations.

Panelli, R. and Larner, W. (2010) 'Timely partnerships? Contrasting geographies of activism in New Zealand and Australia', *Urban Studies*, vol 47, no 6, pp 1343-66.

Panitch, L. and Gindin, S. (2006) 'Feedback: "Imperialism and global political economy": Reply to Alex Callinicos', *International Socialism*, 109 (available at www.isj.org.uk/index.php4?id=175&issue=109).

Panos Institute (2000) *Governing our cities: will people power work?*, London: The Panos Institute.

Paterson, B. (2009) '*Trasformismo* at the World Trade Organization', in M. McNally and J. Schwarzmantel (eds) *Gramsci and global politics: hegemony and resistance,* London: Routledge, pp 42-57.

Pavlov, I.P. (1927) *Conditioned reflexes: an investigation of the physiological activity of the cerebral cortex*, translated and edited by G.V. Anrep, London: Oxford University Press.

Pearce, J. (ed) (2010) *Participation and democracy in the twenty-first century city*, Basingstoke: Palgrave Macmillan.

Peck, J. and Tickell, A. (2002) 'Neoliberalizing space', *Antipode*, vol 34, no 3, pp 380-404.

Perrons, D. and Skyer, S. (2003) 'Empowerment through participation? Conceptual explorations and a case study', *International Journal of Urban and Regional Research*, vol 27, no 2, pp 265-85.

Pierre, J. and Stoker, G. (2000) 'Toward multi-level governance', in P. Dunleavy, A. Gamble, R. Heffernan, I. Holliday and G. Peel eds) *Developments in British politics 6*, Basingstoke, Palgrave, pp 29-44.

Pierson, P. (2000) 'Increasing returns, path dependency and the study of politics', *American Political Science Review*, vol 94, no 2, pp 251-67.

Pimlott, H. (2005) 'From "old left" to "New Labour"? Eric Hobsbawm and the rhetoric of "realistic Marxism"' *Labour/Le travail*, Vol 56, Autumn, pp 175-98.

Plummer, J. (2004) 'Introduction', in J. Plummer. and J. G. Taylor (eds) *Community participation in China: issues and processes for capacity building*, London: Earthscan, pp 1-22.

Polanyi, K. (1957) *The great transformation: the political and economic origins of our time*, Boston, MA: Beacon Paperback.

Pollitt, C. (2003) 'Joined up government: a survey', *Political Studies Review*, vol 1, no, 1, pp 34-49.

Postero, N. (2010) 'Morales' MAS government: building indigenous popular hegemony in Bolivia', *Latin American Perspectives,* vol 37, no 3, pp 18-34.

Poulantzas, N. (2000) *State, power, socialism*, London: Verso, Classics Edition.

Provan, K.G. and Kenis, P. (2008) 'Modes of network governance: structure, management, and effectiveness', *Journal of Public Administration Research and Theory,* vol 18, no 2, pp 229-52.

Putnam, R. (2000) *Bowling alone: the collapse and revival of American community*, New York: Simon and Schuster.

Rabrenovic, G. (2009), 'Urban social movements', in J.S. Davies and D.L. Imbroscio (eds) *Theories of urban politics*, 2nd edn, London: Sage, pp 239-54.

Randall, N.J. (2009) 'Time and British politics: memory, the present and teleology in the politics of New Labour' *British Politics*, vol 4, no 2, pp 188-216.

Rasche, A. and Behnam M, (2009) 'As if it were relevant: a systems theoretical perspective on the relation between science and practice', *Journal of Management Inquiry,* vol 18, no 3, pp 243-55.

Reay, D. (2005) 'Beyond consciousness? The psychic landscape of social class', *Sociology,* vol 39, no 5, pp 911-28.

Rethemeyer, R.K. and Hatmaker, D.M. (2008) 'Network management reconsidered: an inquiry into management of network structures in public sector service provision', *Journal of Public Administration Research and Theory*, vol 18, no 4, pp 617-46.

Retort (2004) 'Afflicted powers: the state, the spectacle and September 11', *New Left Review*, no 2/27, pp 5-21.

Rhodes, R.A.W. (1997) *Understanding governance: policy networks, governance, reflexivity and accountability*, Buckingham: Open University Press.

Rhodes, R.A.W. (1999) 'Foreword: Governance and networks', in G. Stoker (ed) *The new management of British local governance*, Basingstoke: Macmillan, pp xii-xxvi.

Rhodes, R.A.W. (2000a) 'The governance narrative: key findings and lessons from the ESRC's Whitehall Programme', *Public Administration*, vol 78, no 2, pp 345-63.

Rhodes, R.A.W. (2000b) 'Foreword', in G. Stoker (ed) *The new politics of British local governance*, Basingstoke: Macmillan, pp xi-xv.

Rhodes, R.A.W. (2007) 'Understanding governance: ten years on', *Organization Studies*, vol 28, no 8, pp 1243-64.

Rhodes, R.A.W. (2011) 'Thinking on: a career in public administration', *Public Administration*, vol 89, no 1, pp 196-212.

Riedel, J.A. (1972) 'Citizen participation: myths and realities', *Public Administration Review*, vol 32, no 3, pp 211-20.

Rose, N. S. (1999) *Powers of freedom: reframing political thought*, Cambridge: Cambridge University Press.

Rose, S.O. (2003) *Which people's war? National identity and citizenship in war-time Britain, 1939–1945*, Oxford: Oxford University Press.

Rosenberg, J. (2005) 'Globalization theory: a post-mortem', *International Politics*, vol 42, no 1, pp 2-74.

Rothstein, B. and Stolle, D. (2008) 'Political institutions and generalized trust', in D. Castiglione, J. van Deth and G. Wolleb (eds) *Handbook of social capital*, Oxford: Oxford University Press, pp 273-302.

Roy, A. (2009) 'Civic governmentality: the politics of inclusion in Beirut and Mumbai', *Antipode*, vol 41, no 1, pp 159-79.

Savage, M. (2002) 'Social exclusion and class analysis', in P. Branham and L. James (eds) *Social Differences and Divisions*, Oxford: Blackwell, pp 59-100.

Schwarzmantel, J. (2009) 'Introduction: Gramsci in his times and ours', in M. McNally and J. Schwarzmantel (eds) *Gramsci and global politics: hegemony and resistance*, London: Routledge, pp 1-16.

Sinclair, T.J. (2005) *The new masters of capital: American bond-rating agencies and the politics of creditworthiness*, Ithaca, NY: Cornell University Press.

Skelcher, C. (2005) 'Jurisdictional integrity, polycentrism, and the design of democratic governance', *Governance*, vol 18, no 1, pp 89-110.

Skelcher, C. (2007) 'Does democracy matter? A transatlantic research design on democratic performance and special purpose governments', *Journal of Public Administration Research and Theory*, vol 17, no 1, pp 61-76.

Skelcher, C., Mathur, N. and Smith, M. (2005) 'The public governance of collaborative spaces: discourse, design and democracy', *Public Administration*, vol 83, no 3, pp 573-96.

Smith, M. (1991) 'From policy community to issue network: salmonella in eggs and the new politics of food', *Public Administration*, vol 69, no 2, pp 235-55.

Somerville, P. (2004) 'Community governance and democracy', *Policy & Politics*, vol 33, no 1, pp 117-44.

Sorensen, E. and Torfing, J. (eds) (2008) *Theories of democratic network governance*, Basingstoke: Palgrave Macmillan.

Steen, T. and Wayenberg, E. (2003) 'Local governance in Flanders', in B. Denters, O. Van Heffen, J. Huisman and P.J. Klok (eds) *The rise of interactive governance and quasi-markets*, Dordrecht: Kluwer Academic Publishers, pp 261-74.

Stewart, M. (2003) 'Towards collaborative capacity', in M. Boddy (ed) *Urban transformation and urban governance*, Bristol: The Policy Press, pp 76-89.

Stoecker, R. (2003) 'Understanding the development-organizing dialectic', *Journal of Urban Affairs*, vol 25, no 4, pp 493-512.

Stoker, G. (1998) 'Governance as theory: five propositions', *International Social Science Journal*, vol 50, no 155, pp 17-28.

Stoker, G. (ed) (1999) *The new management of British local governance*, Basingstoke: Macmillan.

Stoker, G. (ed) (2000a) *The new politics of British local governance*, Basingstoke: Macmillan.

Stoker, G. (2000b) 'Urban political science and the challenge of urban governance', in J. Pierre (ed) *Debating governance: authority, steering and democracy*, Oxford: Oxford University Press, pp 91-109.

Stoker, G. (2002) 'Life is a lottery: New Labour's strategy for the reform of devolved governance', *Public Administration*, vol 80, no 3, pp 417-34.

Stoker, G. (2004) *Transforming local governance: from Thatcherism to New Labour*, Basingstoke: Palgrave.

Stoker, G. (2011) 'Was local governance such a good idea? A global comparative perspective', *Public Administration*, vol 89, no 1, pp 15-31.

Stone, C.N. (1980) 'Systemic power in community decision making: a restatement of stratification theory', *American Political Science Review*, vol 74, no 4, pp 978-90.

Stone, C.N. (1989) *Regime politics: governing Atlanta*, Lawrence, KS: University Press of Kansas.

Stone, C.N. (2004) 'It's more than the economy after all: continuing the debate about urban regimes', *Journal of Urban Affairs*, vol 26, no 1, pp 1-19.

Stone, C.N. (2009) 'Who is governed? Local citizens and the political order of cities', in J.S. Davies and D.L. Imbroscio (eds) *Theories of urban politics*, 2nd edn, London: Sage, pp 257-73.

Swyngedouw, E. (2005) 'Governance innovation and the citizen: the Janus face of governance-beyond-the state', *Urban Studies*, vol 42, no 11, pp 1991-2006.

Taylor, J.G. (2004) 'The context for community participation in China', in J. Plummer and J. G. Taylor (eds) *Community participation in China: issues and processes for capacity building*, London: Earthscan, pp 23-35.

Taylor, M. (2003) 'Neighbourhood governance: holy grail or poisoned chalice'?, *Local Economy*, vol 18, no 3, pp 190-5.

Taylor, M. (2007) 'Community participation in the real world: opportunities and pitfalls in new governance spaces', *Urban Studies*, vol 44, no 2, pp 297-317.

Teisman, G.R. and Klijn, E.H. (2002) 'Partnership arrangements: governmental rhetoric of governance scheme', *Public Administration Review*, vol 62, no 2, pp 197–205.

Thoburn, N. (2007) 'Patterns of production: cultural studies after hegemony', *Theory, Culture and Society*, vol 24, no 3, pp 79-94.

Thomas, P. (2009) *The Gramscian moment: philosophy, hegemony and Marxism*, Leiden: Brill Academic Publishers.

Thompson, G.F. (2003) *Between hierarchies and markets: the logic and limits of network forms of organization*, Oxford: Oxford University Press.

Thompson, H. (2010) 'The character of the state', in C. Hay (ed) *New directions in political science*, Basingstoke: Palgrave, pp 130-47.

Tilly, C. (1984) *Big structures, large processes, huge comparisons*, New York: Russell Sage Foundation.

Tilly, C. (2001) 'Relational origins of inequality', *Anthropological Theory*, vol 1, no 3, pp 355-72.

Torfing, J. (1999) *New theories of discourse: Laclau, Mouffe and Žižek*, Oxford: Blackwell.

Touraine, A. (1995) *Critique of modernity*, Oxford: Blackwell.

Townshend, J. (2009) 'Giddens's "third way" and Gramsci's "passive revolution"', in M. McNally and J. Schwarzmantel (eds) *Gramsci and global politics: hegemony and resistance,* London: Routledge, pp 156-72.

Tsolakis, A. (2010) 'Opening up open Marxist theories of the state: a historical materialist critique', *The British Journal of Politics & International Relations*, vol 12, no 3, pp 387–407.

Urry, J. (2003) *Global complexity*, Cambridge: Polity Press.

Vigoda, E. (2002) 'From responsiveness to collaboration: governance, citizens and the next generation of public administration', *Public Administration Review*, vol 62, no 5, pp 527-40.

Voloshinov, V.N. (1986) [1929] *Marxism and the theory of language,* Cambridge, MA: Harvard University Press.

Walker, M., Roberts, S. M., Jones, J. P. and Frohling, O. (2008) 'Neoliberal development through technical assistance: constructing communities of entrepreneurial subjects in Oaxaca, Mexico', *Geoforum*, vol 39, no 1, pp 527-42.

Wälti, S., Küjbler, D. and Papadopoulos, Y. (2004) 'How democratic is "governance"? Lessons from Swiss drug policy', *Governance*, vol 17, no 1, pp 83-113.

Wetherly, P. (2000) 'Marxism, 'manufactured uncertainty' and progressivism: a response to Anthony Giddens', *Historical Materialism*, vol 7, no 1, pp 71-97.

White, R.C. (1945) 'Local participation in social security administration', *Public Administration Review*, vol 5, no 2, pp 141-7.

Whyte, W.F. (1943) *Street corner society*, Chicago: Chicago University Press.

Wilson, C. (2008) 'Michel Foucault: friend or foe of the left' *International Socialism*, vol 118 (available at www.isj.org.uk/index.php4?id=431&issue=118).

Wilson, H. (1963) Speech to the Labour Party Conference, Scarborough, 1 October.

Wolin, S.S. (2000) 'Political theory: from vocation to invocation', in J. Frank and J. Tambornino (eds) *Vocations of political theory*, Minneapolis, MN: University of Minnesota Press, pp 3-22.

World Bank (1991) *World development report 1991: the challenge of development*, New York: World Bank.

Wright, J.S.F., Parry, J., Mathers, J., Jones, S. and Orford, J. (2006) 'Assessing the participatory potential of Britain's New Deal for Communities', *Policy Studies*, vol 27, no 4, pp 347-61.

Wyly, E. (2010) '$\sqrt{\text{City}}$', in J.S. Davies and D.L. Imbroscio (eds) *Critical urban studies: new directions*, New York: SUNY Press, pp 9-22.

Zeilig, L. and Ceruti, C. (2008) 'Slums, resistance and the African working class', *International socialism*, no 117 (available at www.isj.org.uk/index.php4?id=398&issue=117).

Zeldin, T. (1994) *An intimate history of society*, London: Minerva.

Žižek, S. (2009) *First as tragedy, then as farce*, London: Verso.

Index

D

G

H

I

J

K

L

M

O

P

Q

R

S